Gay and Lesbian Rights Organizing: Community-Based Strategies

Gay and Lesbian Rights Organizing: Community-Based Strategies has been co-published simultaneously as *Journal of Gay & Lesbian Social Services,* Volume 16, Number 3/4 2004.

The *Journal of Gay & Lesbian Social Services* Monographic "Separates"

Below is a list of " separates," which in serials librarianship means a special issue simultaneously published as a special journal issue or double-issue *and* as a "separate" hardbound monograph. (This is a format which we also call a "DocuSerial.")

"Separates" are published because specialized libraries or professionals may wish to purchase a specific thematic issue by itself in a format which can be separately cataloged and shelved, as opposed to purchasing the journal on an on-going basis. Faculty members may also more easily consider a "separate" for classroom adoption.

"Separates" are carefully classified separately with the major book jobbers so that the journal tie-in can be noted on new book order slips to avoid duplicate purchasing.

You may wish to visit Haworth's website at . . .

http://www.HaworthPress.com

. . . to search our online catalog for complete tables of contents of these separates and related publications.

You may also call 1-800-HAWORTH (outside US/Canada: 607-722-5857), or Fax 1-800-895-0582 (outside US/Canada: 607-771-0012), or e-mail at:

docdelivery@haworthpress.com

Gay and Lesbian Rights Organizing: Community-Based Strategies, edited by Yolanda C. Padilla, PhD, LMSW-AP (Vol.16, No. 3/4, 2004). *Examines successful, tested action strategies designed to end discrimination and achieve social justice for sexual minorities.*

Community Organizing Against Homophobia and Heterosexism: The World Through Rainbow-Colored Glasses, edited by Samantha Wehbi, PhD (Vol. 16, No. 1, 2004). *A guide to using community activism to battle sexual oppression.*

Gay Men's Sexual Stories: Getting It! edited by Robert Reynolds, PhD, and Gerard Sullivan, PhD (Vol. 15, No. 3/4, 2003). *"Fascinating. . . . Explores the diversity in gay men's sexual lives. The stories are in turn moving, funny, sexy, witty, thoughtful, painful, and delightful. They are a joy to read. . . . This book shows the many different ways there are of being sexual–and the many different ways of realizing our humanity." (Jeffrey Weeks, PhD, Professor of Sociology, London South Bank University; Author of* Making Sexual History, Same Sex Intimacies, *and* Sexuality and Society: A Reader*)*

Research Methods with Gay, Lesbian, Bisexual, and Transgender Populations, edited by William Meezan, MSW, DSW, and James I. Martin, MSW, PhD (Vol. 15, No. 1/2, 2003). *"Must reading for all researchers concerned about vulnerable and stigmatized groups. . . . The authors raise significant methodological and ethical issues that researchers studying any vulnerable group, especially LGBT populations, must address. An excellent supplement to any social work or social science research class." (Wynne Sandra Korr, PhD, Dean and Professor, School of Social Work, University of Illinois at Urbana Champaign)*

From Here to Diversity: The Social Impact of Lesbian and Gay Issues in Education in Australia and New Zealand, edited by Kerry H. Robinson, PhD, MA, BA, DipEd, Jude Irwin, BSW, MA, and Tania Ferfolja, MA, BEd (Vol. 14, No. 2, 2002). *"Long awaited . . . challenges the rigid binaries that are produced and reproduced through schooling . . . A collection that will do much to keep anti-homophobia work on the educational agenda. Required reading for educators who must take seriously their responsibility to enhance the quality of school life for sexual minority students." (June Larkin, PhD, Director of Equity Studies, University of Toronto)*

Midlife and Aging in Gay America, edited by Douglas C. Kimmel, PhD, and Dawn Lundy Martin, MA (Vol. 13, No. 4, 2001). *"Magnificent. This is a topic whose time has finally come. This book fills a gaping hole in the GLBT literature. . . . Each chapter is a gem. With its coverage of elder GLBT's who are vision impaired and HIV positive as well as an important chapter on GLBT retirement planning, it makes the literature human and integrated." (Mark Pope, EdD, Associate Professor of Counseling and Family Therapy, University of Missouri, St. Louis)*

From Hate Crimes to Human Rights: A Tribute to Matthew Shepard, edited by Mary E. Swigonski, PhD, LCSW, Robin S. Mama, PhD, and Kelly Ward, LCSW (Vol. 13, No. 1/2, 2001). *An unsparing look at prejudice and hate crimes against LGBT individuals, in such diverse areas as international law, the child welfare system, minority cultures, and LGBT relationships.*

Working-Class Gay and Bisexual Men, edited by George Alan Appleby, MSW, PhD, (Vol. 12, No. 3/4, 2001). Working-Class Gay and Bisexual Men *is a powerfully persuasive work of scholarship with broad-ranging implications. Social workers, policymakers, AIDS activists, and anyone else concerned with the lives of gay and bisexual men will find this informative study as essential tool for designing effective programs.*

Gay Men and Childhood Sexual Trauma: Integrating the Shattered Self, edited by James Cassese, MSW, CSW (Vol. 12, No. 1/2, 2000). *"An excellent, thought-provoking collection of essays. Therapists who work with gay men will be grateful to have such a comprehensive resource for dealing with sexual trauma." (Rik Isensee, LCSW, Author of* Reclaiming Your Life*)*

Midlife Lesbian Relationships: Friends, Lovers, Children, and Parents, edited by Marcy R. Adelman, PhD (Vol. 11, No. 2/3, 2000). *"A careful and sensitive look at the various relationships of [lesbians at midlife] inside and outside of the therapy office. A useful addition to a growing body of literature." (Ellyn Kaschak, PhD, Professor of Psychology, San José State University, California, and Editor of the feminist quarterly journal* Women & Therapy)

Social Services with Transgendered Youth, edited by Gerald P. Mallon, DSW (Vol. 10, No. 3/4, 1999). *"A well-articulated book that provides valuable information about a population that has been virtually ignored...." (Carol T. Tully, PhD, Associate Professor, Tulane University, School of Social Work, New Orleans, Louisiana)*

Queer Families, Common Agendas: Gay People, Lesbians, and Family Values, edited by T. Richard Sullivan, PhD (Vol. 10, No. 1, 1999). *Examines the real life experience of those affected by current laws and policies regarding homosexual families.*

Lady Boys, Tom Boys, Rent Boys: Male and Female Homosexualities in Contemporary Thailand, edited by Peter A. Jackson, PhD, and Gerard Sullivan, PhD (Vol. 9, No. 2/3, 1999). *"Brings to life issues and problems of interpreting sexual and gender identities in contemporary Thailand." (Nerida M. Cook. PhD, Lecturer in Sociology, Department of Sociology and Social Work, University of Tasmania, Australia)*

Working with Gay Men and Lesbians in Private Psychotherapy Practice, edited by Christopher J. Alexander, PhD (Vol. 8, No. 4, 1998). *"Rich with information that will prove especially invaluable to therapists planning to or recently having begun to work with lesbian and gay clients in private practice." (Michael Shernoff, MSW, Private Practice, NYC; Adjunct Faculty, Hunter College Graduate School of Social Work)*

Violence and Social Injustice Against Lesbian, Gay and Bisexual People, edited by Lacey M. Sloan, PhD, and Nora S. Gustavsson, PhD (Vol. 8, No. 3, 1998). *"An important and timely book that exposes the multilevel nature of violence against gay, lesbian, bisexual, and transgender people." (Dorothy Van Soest, DSW, Associate Dean, School of Social Work, University of Texas at Austin)*

The HIV-Negative Gay Man: Developing Strategies for Survival and Emotional Well-Being, edited by Steven Ball, MSW, ACSW (Vol. 8, No. 1, 1998). *"Essential reading for anyone working with HIV-negative gay men." (Walt Odets, PhD, Author,* In the Shadow of the Epidemic: Being HIV-Negative in the Age of AIDS; *Clinical Psychologist, private practice, Berkeley, California)*

School Experiences of Gay and Lesbian Youth: The Invisible Minority, edited by Mary B. Harris, PhD (Vol. 7, No. 4, 1998). *"Our schools are well served when authors such as these have the courage to highlight problems that schools deny and to advocate for students whom schools make invisible." (Gerald Unks, Professor, School of Education, University of North Carolina at Chapel Hill; Editor,* The Gay Teen*)*

Rural Gays and Lesbians: Building on the Strengths of Communities, edited by James Donald Smith, ACSW, LCSW, and Ronald J. Mancoske, BSCW, DSW (Vol. 7, No. 3, 1998). *"This in-*

formative and well-written book fills a major gap in the literature and should be widely read." (James Midgley, PhD, Harry and Riva Specht Professor of Public Social Services and Dean, School of Social Welfare, University of California at Berkeley)

Gay Widowers: Life After the Death of a Partner, edited by Michael Shernoff, MSW, ACSW (Vol. 7, No. 2, 1997). *"This inspiring book is not only for those who have experienced the tragedy of losing a partner–it's for every gay man who loves another." (Michelangelo Signorile, Author, Life Outside)*

Gay and Lesbian Professionals in the Closet: Who's In, Who's Out, and Why, edited by Teresa DeCrescenzo, MSW, LCSW (Vol. 6, No. 4, 1997). *"A gripping example of the way the closet cripples us and those we try to serve." (Virginia Uribe, PhD, Founder, Project 10 Outreach to Gay and Lesbian Youth, Los Angeles Unified School District)*

Two Spirit People: American Indian Lesbian Women and Gay Men, edited by Lester B. Brown, PhD (Vol. 6, No. 2, 1997). *"A must read for educators, social workers, and other providers of social and mental health services." (Wynne DuBray, Professor, Division of Social Work, California State University)*

Social Services for Senior Gay Men and Lesbians, edited by Jean K. Quam, PhD, MSW (Vol. 6, No. 1, 1997). *"Provides a valuable overview of social service issues and practice with elder gay men and lesbians." (Outword)*

Men of Color: A Context for Service to Homosexually Active Men, edited by John F. Longres, PhD (Vol. 5, No. 2/3, 1996). *"An excellent book for the 'helping professions.'" (Feminist Bookstore News)*

Health Care for Lesbians and Gay Men: Confronting Homophobia and Heterosexism, edited by K. Jean Peterson, DSW (Vol. 5, No. 1, 1996). *"Essential reading for those concerned with the quality of health care services." (Etcetera)*

Sexual Identity on the Job: Issues and Services, edited by Alan L. Ellis, PhD, and Ellen D. B. Riggle, PhD (Vol. 4, No. 4, 1996). *"Reveals a critical need for additional research to address the many questions left unanswered or answered unsatisfactorily by existing research." (Sex Roles: A Journal of Research)*

Human Services for Gay People: Clinical and Community Practice, edited by Michael Shernoff, MSW, ACSW (Vol. 4, No. 2, 1996). *"This very practical book on clinical and community practice issues belongs on the shelf of every social worker, counselor, or therapist working with lesbians and gay men." (Gary A. Lloyd, PhD, ACSW, BCD, Professor and Coordinator, Institute for Research and Training in HIV/AIDS Counseling, School of Social Work, Tulane University)*

Violence in Gay and Lesbian Domestic Partnerships, edited by Claire M. Renzetti, PhD, and Charles Harvey Miley, PhD (Vol. 4, No. 1, 1996). *"A comprehensive guidebook for service providers and community and church leaders." (Small Press Magazine)*

Gays and Lesbians in Asia and the Pacific: Social and Human Services, edited by Gerard Sullivan, PhD, and Laurence Wai-Teng Leong, PhD (Vol. 3, No. 3, 1995). *"Insights in this book can provide an understanding of these cultures and provide an opportunity to better understand your own." (The Lavender Lamp)*

Lesbians of Color: Social and Human Services, edited by Hilda Hidalgo, PhD, ACSW (Vol. 3, No. 2, 1995). *"An illuminating and helpful guide for readers who wish to increase their understanding of and sensitivity toward lesbians of color and the challenges they face." (Black Caucus of the ALA Newsletter)*

Lesbian Social Services: Research Issues, edited by Carol T. Tully, PhD, MSW (Vol. 3, No. 1, 1995). *"Dr. Tully challenges us to reexamine theoretical conclusions that relate to lesbians.... A must read." (The Lavender Lamp)*

HIV Disease: Lesbians, Gays and the Social Services, edited by Gary A. Lloyd, PhD, ACSW, and Mary Ann Kuszelewicz, MSW, ACSW (Vol. 2, No. 3/4, 1995). *"A wonderful guide to working with people with AIDS. A terrific meld of political theory and hands-on advice, it is essential, inspiring reading for anyone fighting the pandemic or assisting those living with it." (Small Press*

Addiction and Recovery in Gay and Lesbian Persons, edited by Robert J. Kus, PhD, RN (Vol. 2, No. 1, 1995). *"Readers are well-guided through the multifaceted, sometimes confusing, and frequently challenging world of the gay or lesbian drug user." (Drug and Alcohol Review)*

Helping Gay and Lesbian Youth: New Policies, New Programs, New Practice, edited by Teresa DeCrescenzo, MSW, LCSW (Vol. 1, No. 3/4, 1994). *"Insightful and up-to-date, this handbook covers several topics relating to gay and lesbian adolescents . . . It is must reading for social workers, educators, guidance counselors, and policymakers." (Journal of Social Work Education)*

Social Services for Gay and Lesbian Couples, edited by Lawrence A. Kurdek, PhD (Vol. 1, No. 2, 1994). *"Many of the unique issues confronted by gay and lesbian couples are addressed here." (Ambush Magazine)*

∞ ALL HARRINGTON PARK PRESS BOOKS
AND JOURNALS ARE PRINTED
ON CERTIFIED ACID-FREE PAPER

Gay and Lesbian Rights Organizing: Community-Based Strategies

Yolanda C. Padilla, PhD, LMSW-AP
Editor

Gay and Lesbian Rights Organizing: Community-Based Strategies has been co-published simultaneously as *Journal of Gay & Lesbian Social Services,* Volume 16, Number 3/4 2004.

Harrington Park Press
The Haworth Social Work Practice Press
Imprints of
The Haworth Press, Inc.

Published by

Harrington Park Press®, 10 Alice Street, Binghamton, NY 13904-1580 USA

Harrington Park Press® is an imprint of The Haworth Press, Inc., 10 Alice Street, Binghamton, NY 13904-1580 USA.

Gay and Lesbian Rights Organizing: Community-Based Strategies has been co-published simultaneously as *Journal of Gay & Lesbian Social Services*, Volume 16, Number 3/4 2004.

© 2004 by The Haworth Press, Inc. All rights reserved. No part of this work may be reproduced or utilized in any form or by any means, electronic or mechanical, including photocopying, microfilm and recording, or by any information storage and retrieval system, without permission in writing from the publisher. Printed in the United States of America.

The development, preparation, and publication of this work has been undertaken with great care. However, the publisher, employees, editors, and agents of The Haworth Press and all imprints of The Haworth Press, Inc., including The Haworth Medical Press® and Pharmaceutical Products Press®, are not responsible for any errors contained herein or for consequences that may ensue from use of materials or information contained in this work. Opinions expressed by the author(s) are not necessarily those of The Haworth Press, Inc. With regard to case studies, identities and circumstances of individuals discussed herein have been changed to protect confidentiality. Any resemblance to actual persons, living or dead, is entirely coincidental.

Cover design by Marylouise E. Doyle

Library of Congress Cataloging-in-Publication Data

Gay and lesbian rights organizing : community-based strategies / Yolanda C. Padilla, editor.
    p. cm.
    "Co-published simultaneously as Journal of gay & lesbian social services, volume 16, number 3/4 2004."
    Includes bibliographical references and index.
    ISBN 1-56023-274-9 (hard cover : alk. paper) – ISBN 1-56023-275-7(soft cover : alk. paper)
    1. Gay rights. 2. Gays–Political activity. I. Padilla, Yolanda C. II. Journal of gay & lesbian social services.
HQ76.5.G385 2004
306.76'6–dc22

    2003016595

Indexing, Abstracting & Website/Internet Coverage

This section provides you with a list of major indexing & abstracting services. That is to say, each service began covering this periodical during the year noted in the right column. Most Websites which are listed below have indicated that they will either post, disseminate, compile, archive, cite or alert their own Website users with research-based content from this work. (This list is as current as the copyright date of this publication.)

Abstracting, Website/Indexing Coverage . . . . Year When Coverage Began

- **caredata CD: The social and community care database**
  <http://www.scie.org.uk> 1994
- **CNPIEC Reference Guide: Chinese National Directory
  of Foreign Periodicals** 1995
- **Contemporary Women's Issues** 1998
- **Criminal Justice Abstracts** 1997
- **Education Research Abstracts (ERA) <http://www.tandf.co.uk>** . 2001
- **Environmental Sciences and Pollution Management
  (Cambridge Scientific Aabstracts Internet Database Service)
  <http//:www.csa.com>** . . . . *
- **ERIC Clearinghouse on Urban Education (ERIC/CUE)** 1995
- **Family Index Database <http://www.familyscholar.com>** 2001
- **Family Violence & Sexual Assault Bulletin** 1999
- **Gay & Lesbian Abstracts <http://www.nisc.com>** 1999
- **GenderWatch <http://www.slinfo.com>** 1999
- **HOMODOK/"Relevant" Bibliographic Database** 1995
- **IBZ International Bibliography of Periodical Literature
  <http://www.saur.de>** 1996
- **IGLSS Abstracts <http://www.iglss.org>** 2000

(continued)

- *Index Guide to College Journals (core list compiled by integrating 48 indexes frequently used to support undergraduate programs in small to medium sized libraries)* . . . 1999
- *Index to Periodical Articles Related to Law* 1994
- *Lesbian Information Service* <http://www.lesbianinformationservice.org>. 2003
- *OCLC Public Affairs Information Service* <http://www.pais.org> . . 1995
- *Psychological Abstracts (PsycINFO)* <http://www.apa.org> 2001
- *Referativnyi Zhurnal (Abstracts Journal of the All-Russian Institute of Scientific and Technical Information– in Russian)* 1994
- *Social Services Abstracts* <http://www.csa.com>. 1999
- *Social Work Abstracts* <http://www.silverplatter.com/catalog/swab.htm> 1994
- *Sociological Abstracts* <http://www.csa.com> 1994
- *Studies on Women & Gender Abstracts* <http://www.tandf.co.uk> 1994
- *Violence and Abuse Abstracts: A Review of Current Literature on Interpersonal Violence (VAA)* 1995

* **Exact start date to come.**

Special Bibliographic Notes related to special journal issues (separates) and indexing/abstracting:

- indexing/abstracting services in this list will also cover material in any "separate" that is co-published simultaneously with Haworth's special thematic journal issue or DocuSerial. Indexing/abstracting usually covers material at the article/chapter level.
- monographic co-editions are intended for either non-subscribers or libraries which intend to purchase a second copy for their circulating collections.
- monographic co-editions are reported to all jobbers/wholesalers/approval plans. The source journal is listed as the "series" to assist the prevention of duplicate purchasing in the same manner utilized for books-in-series.
- to facilitate user/access services all indexing/abstracting services are encouraged to utilize the co-indexing entry note indicated at the bottom of the first page of each article/chapter/contribution.
- this is intended to assist a library user of any reference tool (whether print, electronic, online, or CD-ROM) to locate the monographic version if the library has purchased this version but not a subscription to the source journal.
- individual articles/chapters in any Haworth publication are also available through the Haworth Document Delivery Service (HDDS).

Gay and Lesbian Rights Organizing: Community-Based Strategies

CONTENTS

About the Contributors   xv

Foreword   xxi
   Urvashi Vaid

BUILDING COALITIONS AND CHANGING COMMUNITIES

Organizing for Change: One City's Journey Toward Justice   1
   Erlene Grise-Owens
   Jeff Vessels
   Larry W. Owens

One Community's Path to Greater Social Justice:
   Building on Earlier Successes   17
   Melanie D. Otis

Coalition Building and Electoral Organizing
   in the Passage of Anti-Discrimination Laws:
   The Case of Connecticut   35
   John Bonelli
   Louise Simmons

Organizing to Amend Antidiscrimination Statutes in Maryland   55
   Daphne L. McClellan
   Geoffrey L. Greif

VISIONS OF COMMUNITY FOR GLBT YOUTH

Resisting Fragmentation, Living Whole: Four Female
   Transgender Students of Color Speak About School   69
   Nova Gutierrez

Building Community for Toronto's Lesbian, Gay, Bisexual,
  Transsexual and Transgender Youth 81
    Bev Lepischak

Building Community-Based Alliances
  Between GLBTQQA Youth and Adults in Rural Settings 99
    Carol A. Snively

Grassroots Meet Homophobia: A Rocky Mountain Success Story 113
  Audrey Olsen Faulkner
  Ann Lindsey

INNOVATIVE STRATEGIES FOR A NEW ERA

The Importance of GLBT Think Tanks
  to Our Agenda of Equality and Liberation 129
    Sean Cahill

Assessing Health and Social Service Needs
  in the GLB Population: The Norwegian Experience 147
    Berge-Andreas Steinsvåg
    Bjørg Sandkjær
    Ingvill Størksen

'Trans'cending Barriers:
  Transgender Organizing on the Internet 165
    Eve Shapiro

"AM/FM Activism": Taking National Media Tools
  to a Local Level 181
    Kristen Schilt

A Gay and Lesbian Congregation Seeks Social Justice
  for Other Marginalized Communities 193
    Lon B. Johnston
    David Jenkins

From Movement Demands to Legislation:
  Organizing in the LGBT Community in Mexico City 207
    Mirka J. Negroni

Index 219

ABOUT THE EDITOR

Yolanda C. Padilla, PhD, LMSW-AP, is Associate Professor at the School of Social Work, University of Texas at Austin. Dr. Padilla is co-author of "Psychosocial Support for Families of Gay, Lesbian, Bisexual, and Transgender People," forthcoming in *Sexual Orientation and Gender Identity in Social Work Practice* (Columbia University Press) and "Gays and Lesbians in American Society: Policy and Practice Issues" in *Teaching Social Policy: Model Course Outlines and Modules* (Council on Social Work Education, 2003). Her research areas of interest focus on gay rights and policy development and GLBT youth in family, organizational, and community contexts. She is currently serving on the Commission on Sexual Orientation and Gender Expression of the Council on Social Work Education and the Special Interest Committee on Gay/Lesbian/Bisexual Issues of the National Association of Social Workers/Texas, and is involved in several local gay activist organizations. In addition to her work in gay and lesbian studies, Dr. Padilla specializes in poverty and social welfare policy. Dr. Padilla holds a dual doctoral degree in social work and sociology from the University of Michigan.

About the Contributors

John Bonelli, MSW, is currently Director of Policy and Community Organizing for the Connecticut Positive Action Coalition, an AIDS advocacy organization. He is also an adjunct professor at the University of Connecticut School of Social Work. He helped establish People for Change and ran for Hartford City Council in 1989 on the People for Change slate. He was co-director of the Connecticut Coalition for Lesbian and Gay Civil Rights and has a long history of activism in Connecticut and the Northeast on issues ranging from gay rights to homelessness to AIDS and many other issues.

Sean Cahill, PhD, is Director of the Policy Institute of the National Gay and Lesbian Task Force, a think tank that conducts research, policy analysis, and strategy development on issues of concern to GLBT people. Since joining NGLTF in 1999, Cahill has led research efforts in a number of areas, including racial and economic justice issues, aging, and family policy. He coauthored, with Research Director Kenneth Jones, *Leaving Our Children Behind: Welfare Reform and the GLBT Community* (2001). Cahill holds a doctorate in political science from the University of Michigan. His dissertation examined anti-gay discourse in U.S. politics.

Audrey Olsen Faulkner, ACSW, MSW, PhD, is Faculty Emerita from Rutgers University School of Social Work and is presently a faculty member at The Union Institute and University. She has over 45 years of experience as a social work community organizer, researcher, policy analyst, and teacher. Her professional and community volunteer work has focused on excluded groups–the poor, the aged, people of color, women, and more recently, the GLBT community. Her most recent book is *Development and Diversity*, published by The Haworth Press. In 2000 she coedited a special issue of *Affilia*, "Women and the New American Welfare." She is a recipient of a Lifetime Achievement Award in Community Organization from the Association of Community Organization and Social Administration.

Geoffrey Greif is Associate Dean and Professor at the University of Maryland School of Social Work. He received his MSW from the University of

Pennsylvania and his DSW from Columbia University. He is the author of more than 80 articles and chapters and eight books. His most recent book is *Overcoming the Odds: Raising Academically Successful African American Females* (co-authored). In 2001, he chaired the Governor's Special Commission to Study Sexual Orientation Discrimination in Maryland.

Erlene Grise-Owens, EdD, LCSW, is Associate Professor in the School of Social Work at Spalding University. She has taught social work and held administrative roles, including Director of Field Education, for almost 10 years. Her practice experience includes child welfare, clinical social work, and faith-based contexts. She serves on the editorial board of *Family Ministry*. Her publication topics include gender equity, leadership, and religion and spirituality. Most recently, she wrote a chapter, "To leave or not to leave," for a sourcebook on religion and spirituality decision cases, published by the Council on Social Work Education.

Nova Gutierrez, MA, is a Chicana feminist educator, artist, activist, writer, and scholar who lives in West Harlem. She has an MA in gender studies and feminist theory from the New School for Social Research, and is a Gates Millennium Scholar pursuing an EdD in International Educational Development: Gender Studies from Teachers College Columbia University. She is a contributor to the forthcoming anthology *This Bridge We Call Home: Envisioning the Spirit of This Bridge Called My Back*, by AnaLouise Keating and Gloria Anzaldua (Routledge Press, 2002). She taught for a short time at the alternative school for gay, lesbian, bisexual, and transgender youth described in this article.

David A. Jenkins, BS, MSW, PhD, LMSW-ACP, is Associate Professor of Social Work at Texas Christian University. He serves as Chair of the National Association of Social Workers/Texas Special Interest Committee on Gay, Lesbian, and Bisexual Issues. He also serves on the Council on Social Work Education Committee on Sexual Orientation and Gender Expression. At TCU, Jenkins serves as Co-chair of the eQ Alliance, a student organization that reaches out to sexual minorities.

Lon B. Johnston, BA, MSSW, PhD, LMSW-ACP, is Assistant Professor of Social Work at the University of Texas at Arlington. In 2001, he was selected to deliver the Federico Memorial Lecture for the Association of Baccalaureate Social Work Program Directors. Johnston was recently nominated for the Chancellor's Award for recognition of excellence in teaching and research at UT Arlington, and he has been the recipient of three other teaching and leadership awards during his teaching career. Johnston has been a James Still Fellow in the Faculty Scholars Program at the University of Kentucky.

Bev Lepischak, MSW, is a Program Coordinator in the Pride & Prejudice program at Central Toronto Youth Services in Toronto, Canada. Since 1997, she has been the Project Supervisor for Supporting Our Youth. A social worker by profession, Bev has provided education and training to thousands of health and social service providers and educators across Ontario about issues relevant to lesbian, gay, bisexual, transsexual, and transgender youth. For the past five years, Bev has also taught a course in Sexual Diversity at the School of Social Work at York University in Toronto.

Ann Lindsey, MSW, has been in social work practice since 1983 in a range of fields: public assistance, child protection, juvenile probation, developmental disabilities. Her undergraduate degree is from the University of Wyoming in Social Work. Ann received her MSW in May 2001 from Colorado State University. Ann's focus in social work is on macropractice and social change efforts. Currently, she is living in the province of Alberta, Canada.

Daphne McClellan, PhD, is Assistant Professor at the University of Maryland, Baltimore County. She received her MSW from the University of Oklahoma and her PhD from the Florence Heller School of Social Welfare at Brandeis University. Her research focuses primarily on GLBT families. Her most recent publications are "The Other Mother and Second Parent Adoption" published in the *Journal of Gay & Lesbian Social Services* and "Religious Minorities: Empowerment Through Reconciliation," a book chapter in *Strategies to Overcome Oppression and Discrimination for Marginalized Groups.*

Mirka J. Negroni, MA, has a bachelor of arts in psychology from Harvard University and a master's in public administration from Baruch College at the City University of New York. She currently works as an Associate Researcher at the National Institute for Public Health, Cuernavaca, Morelos, Mexico. Before moving to Mexico, Ms. Negroni worked at the International Gay and Lesbian Human Rights Commission in San Francisco, California. Ms. Negroni currently serves as Co-chair of the National Latina/o Lesbian, Gay, Bisexual and Transgender Organization, LLEGÓ. She served as editor of the Spanish version of UNSPOKEN RULES and has cowritten various articles and chapters on qualitative research on HIV/AIDS in Mexico and Central America.

Melanie D. Otis, PhD, is Assistant Professor and Director of Undergraduate Studies in the College of Social Work, University of Kentucky, Lexington, Kentucky. She has taught social work at the University of Kentucky for six years in both the graduate and undergraduate programs. The majority of her research focuses on social movements, social justice, and

LGBT concerns. Additionally, Dr. Otis does consultation and program evaluation for agencies and organizations working to develop social capital and community assets. She has worked as a social activist in the Lexington-Fayette County community since 1986.

Larry W. Owens, MSW, CSW, is a graduate of the Carver School of Social Work, The Southern Baptist Theological Seminary, Louisville, Kentucky. He holds a BS in psychology from Gardner-Webb University. He has 20 years of social work experience, primarily in child welfare. Currently, he is the Associate Director of Residential Services at Home of the Innocents in Louisville. Owens has served on numerous local, state, and national boards and committees, including the National Association of Social Workers and the Children's Alliance, and he is a peer reviewer for the Council on Accreditation.

Bjørg Sandkjær is a project manager in Kontekst Kommunikasjon, a consultancy firm in the health and human services in Oslo, Norway. A demographer, her research interests include reproductive health, both practical implementation and policy, and work with all aspects of HIV. She is presently working on health promotion strategies for lesbian, gay, and bisexual youth. She has a master's degree in demography from the London School of Economics.

Kristen Schilt, MA, is a graduate student in the Department of Sociology at the University of California, Los Angeles. Her MA is from the University of Texas at Austin and focuses on radical feminist subcultures. Her doctoral work explores the experience of transsexuals who openly transition on the job. She has a forthcoming article about music and feminism in *Popular Music and Society.*

Eve Shapiro, MA, has a master's degree in sociology and is currently a PhD candidate in sociology at the University of California at Santa Barbara. She is the author of "Trans Movements: From Gender Clinics to Internet Organizing," forthcoming in *Transgender Rights: Culture, Politics, and Law* by Currah, Juang, and Minter (University of Minnesota Press, forthcoming).

Louise Simmons, PhD, is Associate Professor at the University of Connecticut School of Social Work where she directs the Urban Semester Program and teaches community organization. She helped build the People for Change party in Hartford and was elected on the People for Change slate to the Hartford City Council from 1991 to 1993. Her research includes work on community-labor alliances, the challenges of progressive office holders, and the impact of welfare reform. She is the author of *Organizing in*

Hard Times: Labor and Neighborhoods in Hartford, published by Temple University Press, 1994.

Carol A. Snively, PhD, is Assistant Professor of Social Work at the University of Missouri-Columbia. Her research focuses on youth involvement in community change, effective helping strategies for minority youth, and the use of art making as a tool in community organization. She volunteers as an advisory board member for the local community-based, gay-straight, youth-adult alliance that is described in her manuscript. Before working in academia, Dr. Snively worked for 15 years as a registered/board certified art therapist and licensed social worker with youth and their families in mental health and addiction treatment.

Berge-Andreas Steinsvåg, MA, is the manager of Kontekst Kommunikasjon, a consultancy firm in the health and human services in Oslo, Norway. He is a licensed social worker and has a master's degree in communication from DePaul University, Chicago. Important themes in his work are challenged youth, and how to best reach disadvantaged groups. He is now working on strategies for a meaningful life for disabled youth.

Ingvill Størksen is a project manager in Kontekst Kommunikasjon, a consultancy firm in the health and human services in Oslo, Norway. With a degree in comparative politics from the University of Bergen, she has focused her research on policies related to homosexuality and the development of these in different cultural contexts. Presently, she is working on developing strategies for suicide prevention among gay men, lesbian women, and bisexual persons.

Urvashi Vaid is a longtime activist in the LGBT movement and former Director of the Policy Institute of the National Gay and Lesbian Task Force. She is the author of *Virtual Equality: The Mainstreaming of Gay and Lesbian Liberation* (Anchor Books) and co-editor of *Creating Change: Public Policy, Sexuality and Civil Rights* (St. Martin's). Ms. Vaid is currently the Deputy Director of the Governance and Civil Society Unit in the Peace and Social Justice Program of the Ford Foundation.

Jeff Vessels, MSW, is a graduate of the Kent School of Social Work, University of Louisville, where he now teaches social policy classes part time. He holds a BA in English from Brescia University. He has been the Executive Director of the American Civil Liberties Union of Kentucky since 1999. Previously, he was Administrator at Jefferson County Department for Human Services and Supervisor of HIV Prevention for the Kentucky Department for Health Services. He co-founded the Owensboro Gay Alliance in 1983 and the Louisville Youth Group, a social support organization for lesbian, gay, bisexual, and transgender youth in 1990.

Foreword

The progress of social movements is rarely linear. Movements are marked by periods of cataclysmic change and incrementalism, setbacks and surprising advances. What sustains their progress is grassroots action–the broad set of practices that get grouped under the term organizing. Grassroots organizing can involve public education strategies (like tabling at a supermarket), door to door canvassing, electoral activity, leadership training, or specific campaigns to change policies. It can encompass research, analysis, direct action tools as well as mobilizing strategies that enable constituent voices to be heard in the legislative arena.

Through more than five decades, the gay, lesbian, bisexual and transgender (GLBT) rights movement has won several major victories. Over terrain that remains bitterly contested in the fields of sexuality and religion, the GLBT movement has steadily redefined sexuality out of the realm of illness or shame where it never belonged and into the realm of health and well-being where it appropriately resides. Legal challenges brought by GLBT people facing discrimination and exclusion have transformed civil rights, criminal law, and family law. Cultural visibility has been realized because millions of people came out and live open and unashamed lives. This visibility, in turn, makes legislation for gay and lesbian equality possible.

Most dramatically, GLBT communities are no longer regarded as political pariahs but as a constituency whose votes and money are actively courted. Political access is a remarkable achievement, an amazing thing for a people who, just ten years ago, could not get a meeting with high level federal officials, much less dream that a President would speak at a GLBT political event. No doubt, the gain of political access has proved frustrating–as both the Clinton and Bush Administrations

---

Urvashi Vaid is affiliated with the Ford Foundation, 320 East 43rd Street, New York, NY 10017 USA.

[Haworth co-indexing entry note]: "Foreword." Vaid, Urvashi. Co-published simultaneously in *Journal of Gay & Lesbian Social Services* (Harrington Park Press, an imprint of The Haworth Press, Inc.) Vol. 16, No. 3/4, 2004, pp. xxvii-xxx; and: *Gay and Lesbian Rights Organizing: Community-Based Strategies* (ed: Yolanda C. Padilla) Harrington Park Press, an imprint of The Haworth Press, Inc., 2004, pp. xxi-xxiv. Single or multiple copies of this article are available for a fee from The Haworth Document Delivery Service [1-800-HAWORTH, 9:00 a.m. - 5:00 p.m. (EST). E-mail address: docdelivery@haworthpress.com].

© 2004 by The Haworth Press, Inc. All rights reserved.

paid lip service to inclusion but opposed key policy changes that would guarantee GLBT equality, such as nondiscrimination in all aspects of life (including military service), support for same-sex marriage, and adoption rights.

Thus, broad victories set the national backdrop for this book's examination of GLBT organizing, but the bulk of GLBT activism today takes place, as it always has, in the place where Eleanor Roosevelt once stated human rights began, "the small places close to home." Local and state activism remains the vibrant center of the movement–a fact demonstrated by the emergence of thousands of grassroots GLBT organizations in every corner of this country, and the steady progress these local groups have made. The liveliness of the movement is evident in the energetic growth of annual conferences like the National Gay and Lesbian Task Force (NGLTF) Creating Change Conference, which routinely gathers 2,500 activists each November. Statewide GLBT organizations or networks are active in every state and deal annually with literally hundreds of state level bills addressing sexuality, HIV, health policy, welfare, civil rights, and other issues of concern to GLBT communities. A growing number of GLBT elected and appointed officials nationwide bring a new voice and style of political leadership–one built on coalition politics and inclusive values. And four national Marches on Washington from 1979 to the mid-1990s have shown the growing diversity of the GLBT community.

Underlying all of these developments is the steady and determined community-based activism at the grassroots, which the articles in this volume describe. The stories told here are not widely known even in the communities in which they occurred–GLBT political history remains a secret archive. It is rarely covered in mainstream media, and its heroes are unsung. In fact, as this volume details, activists in rural Colorado, Missouri and Kentucky have won exciting civil rights battles, advanced public acceptance of homosexuality and gender variance, and created a more welcoming space for GLBT people. Indeed, the coalitions built among GLBT people, faith-based leaders, and communities of color in small cities like Louisville and Hartford are far deeper and stronger than coalitions that exist in major gay centers like New York, Boston, or Atlanta.

The case studies in this book also suggest the elements of winning strategies–even against a strong and relentless opposition. Among these successful approaches are strategic, issue-focused, local organizing campaigns; political alliances across race and class; personal relationships among leaders at the community level; the engagement of people most affected by discrimination and exclusion in designing services and solutions; increased political participation; and public education.

Several other lessons can be abstracted from the cases studied in this book. These include the need for a GLBT agenda that encompasses race, class, gender as well as sexuality; the importance of coalitions with other social justice constituencies; the accessibility of the state-level policy environment to GLBT people; and the need to engage homophobic arguments intellectually, culturally and morally.

First, these studies suggest that winning campaigns for change are those that offer a broad and inclusive vision of what the GLBT movement is trying to achieve. A narrow focus on sexuality alone is less effective than a framework that enables the movement to explain why the change being sought will benefit all members of the community in general, in addition to helping GLBT people in particular. The story of the Rightville, Colorado, school-reform effort, for example, suggests that activists made progress when they placed the harassment facing GLBT youth into an overall framework of a right to safety that all children should enjoy. The larger frame did not erase the particular problems facing GLBT youth at all; instead, it placed the problem in a context that religious conservatives and liberal allies could not ignore.

A related truth revealed through these case studies is that successful policy campaigns depend on the existence of alliances between GLBT people and other constituencies. Activists have turned civil rights losses into victories because they established long-term and reciprocal relationships with other constituencies for change in the city–constituencies such as progressive religious leaders, communities of color, and progressive democrats, among others. The models of organizing used in Hartford and Louisville have much to teach organizers in other cities.

Third, this volume underscores the fact that local and state-level activism can advance even when federal action for GLBT rights has stalled. This notion of progress at the state level exceeding progress at the national runs counter to the history of civil rights legislation in this country. However, a few factors make it true. For one, conservatives are dominant at the national level and have stymied GLBT efforts to make gains in Congress. Meanwhile, the devolution of authority to the state level from the federal over the last twenty years has created greater opportunities for local action over matters of welfare, health care, and education policy. This shift holds promise for emerging constituencies like GLBT people, Latinos, and African-Americans, who can band together to exert new power over local elections and officials. Finally, the GLBT movement's focus on community building leaves the movement with a real base and potential resources that are better organized into local networks than they are into national ones. Harnessing the energies of youth organizations, community centers, anti-violence groups, social clubs as well as health and social service agencies has enabled urban GLBT communities to build greater political power.

Fourth, this volume surfaces the truth that politics, legislative advocacy, litigation, and federal arenas are not the only forums for GLBT activism. The battle against homophobia requires an engagement with the arguments deployed against GLBT equality. In making these arguments, the role of think tanks and policy analysis is critical, for the reasons that Sean Cahill so carefully explains. But defamation and misinformation must also be challenged in the public square through media and cultural organizations. Indeed, the success of the Gay and Lesbian Alliance Against Defamation (GLAAD) has been one of the unique strategic victories of the GLBT movement to date. This volume touches on the central role that pro-GLBT religious organizations play–in the lives of many in GLBT communities, as well as in challenging the characterization of homosexuality as immoral and sinful–through a description of one of the largest pro-gay congregations in the country.

Ultimately, the case studies in this book tell a hopeful and inspiring story. People at the local level are making progress on GLBT equality. It is the accumulated impact of local practice that gives the GLBT movement its energy and resilience. Whatever its form, grassroots organizing–defined as the varying processes through which people work with each other to articulate their concerns and enact policy change–is the muscle behind the political transformation of GLBT life that we experience today.

Urvashi Vaid
Ford Foundation

BUILDING COALITIONS AND CHANGING COMMUNITIES

Organizing for Change: One City's Journey Toward Justice

Erlene Grise-Owens
Jeff Vessels
Larry W. Owens

Erlene Grise-Owens, EdD, MSW, MRE, is Associate Professor, Spalding University, School of Social Work, 851 South Fourth Street, Louisville, KY 40203.

Jeff Vessels, MSSW, is Executive Director, American Civil Liberties Union of Kentucky (ACLU), 425 W. Muhammad Ali Boulevard, Suite 230, Louisville, KY 40202.

Larry W. Owens, MSW, is Associate Director of Residential Services, Home of the Innocents, 485 E. Gray Street, Louisville, KY 40202.

The National Gay and Lesbian Task Force recognized the Fairness Campaign and the Kentucky Fairness Alliance for their work on the passage of nondiscrimination ordinances in three Kentucky communities. Jeff Vessels participated at varying levels throughout the grassroots campaign described in this article and has served as director of the American Civil Liberties Union of Kentucky since 1999.

[Haworth co-indexing entry note]: "Organizing for Change: One City's Journey Toward Justice." Grise-Owens, Erlene, Jeff Vessels, and Larry W. Owens. Co-published simultaneously in *Journal of Gay & Lesbian Social Services* (Harrington Park Press, an imprint of The Haworth Press, Inc.) Vol. 16, No. 3/4, 2004, pp. 1-15; and: *Gay and Lesbian Rights Organizing: Community-Based Strategies* (ed: Yolanda C. Padilla) Harrington Park Press, an imprint of The Haworth Press, Inc., 2004, pp. 1-15. Single or multiple copies of this article are available for a fee from The Haworth Document Delivery Service [1-800-HAWORTH, 9:00 a.m. - 5:00 p.m. (EST). E-mail address: docdelivery@haworthpress.com].

Journal of Gay & Lesbian Social Services, Vol. 16(3/4) 2004
http://www.haworthpress.com/store/product.asp?sku=J041
© 2004 by The Haworth Press, Inc. All rights reserved.
10.1300/J041v16n03_01

SUMMARY. This article illustrates a multilevel process of organizing for gay, lesbian, bisexual, and transgender rights carried out by concerned citizens in Louisville, Kentucky. It describes how a grassroots campaign, the Fairness Campaign, lobbied successfully for a local ordinance protecting GLBT rights in Louisville. Broader implications for advocacy and organizing efforts include an understanding that significant change requires coalition building and systemic intervention, that organizers need to be ready to take advantage of key opportunities to take action, and that action must be sustained even beyond victory. *[Article copies available for a fee from The Haworth Document Delivery Service: 1-800-HAWORTH. E-mail address: <docdelivery@haworthpress.com> Website: <http://www.HaworthPress.com> © 2004 by The Haworth Press, Inc. All rights reserved.]*

KEYWORDS. Advocacy, organizing, grassroots campaign, GLBT rights, Louisville, Kentucky

Using a case study format, this article illustrates how concerned citizens in one city organized at multiple levels for gay, lesbian, bisexual, and transgender (GLBT) rights. A confluence of events in Louisville, Kentucky, over almost two decades resulted in significant strides for the GLBT population and, thus, the city as a whole. The story describes how a grassroots organization, the Fairness Campaign, lobbied successfully for an ordinance establishing GLBT rights in housing, employment, and public accommodations. Amidst this campaign, the firing of a lesbian employee at a child welfare agency ignited a firestorm of support for GLBT rights within the local community. This incident was pivotal in the Fairness Campaign's success in securing the ordinance protecting GLBT rights. This article relates both the events that transpired in this one city and the "stories" of some of the persons involved, based on interviews with several leaders of the Fairness Campaign, as well as public media accounts and other relevant documents. The article describes various strands of action that came together to form a strong cord of change. It concludes with a summary of "lessons learned," based on community organizing strategies that can be applied in other contexts.

BEGINNING A JOURNEY TOWARD JUSTICE

Louisville, Kentucky, is situated in Jefferson County, on the Ohio River, bordering Indiana. With a county and city combined population of almost 700,000, metro Louisville is the largest city in the state. Most Louisville residents see Louisville as "special," pointing to "our outstanding park system, excellent arts and cultural attractions, affordable cost of living, [and] low crime rate" (Higdon, 2002, D4). Made up of distinct neighborhoods, Louisville is described by locals as a "big small town." Education, health, and social services comprise the primary industry in Louisville, and manufacturing the second. Louisville has a strong web of social services and internationally recognized medical facilities–some of which are associated with the large state university. Louisville has a particularly diverse faith make-up, including two seminaries (Presbyterian and Southern Baptist); two historic Catholic universities; the Presbyterian U.S.A. National Headquarters; strong Catholic, Jewish, Presbyterian, and Southern Baptist communities, along with Mormon, Muslim, and myriad religions. With a population of approximately 63 percent white and 33 percent African American, Louisville also has a burgeoning immigrant and refugee community–one of the fastest growing in the country.

Louisville is a community of radical fundamentalists, radical liberals, and every stripe in between those two extremes. Louisville has a civil rights history of virulent segregationists, heroic activists, and those along the continuum. As this snapshot of Louisville illustrates, the city provides both a unique and universal context for local gay rights activism. Button, Rienzo, and Wald (1997) report that over the past two decades GLBT mobilization has become a significant social movement, but that much of this work transpires at the community level. Although the movement varies from city to city, a primary goal is to "create or change various laws and policies in order to secure basic civil rights for gays and lesbians" (Button, Rienzo, & Wald, 1997, 58). Hence, the unique story of Louisville's journey toward justice has universal applications.

As part of a larger civil rights movement, the GLBT community in Louisville and Jefferson County became visibly organized and engaged in political advocacy in the early 1980s. In 1983, a small ad hoc grassroots organization, called the Greater Louisville Human Rights Coalition (GLHRC), formed. GLHRC, begun by lesbians and gay men already engaged in combating racism, began pressuring elected officials and public agencies to address discrimination against GLBT persons in employment, housing, and public accommodations. GLHRC's proposal to extend equal rights protections gained endorsement of the Louisville/Jefferson County Human Relations Commission and several members of Louisville's city council, the Board of Aldermen (Fairness Campaign, n.d.). However, the effort mired in claims that such discrimination did not occur, making legal protection unnecessary. In fact, people who lost jobs or were refused housing or public services were afraid to "out" themselves (call attention to their sexual orientation) in the process, fearing yet more discrimination. Thus, there was little visible evidence of discrimination. Nevertheless, these early advocacy efforts laid the foundation for more extensive future organizing.

After several years marked by lack of action on the part of city officials, GLHRC's agenda evolved into the first Louisville GLBT rights march, the March for Justice, in June 1987. About 300 people walked to the steps of the Jefferson County courthouse. At that first march, only a handful of GLBT people were willing to be visible or quoted by name in local print and electronic media, because of fear of losing their jobs and homes. The media agreed to show the faces of, or speak to, only a few designated spokespersons. Television accounts of the march consisted of images of marchers' feet as they passed by cameras sitting on the ground. While no concrete policy changes occurred, this first march generated empowerment and visibility. The experience marked a new plateau of possibilities for the GLBT community and supporters. However, this march also prompted more opposition, including death threats against some of the organizers and participants.

In ensuing years, political and social action in the GLBT community in Louisville grew. GLBT rights organizations at the University of Louisville were established. In conjunction with the broad-based Progressive Student's League, the Gay and Lesbian Student Union was formed and later developed into the Gay and Lesbian Or Bisexual Alliance (GLOBAL). The Louisville chapter of Parents and Friends of Lesbians and Gays (PFLAG) and Louisville Youth Group (for self-identified GLBT youth) were established. Other social organizations were formed by Lutherans, Presbyterians, Southern Baptists, Catholics, Jews, and others to provide venues for GLBT people of faith to affirm their faith.

In 1990 a highly publicized hate crime incident propelled pressure to pass a local Hate Crimes Ordinance, which covered race, religion, ethnicity, and sexual orientation. Introduced by a black member of the Louisville Board of Aldermen, this measure was supported by a broad coalition of justice organizations–led by the Kentucky Rainbow Coalition and the Kentucky Alliance Against Racist and Political Repression. Key to this effort was the decision by the diverse coalition to retain inclusive language. In November 1991 the Louisville Board of Aldermen passed, by a vote of 7 to 4, an anti-hate crimes law that included sexual orientation–the first major victory for gay rights in Louisville and the state of Kentucky. This victory was an important catalyst in creating a more formal organization focused on GLBT rights–within the continued context of broad-based justice efforts.

The March for Justice had become an annual event. At the 1991 March for Justice, GLBT leaders announced the formation of a grassroots organization, the Fairness Campaign. The name "Fairness" was strategically selected as a term that would promote GLBT rights as a collaborative issue of equality–which the broader public could embrace. The message was simple: Fairness means stopping discrimination, and all discrimination is wrong (D. Farrell, personal communication, November 29, 2001). The Fairness Campaign advocated for a "Fairness Amendment" to change the city's laws regarding employment, housing, and public accommodations discrimination. The local Human Relations Commission reaffirmed unanimous support for the ordinance (Muhammad, 1991).

In December, the first public hearing on the Fairness Amendment took place. It lasted more than five hours and was the first time a law-making body in Kentucky had held such a hearing. The hearing galvanized support in three ways. First, this event demonstrated the connection between gay rights and other basic civil rights activism when a Fairness Campaign representative read a list of dozens of organizations outside the GLBT community who supported the Fairness Amendment. The organizations represented a broad range of groups, including union locals, anti-racist organizations, women's rights groups, and affordable housing coalitions. Second, it gave a face to the GLBT rights movement and empowered GLBT people by allowing them to publicly tell their stories of discrimination. Finally, this forum revealed some of the opposition's unfounded arguments against the passage of gay rights protections, forcing the general public to grapple with its own attitudes (C. Kraemer, personal communication, November 2, 2001).

As the push for a vote on the Fairness Amendment continued, the Fairness Campaign created a political action committee, C-FAIR (Committee for Fairness and Individual Rights). The goal of C-FAIR was to support friendly candidates with contributions and volunteers. In addition, the Fairness Campaign supported the formation of a coalition of religious leaders (Religious Leaders for Fairness), which could counter opposition arguments grounded in religious terms (Muhammad & Baker, 1991). The religious leaders included representatives from Presbyterian, Catholic, Methodist, United Church of Christ, Baptist, Jewish, and other faiths. This coalition largely stemmed from the more informal faith-based social organizations–noted earlier–that had been meeting over the years.

The Louisville Board of Aldermen introduced the Fairness Amendment on November 12, 1991. As a December 23 vote grew near, the Fairness Campaign organized rallies and candlelight vigils. However, when a supportive Alderman suddenly switched his position, under apparent pressure from his employer, the Board of Aldermen failed to take a vote on the Fairness Amendment (McDonough & Hershberg, 1991).

STRATEGIES, STEPS, AND STYLE:
MOVING TOWARD FAIRNESS

Disappointed, but undaunted, the Fairness Campaign prepared for a long battle. The opening of its headquarters on a very visible Louisville thoroughfare in March 1992 provided the Campaign with both legitimacy and logistical space. In addition, the Campaign changed from a confrontational and sometimes militant style to a "more sophisticated and less confrontational style" (Stewart, 1995, p. A1). Previously, the Campaign had used more adversarial approaches such as aggressively confronting politicians. Switching from combat boots to business suits, Carla Wallace, the Fairness Campaign's Co-coordinator, stated the Campaign sought to "create a more peaceful atmosphere in which it could rationally discuss discrimination" (Stewart, 1995, p. A1). In ensuing years, the organization grew as a political entity and decided to build upon the partial successes that it had enjoyed in past years. Four strategies used by the Fairness Campaign played a key role in its growing effectiveness.

First, the Fairness Campaign headquarters provided a myriad of vehicles for GLBT people and their supporters to participate at varying levels. The first paid staff person was hired in 1993, primarily to coordinate the growing volunteer base (in 1996, a half-time staff person was added). The March for Justice continued annually and consistently grew in size. The Fairness Ordinance came up for a vote several times before it was ultimately approved, and before each vote the Fairness Campaign organized public hearings. Supporters wearing t-shirts and buttons supporting Fairness attended every Board of Aldermen meeting from 1992 forward, even when the issue wasn't on the agenda, to remind the Board that the issue was still present. Postcards were available for supporters to sign and send to their Alderman or Alderwoman. Hundreds expressed support by posting "Fairness Does a City Good" and "Fairness = Everyone" yard signs throughout the city and county, beginning in 1997. Finally, to prepare volunteers for ongoing work, the organization trained participants in lobbying.

A second strategic focus of the Fairness Campaign was a public education campaign to increase the visibility of GLBT people, expose discrimination, and expand the support for the Fairness Amendment. "Hate Hurts" ads on city buses and radio ads were begun, and a "Fairness: No More, No Less" banner was displayed regularly in the Kentucky Derby Parade. Twice, full-page signature ads in the local newspaper included the names of more than 1,000 individuals in support of the Fairness Campaign, including some prominent civic and business leaders. In 1993, the Fairness Campaign joined the statewide Kentucky Fairness Alliance (KFA) in sponsoring informational booths at the Kentucky State Fair. The mission of the KFA is to do statewide lobbying, public education, community organizing, and leadership development for broader GLBT rights and establish coalitions with other justice organizations.

In an effort to expand public education, in 1994 Fairness supporters began going door-to-door to deliver educational materials and discuss the ordinance with Louisville residents. A broad range of Fairness Campaign spokespersons appeared in the media, so that people in the broader community were more likely to see representatives who looked like them (J. Rodgers, personal communication, November 29, 2001). Furthermore, Fairness Campaign members developed important relationships with key community leaders, including the Alderman president–using both statistics and stories to raise awareness of the oppression of GLBT persons. The organization strategically created a public awareness campaign to pass the amendment, rather than making political deals behind closed doors with elected officials. The intent was to empower GLBT people and their supporters in order to create lasting changes and anchor the struggle for GLBT rights in the broader movement for justice. According to its leaders, the Fairness Campaign was not just about passing a law, but about creating a movement to sustain and build upon the law once it passed (D. Farrell & J. Rodgers, personal communication, November 29, 2001). Public education efforts seemed to pay off: A 1996 poll found that 65 percent of Louisvillians favored the Fairness Amendment (McDonough, 1996).

A third tactic of the Fairness Campaign was to actively engage in political races. The Campaign focused on "winnable" elections of supporters, rather than diffusing energy toward defeating detractors. The Committee for Fairness and Individual Rights raised money and dispatched volunteers for supportive Alderman candidates, made endorsements, and issued voter information cards. Voter registration drives were coordinated with a local GLBT community newspaper and with bars catering to GLBT people. In 1993, an openly gay man and cofounder of the Fairness Campaign, Ken Herndon, ran a surprisingly close race against one of the more anti-Fairness Aldermen. In later elections, some Alderman candidates who were publicly pro-Fairness won surprising victories. The Fairness Campaign's support was pivotal: One pro-Fairness candidate won by fewer than 20 votes. As evidence of its growing impact, in 1998, C-FAIR received completed questionnaires regarding Fairness support from 70 candidates, interviewed 50, and endorsed 25.

Fourth, as a core strategy, the Fairness Campaign built bridges between Fairness and other civil rights movements. From the outset, the Fairness Campaign linked with other civil rights organizations, drawing parallels to other justice movements. A broad coalition of civil rights leaders held a pro-Fairness news conference in 1995. For its part, the Fairness Campaign also joined anti-racist actions in the community and held "dismantling racism" workshops. As a visible ally, the Campaign held fundraisers jointly with other GLBT organizations, the Kentucky Alliance Against Racist and Political Repression, the American Civil Liberties Union of Kentucky, and others (Fairness Campaign, n.d.). This coalition building and involvement in the broader struggles for justice–in particular the battle against racism–was key. (A more comprehensive description of this distinctive aspect of the Fairness Campaign's success in community organizing is provided by Stults, 1999/2000.)

In spite of concerted efforts and strategies, in 1992 the Fairness Amendment was defeated 8 to 4. One month after the defeat of the amendment, the Kentucky Supreme Court ruled that the state's sodomy law was unlawful under the state's Constitution, thus eliminating some opponents' arguments that the Fairness Amendment would encourage illegal activity. Nevertheless, a scaled-back version of the amendment, covering only employment discrimination, failed 7 to 4 in 1995, after which 23 supporters were arrested in an act of civil disobedience. In 1997, the legislation failed on a vote of 7 to 3 with two abstentions. Another 52 supporters were arrested in peaceful protest after the 1997 vote (Fairness Campaign, n.d.).

Although building community support, the Campaign seemed stymied at the political level. Nevertheless, the Fairness Campaign decided to push for votes of the Board of Aldermen, even when it anticipated defeat, in order to create a public record and continue to build visibility of the issue. Up to this point, some Board members maintained that they did not support the amendment because they saw no compelling evidence that discrimination was occurring. A 1998 event turned the tide.

PIVOTAL EVENT: LOCAL AGENCY FIRES A LESBIAN EMPLOYEE

On October 23, 1998, Kentucky Baptist Homes for Children (KBHC), fired an employee, Alicia Pedreira, explicitly because she was lesbian (Barbee, 1998). Subsequent media coverage of the firing provided prominent attention to discrimination based on sexual orientation. Pedreira's story soon became common knowledge in Louisville and Jefferson County and garnered significant national attention. A *New York Times Magazine* article and a local alternative newspaper, the *Louisville Eccentric Observer (LEO)*, provided comprehensive accounts of Pedreira's story (Jones, 1998; Press, 2001). This incident became a pivotal point for the Fairness Campaign by putting a face on discrimination, whereas in previous discrimination reports employers avoided the issue of sexual orientation by saying they fired GLBT employees for other reasons, such as tardiness. Pedreira's case was blatant–and timely. Pedreira and her partner's willingness to be public about KBHC's actions raised critical awareness and inspired others to speak publicly about incidents of discrimination that they had endured (C. Kraemer, personal communication, November 2, 2001).

During the same month as Pedreira's firing, an openly gay Wyoming college student, Matthew Shepard, was tied to a fencepost and beaten to death in a hate crime that shocked the nation. Shepard's death was a stark image of the brutal reality of anti-GLBT hate and discrimination. This juxtaposition of events was profound (Poynter, 1998).

PARTNERS ON THE JOURNEY:
A COMMUNITY RESPONDS

Segments of the Louisville community supported the discriminatory actions of the Kentucky Baptist Homes for Children and opposed the Fairness Amendment. Some conservative Christian groups spoke out against the ordinance. For example, a black religious leader denounced the amendment, suggesting that it would somehow diminish the rights of racial minorities (Scanlon, 1999). However, much of the community reacted negatively to Pedreira's firing and spoke out in favor of the Fairness Ordinance. Reverend Jesse Jackson (1999) wrote a letter to the Louisville *Courier-Journal* to support the amendment and assailed the local minister's race-based opposition. Local civil rights leaders and religious leaders for Fairness spoke publicly of their support (Fairness Campaign, n.d.). The Fairness Campaign's earlier efforts in forming coalitions with these leaders resulted in a powerful "united front" for justice. Much of the local social service community was also critical of KBHC's actions, and the schools of social work in two local universities discontinued student field placements with KBHC. All in all, these actions were seen as significant support for the goals of the Fairness Ordinance (e.g., Barbee, November 18, 1998).

SUCCESS AT LAST:
FAIRNESS ORDINANCE PASSES

With the myriad of advocacy efforts, the prominent media attention of Pedreira's firing and Shepard's death, and the groundswell of community support, the opportunity was ripe for passing the Fairness Ordinance. One obstacle remained: one critical vote was needed. The president of the Board of Alderman, Steve Magre, had opposed the Fairness Ordinance. In order to address Magre's concerns, GLBT youth met with him and told their stories of fear and discrimination. Moreover, the Fairness Campaign successfully lobbied at least one local religious leader to issue a statement supporting the amendment as a human rights and justice issue, virtually reversing his 1992 public statement opposing the amendment (Scanlon & Murphy, 1995).

On January 12, 1999, only days after two pro-Fairness Aldermen and one pro-Fairness Alderwoman were sworn into office, the Fairness Amendment was reintroduced. The new pro-Fairness votes joined with three pro-Fairness votes already secure on the Board. Finally, the Board president "had a change of heart" (Nord, 1999, p. B6) and changed his vote to "Yes," thus providing the seventh vote needed for the simple majority on the 12-member board. The Board president announced that he became convinced that "there are instances of discrimination in employment that are morally wrong" (Nord, 1999, p. B6). The Fairness Ordinance passed on January 26, 1999, forbidding sexual orientation and gender identity discrimination in employment (McDonough & Shafer, 1999).

What caused Magre's "change of heart?" Why did the ordinance pass, after three failed attempts? Tina Ward-Pugh (personal communication, November 5, 2001), chair of the Louisville Board of Aldermen's Committee on Fairness, delineated several factors. First, political compromise: Alderman Magre would only support the employment amendment and a compromise was reached. Second, personal relationships: Magre had come to know GLBT persons. Surveys indicate that those who personally know someone who is gay will more likely favor gay rights (Button, Rienzo, & Wald, 1997). Third, timing of pivotal events: Pedreira's firing and Shepard's death brought timely and startling attention to the issue. Finally, incremental efforts: the Fairness Campaign's efforts were building to a crescendo of support, with the less confrontational tactics being seen as more palatable to local politicians.

Following the victory in Louisville, two of the three members of the Jefferson County Fiscal Court announced that they were interested in passing a countywide ordinance. Heretofore, the Fairness Campaign had not specifically targeted the county because the Campaign mirrored the history of other civil rights legislation, which started with the city and then moved out into the county. But, when Fairness leaders saw that the City of Louisville was moving toward passage of the Fairness Ordinance, they expanded the focus to the county ordinance (Shafer, 1999). Although no concentrated base building had been done in the county, the organizing efforts in the city produced spillover effects in the county. Many Fairness supporters who were county residents saw an opportunity to press their local officials to pass a Fairness Ordinance. An atmosphere had been created in which it was politically expedient to support an ordinance. The Campaign and its justice allies accentuated the need for consistency in civil rights throughout the city and county and played on the historic competitiveness between city and county government to outshine each other (C. Kraemer, personal communication). After a series of public hearings, the three County Commissioners "upped the ante" and proposed an ordinance broader than the city ordinance, offering protection not only in employment, but in housing and public accommodations, as well. The county ordinance passed in October 1999 by a vote of 3 to 1, with the County Judge/Executive casting the only negative vote. In mid 2001, the Kentucky Court of Appeals ruled that the broader county ordinance applies to Louisville and the other cities within Jefferson County. In addition to the passage of the ordinance in Jefferson County, two other Kentucky communities–Lexington-Fayette County and Henderson–also passed Fairness ordinances in 1999, following the Louisville success (Poynter, 1999).

MAINTENANCE AND MORE: KEYS TO ONGOING SUCCESS

The above discussion portrays the multifaceted efforts to organize for GLBT rights. All the efforts were important in the struggle for fairness and justice. The successes of these efforts are to be celebrated. However, the story does not end there. Ongoing efforts are necessary both to continue the progress and to retain the ground gained. For example, the city of Louisville will merge with Jefferson County in 2003. A new governing body, the Metro Council, will be elected. In order to retain the Fairness Ordinance inclusive of employment, housing, and public accommodations that has been approved for the merger, fairness-friendly candidates must be elected to the Metro Council. Moreover, in the race for the Metro mayor, the candidates' platform statements must be examined in light of fairness issues. Thus, the Fairness Campaign and other entities must continue to advocate for political candidates who will secure fairness.

The Fairness Ordinances have already faced legal challenges. Supported by a law firm founded by televangelist Pat Robertson, a Louisville gynecologist, J. Barrett Hyman, filed suit to overturn the Louisville and Jefferson County Fairness Ordinances (Schaver, 1999). Hyman claimed that by barring him from discriminating on the basis of sexual orientation and gender identity in his medical business, the ordinances would punish him for his religious beliefs. The ACLU intervened on behalf of the Fairness Campaign and sent two of its members to help the Louisville and Jefferson County governments defend the ordinances. As with Pedreira's case, defense of the ordinances took on national prominence, calling into question whether individual religious beliefs "trump" gay rights laws. Similar legal challenges had previously been filed elsewhere around the country, but courts dismissed them on technical grounds. In an unprecedented move, the U.S. Department of Justice filed a friend-of-the-court brief in 2000, siding with the ACLU and citing concerns that if Hyman prevailed, the government's ability to enforce a broad range of civil rights laws would be jeopardized. On March 21, 2001, a federal court dismissed Hyman's lawsuit. However, Hyman appealed the decision to the U.S. Court of Appeals for the Sixth Circuit (Fairness Campaign, n.d.). At this writing, the case is set for oral arguments. Other legal challenges could be forthcoming. Ongoing efforts must be made to ensure that fairness-friendly judges are installed. Organized efforts at all levels are necessary to guard the progress made and build toward increased justice.

LESSONS LEARNED FROM THE JOURNEY: IMPLICATIONS FOR ORGANIZING FOR CHANGE

The story of Louisville's struggle for GLBT rights provides lessons for broader contexts. The following discussion synthesizes six themes that emerged–lessons learned that have implications for organizing for change. Although these lessons evolved inductively through a local movement that did not use any one specific model of community organizing, the themes reflect classic guidelines developed by activists, such as those proposed by Saul Alinsky (1971).

Lesson #1: Small, consistent steps can lead to large, significant strides. In *Rules for Radicals* (1971), Alinsky emphasized that activism is "thwarted by the desire for instant and dramatic change" (p. xx). This city's story took place over almost two decades. The movement began in the early 1980s with a handful of people. Most of the persons who participated in the first March for Justice in 1987 were afraid to be visible. Furthermore, in one alderman election fewer than 20 votes determined that a fairness-friendly candidate would be elected. Those who voted made a small but critical effort for GLBT rights. Persistent and consistent steps led to slow, yet solid, success.

Lesson #2: Significant change requires systemic intervention. Examining the history and complexity of how change occurred in this city leads to systemic understanding. As Alinsky (1971) aptly observed, "everything is functionally interrelated" (p. 15). All the efforts made in passing the Louisville ordinance melded to create the desired change. The advocacy and education efforts of the Fairness Campaign were linked with political strategies focusing on winnable races and building political relationships. Personal relationships impacted the policymaking process. The reaction of the community to the pivotal event of Pedreira's firing pressured politicians to act. The acts of protest, advocacy, and education–both within the systems and outside the systems–were complementary. Political compromises were as important as the unrelenting advocacy efforts. Legal interventions, coalition building, education efforts, relationship nurturing, political engagement, advocacy strategies, compromises, and protests–all these parts and more came together to create change.

Lesson # 3: The personal is political and the political is personal. A classic cornerstone of Alinsky's (1971) approach was that social change happens through personal relationships and experiences. Fairness Campaign members fostered relationships with politicians that led to increased understanding, through respectful relationships. Clearly, personal lives and political processes are connected. Another Alinsky axiom is that "all our welfares" are interdependent (p. 23). In its core organizing, the Fairness Campaign accented the commonalties of all types of injustice and developed relationships with people in other justice movements. With this approach, justice-seeking communities inoculate themselves against the divide-and-conquer tactics that often are used by opponents. Understanding the systemic nature of oppression leads to the realization that coalition building is needed. Understanding and utilizing this connection leads to changes in social policies, human lives, and community cultures.

Lesson #4: Adaptation, patience, perseverance, planning, and a few lucky breaks bring success. Alinsky (1971) asserts that activists must be "resilient, adaptable to shifting political circumstances, and sensitive enough to the process . . . to avoid being trapped by their own tactics" (p. 6). He also notes, "to the organizer, compromise is a key and beautiful word" (p. 59). In this city's story, success required changes in strategies, political compromises, and adaptations every step of the way. The goals were not reached quickly or easily. The successful passing of the Fairness Ordinance required years of planning and perseverance. While it was not planned or orchestrated, the Pedreira firing came at an ideal juncture. The Fairness Campaign laid the groundwork and had the mechanisms in place when the opportunity arose to present the Fairness Ordinance again. Consistent with Alinsky's framework, Fairness built a "mass power base" (p. 113) and, thus was poised to use timing, "an essential of organizing" (p. 158), to promote passage of the ordinance.

Lesson # 5: Success must be maintained with continued action. After so much hard work, it is tempting to become complacent with the progress made. However, the success can be gradually eroded by lack of continued attention, or the success can be shot down by persistent detractors. Part of the character of the Fairness Campaign is its commitment to long-term investment and multilevel involvement. For instance, by providing vehicles for all supporters to work on behalf of the legislation, the Fairness Campaign ensures that everyone shares in the commitment to achieving and maintaining the success. Moreover, as a result of skills-building, supporters now have concrete tools to build additional successes. Two classic "rules" from Alinsky mirror this lesson. Alinsky noted that activists must "keep the pressure on" (p. xxiii) and that a single issue is a "fatal strait jacket" (p. 120). Issues must be couched both in specific terms and broader contexts so that constituents do not quit after one victory (or loss), but continue the process of pursuing justice.

Lesson #6: Do not lose sight of the desired goal. Just as it is tempting to become complacent in success, it is even more tempting to lose sight of desired goals when success seems intangible–which can result in losing hope or resorting to ineffective measures. For example, while it can be tempting to spend energy countering or deflecting opponents' arguments, it is more effective to address them factually in moving forward with planned strategies toward specific objectives. Oftentimes, opponents' unfounded arguments actually benefit supporters, because these characteristics stand in stark contrast to a measured, well-reasoned, and researched approach of supporters. As Alinsky (1971) discovered, activists can practice "political jujitsu" (p. 152), allowing opponents to create their own defeat.

A significant symbol of the success of the efforts for GLBT rights in this city is that in the first steps toward fairness, the 1987 March for Justice, only the feet of most of the marchers could be shown publicly. Those feet have trod a long journey and have been joined by many others along the way. Now, years later, both the feet and faces for fairness are more publicly prominent. The journey continues.

REFERENCES

Alinsky, S. (1972). *Rules for radicals: A pragmatic primer for realistic radicals.* New York: Random House.

Barbee, C. D. (1998, November 18). Baptist youth home fires lesbian worker. *The Courier-Journal,* pp. A1, A6.

Barbee, C. D. (1998, November 25). Protesters decry Baptists' firing of lesbian employee. *The Courier-Journal,* p. B1.

Button, J. W., Rienzo, B. A., & Wald, K. D. (1997). *Private lives, public conflicts: Battles over gay rights in American communities.* Washington, DC: Congressional Quarterly Press.

Fairness Campaign (n.d.). Fairness campaign timeline. Retrieved November 15, 2001, from <http://fairness.org/time_line/time_linc.htm>.

Higdon, S. (2002, August 18). Louisville: Becoming special [editorial]. *The Courier Journal,* p. D3.

Jackson, J. (1999, January 26). Fairness ordinance 'is needed' [Letter to the editor]. *The Courier Journal,* p. A8.

Jones, M. (1998, November 18). Every picture tells a story. *LEO (Louisville's Eccentric Observer),* pp. 11-14.

McDonough, R. (1996, July 12). Bluegrass state poll. Many would welcome homosexuals as neighbors. Gay-rights law backed in metro area survey. *The Courier Journal,* p. A1.

McDonough, R., & Hershberg, B. Z. (1991, December 11). Bank memo says Bather now opposes gay-rights law–He denies content or being pressured. *The Courier-Journal,* p. A1.

McDonough, R., & Shafer, S. S. (1999, January 27). Gay-rights ordinance passes–Aldermen vote 7-5 to outlaw job discrimination. *The Courier-Journal*, p. A1.

Muhammad, L. (1991, November 13). Hate crimes bill passes–Ordinance includes protection for gays. *The Courier-Journal*, p. A1.

Muhammad, L., & Baker, K. (1991, November 15). City amendment would protect gays from housing, job discrimination. *The Courier-Journal*, p. B2.

National Association of Social Workers (1996). *Code of ethics*. Washington, DC: Author.

Nord, T. (1999, January 24). 3 changes gave gay-rights effort new hope. Compromise, new aldermen altered outlook. *The Courier-Journal*, pp. B1, B6.

Plaintiff's Brief, *Alicia Pedreira et al. v. Kentucky Baptist Homes for Children*, Commonwealth of Kentucky et al. (2000, April 17). U.S. District, Western Division of Kentucky, Court 00-CV-210.

Poynter, C. (1998, October 14). 'This could be my son' Slain gay student mourned. *The Courier-Journal*, p. A1.

Poynter, C. (1999, October 8). Kentucky gay-rights battle Anti-bias ordinances fuel political, religious debate. *The Courier-Journal*, p. A1.

Poynter, C. (2000, June 29). Baptist Homes rejects new state contract. *The Courier-Journal*, p. A1, A8.

Poynter, C. (July 25, 2001) Baptist Homes' firing of lesbian is upheld. But suit to proceed on issues of group getting state funds. *The Courier-Journal*, pp. A1,10.

Press, E. (2001, April 1). Faith-based furor. *New York Times Magazine*, p. 62-65.

Scanlon, L. (1999, January 20). Black pastor fights protection for gays. Minister says issue is not like fight for racial equality. *The Courier-Journal*, p. A8.

Scanlon, L., & Murphy, T. (1995, March 25). Gay-rights debaters share the air–but not points of view. *The Courier-Journal*, p. A1

Schaver, M. (1999). Gay-rights ordinances challenged. *The Courier-Journal*, p. B1.

Shafer, S.S. (1999, January 14). Gay-rights issue spreads to county. *The Courier-Journal*, pp. B1-B2.

Stewart, N. (1995, March 14). Gay-rights group tones down tactics. *The Courier-Journal*, p. A1.

Stults, K. (1999/2000, Winter). Moving mountains for fairness. *Southern Exposure*, 26-32.

One Community's Path to Greater Social Justice: Building on Earlier Successes

Melanie D. Otis

SUMMARY. Across the nation, lesbian, gay, bisexual, and transgender communities are facing the challenge of advancing civil rights on the local and state levels. One community successfully met that challenge with the passage of the Fairness Ordinance in Lexington-Fayette County, Kentucky, in 1999. Although the opposition characterized the Fairness Alliance as a "million dollar operation out of Washington," the National Gay and Lesbian Task Force (NGLTF) recognized the work of the Alliance as a model of local grassroots organizing with its Creating Change Award. This case study examines that campaign and the strategies the Fairness Alliance used, including effective lobbying and coalition building between the LGBT community and business, civic, political, community, and religious leaders. *[Article copies available for a fee from The Haworth Document Delivery Service: 1-800-HAWORTH. E-mail address: <docdelivery@haworthpress.com> Website: <http://www.HaworthPress.com> © 2004 by The Haworth Press, Inc. All rights reserved.]*

Address correspondence to: Melanie D. Otis, PhD, MSW, 651 Patterson Office Tower, College of Social Work, University of Kentucky, Lexington, KY 40506-0027 (E-mail: mdotis00@uky.edu).

[Haworth co-indexing entry note]: "One Community's Path to Greater Social Justice: Building on Earlier Successes." Otis, Melanie D. Co-published simultaneously in *Journal of Gay & Lesbian Social Services* (Harrington Park Press, an imprint of The Haworth Press, Inc.) Vol. 16, No. 3/4, 2004, pp. 17-33; and: *Gay and Lesbian Rights Organizing: Community-Based Strategies* (ed: Yolanda C. Padilla) Harrington Park Press, an imprint of The Haworth Press, Inc., 2004, pp. 17-33. Single or multiple copies of this article are available for a fee from The Haworth Document Delivery Service [1-800-HAWORTH, 9:00 a.m. - 5:00 p.m. (EST). E-mail address: docdelivery@haworthpress.com].

Journal of Gay & Lesbian Social Services, Vol. 16(3/4) 2004
http://www.haworthpress.com/store/product.asp?sku=J041
© 2004 by The Haworth Press, Inc. All rights reserved.
10.1300/J041v16n03_02

KEYWORDS. Lesbian and gay, social justice, contemporary social movements, grassroots organizing, case study

A great deal has happened in the last 30 years in the arena of lesbian, gay, bisexual, and transgender (LGBT) civil rights and social and political activism. One of the key changes that began in the mid 1970s was an increasing focus on the pursuit of social justice (Rawls, 1999). The shift to the pursuit of a broad social justice agenda through political action also meant a significant shift in the nature of tactics and resources utilized by LGBT activists (Werum & Winders, 2001). While the existence of numerous books, magazines, newsletters, and social action Websites make it clear that the battle of LGBT rights is no longer in the closet, for activists in middle-America, the strides made in predominantly metropolitan East Coast/West Coast communities often mean little. In fact, the dearth of concrete data from small towns and cities across the nation may become a tool for the opposition, citing the absence of information as an indication that the civil rights concerns raised are an urban, coastal problem–not a local one. It is against this backdrop of limited empirical evidence and seeming invisibility that many social activists in small towns stage their efforts to achieve social justice.

This case study provides an example of how one community took that next step toward greater social justice by effectively lobbying the local government for the passage of a comprehensive ordinance protecting the civil rights of LGBT people in employment, housing, and public accommodations. A long history of LGBT activism in the state, and a recent victory on a local nondiscrimination ordinance in another local community, Louisville, Kentucky, paved the way for the campaign highlighted here. The focus of this article is on the implementation of lessons learned, and how these lessons led to success in a matter of months, rather than years, for this particular initiative. Specifically, the discussion focuses on the Kentucky Fairness Alliance's (KFA's) implementation of contemporary social movement strategies and tactics for social change, with particular emphasis on concepts addressed in the community organizing literature (Fisher, 1993), such as the roles of timing, community education, media engagement, coalition building, and lobbying as tools for effective social action.

BACKGROUND

Community Climate

Kentucky is predominantly a rural state, with numerous small towns and tiny communities scattered across farmland in the central and western part of the state and tucked away in the Appalachian Mountains along the eastern border of the state. The home of the state's land grant university, Lexington is the second largest city with a 2000 Census population of approximately 260,000 (Louisville, population 680,000, is Kentucky's largest city) (U.S. Census Bureau, 2000). In addition to the approximately 31,000 students and 20,000 university employees who make up a substantial portion of the county's residents, Lexington is dominated by employment in service industries, the horse industry, and a variety of professions.

University communities are often more diverse than other areas in the state in which they are located. As a state, Kentucky's demography suggests limited ethnic/racial diversity, with a population that is 90 percent white and 7.3 percent black. The majority of non-white residents live in the major cities of Louisville and Lexington. In Fayette County, however, the 2000 Census indicates a slightly more diverse population, with 81 percent of residents being white, 13.5 percent black, and 5.5 percent Latino, Asian, American Indian, or Pacific Islander (U.S. Census Bureau, 2000).

LGBT Community

As one of two large cities with an established LGBT community, Lexington is a refuge for many LGBT people growing up in rural areas of the state. Not surprisingly, many young people are drawn to the community because of the potential for anonymity and the available LGBT resources. This is not a factor unique to Kentucky. As communities such as Lexington began to develop resources, more individuals opt to relocate in larger communities in their home state, rather than making the significant, and often solitary, journey to places like San Francisco, New York City, Los Angeles, and Atlanta.

It may be the combination of this new migration and the development of community resources that led to a surprising announcement on the Oprah Winfrey show in the early 1990s. Shortly after the 1990 census was released, Oprah Winfrey announced on her television talk show that Fayette County, Kentucky, had the largest percentage of lesbians and gay men of any city its size in the country. The comments came as a result of Census reports identifying the number of cohabitating, same-sex couples in country. While the evidence was sketchy, it also said something about the impact of the community-wide campaign to encourage people to take advantage of the opportunity to have their same-sex relationships counted ("Standup and be counted," 1990).

One of the oldest continuously operating businesses on the main street of downtown Lexington is an LGBT bar that opened in 1970. Other LGBT bars and restaurants have come and gone from the center of downtown over the past 30 years, with two or more in operation at any given time. Although the relevance of the gay bar to the development of the LGBT communities is often noted (Adam, 1997; Cruikshank, 1992), the centrality of such establishments is a part of the unique climate in which the LGBT presence exists in the larger Lexington community.

The presence of the LGBT community is further evidenced by their active role in the annual Fourth of July parade. Since 1992, a notable contingent of marchers from the LGBT community has participated in the parade–at times having one of the largest groups in the parade with 150 to 200 participants. Members of the major local LGBT activist organization in central Kentucky, the Kentucky Fairness Alliance (KFA)-Bluegrass, have also participated in the annual Martin Luther King Day, Jr., parade, St. Patrick's Day parade, and other community events.

Local History

An earlier victory for LGBT rights in the state of Kentucky set the stage for the struggle for a local ordinance in Lexington-Fayette County. In 1991, a small collective of people in Louisville, the state's largest city, began a movement to pursue the passage of a civil rights ordinance protecting LGBT people in that community. The grassroots effort in Louisville, the Fairness Campaign, achieved a major success in January 1999, with the passage of a local ordinance protecting LGBT people in the area of employment. The article by Erlene Grise-Owens and her co-authors in this volume provides the background of the eight-year struggle for the passage of the ordinance in Louisville. The case that follows provides an example of how lessons learned from the Fairness Campaign in Louisville were put to the test in the six-month campaign that led to the successful passage of a comprehensive civil rights ordinance in the central Kentucky community of Lexington.

On June 22, 1999, the Lexington-Fayette Urban County Human Rights Commission submitted the Fairness Ordinance for consideration by the city council. On July 8, 1999, the city council Local Ordinance 199-94 (Fairness Ordinance) with a vote of 12 to 3. The ordinance, subsequently referred to as the Fairness Ordinance, added protection based on real or perceived sexual orientation or gender identity, to existing civil rights protection related to housing, employment, and public accommodations. At the time of its passage, the language and civil rights protection accorded to citizens of the Lexington-Fayette County community was among the most inclusive in the nation (Mulvihill, 1999, July 9). The passage of the Fairness Ordinance marked the first change in civil rights protection in the community since the 1960s. The significance of the event was noted by the Lexington-Fayette Urban County Human Rights Commission as well as members of the city council.

THE KENTUCKY FAIRNESS ALLIANCE

The Kentucky Fairness Alliance is a grassroots organization that seeks to address LGBT rights across the state. On its Website the KFA indicates that its mission is "to advance equality for lesbian, gay, bisexual, and transgender people through leadership development, public education, and by encouraging participation in the democratic process" (Kentucky Fairness Alliance, n.d.). The KFA has its roots in the eight-year battle in the state's largest city, Louisville, over the passage of their local ordinance protecting gay and lesbian people in employment. The organization in Louisville started out as a loosely configured group of LGBT community leaders and activists who took on the day-to-day battle of convincing the local alderman to consider inclusion of sexual orientation in the city's list of protective categories. The commitment of those individuals brought the attention of the local media and a growth in the number of KFA supporters. Finally, in January 1999, the alderman voted to include employment protection based on sexual orientation in the existing local ordinance. On the heels of that victory, activists in the Lexington-Fayette County community decided to increase their efforts to move forward a local initiative.

Residents of the Lexington-Fayette County community make up the working core of the central Kentucky chapter of the KFA, known as KFA-Bluegrass. As a chapter, however, the group includes 16 counties in all. With the exception of Fayette County, these areas are primarily rural, with the largest county seat having a population of slightly less than 20,000.

THE FAIRNESS CAMPAIGN

Although a long history preceded the actual pursuit of a local ordinance in the Lexington-Fayette County community, the public spotlight on the campaign was fairly brief and strategically focused. On June 22, 1999, the local Human Rights Commission, charged with the responsibility of protecting the civil rights of community residents, unanimously voted to pursue a change in the local civil rights ordinance to include LGBT citizens. Seventeen days passed from that moment to the final vote of the city council on July 8, 1999. Angry opponents of the Fairness Ordinance who believed the community had been taken over by national LGBT rights organizers lamented that their own forces were no "match for the 'machine' that had been released" (Ostrander, 1999). Members of KFA, however, knew the successful campaign was the result of months of planning and preparation for the battle ahead. KFA was accused of utilizing national dollars to conduct the necessary work for effective lobbying. The reality, however, was that the campaign was conducted with a very modest budget and very careful planning–and the tireless efforts of numerous volunteers. From the selection of the name of the campaign to the development of press kits and community education packets, KFA-Bluegrass waged a thoughtful and productive campaign informed by the previous work undertaken in Louisville.

Structure and Process

The strengths-based perspective recognizes that individuals bring with them knowledge and skills that can be tapped to reach the goals of an organization or group (Saleebey, 1997). Ultimately, the success of an organization's efforts greatly depends on its ability to make the most of the strengths of its supporters. Like most grassroots organizations, KFA is a collection of volunteers who have come together for a common purpose. The small collective that made up the core of KFA-Bluegrass brought together representatives of social work, law, medicine, academia, architecture, journalism, students, and local entrepreneurs. Research has shown that those who take on active roles in grassroots organizations are often adding their activism to an already packed work and personal schedule (Taylor & Raeburn, 1995). Members of KFA-Bluegrass were no different. Finding ways to move forward with the activities necessary to bring the ordinance to a vote meant capitalizing on the skills and resources of the members. As theoretical discussions on community organizing indicate (Schwartz & Paul, 1992), when the needs moved beyond the capacity of the core members of the organization, other community resources were tapped.

In addition to the steering committees that guide the state organization and KFA-Bluegrass, there exists a growing number of supporters that are often referred to as "Friends of Fairness." These individuals are included in a database of postal and e-mail addresses and phone numbers. The database allows KFA to have fairly quick contact with its membership. Through e-mail listservs, mailing campaigns, and action alerts that trigger volunteer-driven phone trees (Hick & McNutt, 2002), KFA is able to mobilize its membership fairly quickly when needed.

The Pursuit of Social Justice:
Making It Possible for Community Leaders to Do the Right Thing

No matter what their position on an issue, politicians are, first and foremost, elected officials. The tenuousness of that position is never far from their minds, particularly when an election is imminent. Any organization seeking to move forward a piece of legislation, whether it is a local, state, or national mandate, must attend to the reality of that issue. The gravity of that fact is particularly weighty when the legislation addresses the needs of the LGBT community in a small city in the Bible-belt. Although the outcome of the next election is at stake, for the conscientious civil servant, doing the "right thing" also matters. Many members of the LGBT community (for example, social workers, civic leaders, lawyers) know the civil rights, economic, social, political, and religious arguments that make the right thing seemingly obvious, and defensible. They've spent hours gathering facts and data to make the argument that local politicians have quietly hoped the question would not come up. In the absence of factual information and faced with a mandate to decide, members of the religious right will pose convincing arguments. These are the arguments for which LGBT activists and supporters must be prepared.

An awareness of this fact led members of KFA to begin by educating members of the city council. Each council member was visited by representatives of the LGBT community who were also constituents in the councilperson's district. KFA representatives used social movement methods (Klandermans, 1992), such as sharing data from other communities that had successfully passed such an ordinance.

COMMUNITY EDUCATION AND VISIBILITY

Timing

A substantial area of extant contemporary social movement literature has addressed the role of timing in understanding the ebb and flow, successes and failures of a myriad of social movement initiatives. Historically, the moment may have been somewhat serendipitous. Today, many social movement organizations have learned to gauge windows of opportunity and when it may be most fortuitous to mobilize resources (Vago, 1989).

When the Louisville Fairness Campaign (www.fairness.org) successfully lobbied for the passage of a local ordinance addressing LGBT employment rights, members of state and local KFA knew the time was right to pursue a similar ordinance in the Lexington-Fayette County community. The organization and its supporters were prepared to act.

Working with the Media

Working effectively with the media is a challenge for any social movement organization. The message of the organization and the constraints of various media formats are often incongruent. Individuals who have had little experience working with the media may find their message lost in the framing of local media and the demands of a particular media format. The key to making the most of media coverage is in taking a proactive approach–crafting a message that readily lends itself to journalists' use. Often, a carefully crafted message may become the bulk of a newspaper article, and a clear, concise statement of purpose can become the key quote in a television news report. As efforts to move the local ordinance toward a hearing and vote continued, KFA-Bluegrass relied on a number of grassroots organizing methods (Kahn, 1982; McCarthy, 1994) by issuing carefully timed press releases and providing opportunities for media sound bites.

From an organizational standpoint, several factors are important (Gitlin, 1980). First, journalists like to identify spokespeople for a cause. In the absence of a clearly defined organizational spokesperson, journalists will often bring one to the forefront. The person may be someone they have seen at more than one event, or simply someone who proved willing to respond to questions. For the organization, such actions may pose a major problem, especially when the individual has a message that is either incongruent with the organization's mission or inconsistent. Further, unless one has some training or practice working with the media, the tendency is to want to provide as much information as possible. The outcome, however, is less informative. Journalists are generally looking for sound bites and interesting quotes, depending on their medium. What seems like a wealth of important information on the issue at hand may result in a focus on a seemingly minor detail–the core of the message often being lost. Members of KFA-Bluegrass recognized the potential pitfalls and took a number of steps to ensure that the message that went into the public realm was clear and consistent. First, one lesbian and one gay spokesperson for the organization were identified. Their names and contact information were distributed to targeted members of local and state media agencies in a press release. Second, one or both of these representatives were available at any event related to the potential ordinance. And finally, both spokespeople, as well as a number of other members of the organization, participated in training to increase their effectiveness in addressing members of media. The end result was a clear, consistent, and polished message that kept the fundamental issue of civil rights at the forefront of all discussions about the proposed ordinance.

The importance of language and the role that it plays in working with the media cannot be overstated. When the name "Fairness Campaign" was selected it was with a clear understanding of the prominence the name would have in media coverage. While it clearly conveyed the goal of the campaign–to support the fair and just treatment of all citizens in the community–it also provided an interesting antithesis for opponents who were often referred to as the anti-Fairness position. Further, the name conveyed the important message that this was a discussion of social justice, not of perspectives on sexual orientation. The fact that the language resonated with the community as a whole became evident as the local city council quickly began to refer to the proposal as the Fairness Ordinance.

The Role of Research

The problem with attempting to argue facts in relation to any LGBT concern is that the research is limited, and, arguably, nonrepresentative (Otis & Skinner, 1996). For people living in middle-America, this creates a difficult platform from which to argue civil rights. Opponents want to suggest that it is not an issue for their community. They call for evidence of the presence of a relevant number of LGBT people in the community, or statistics on the existence of discrimination or victimization of LGBT people that would support the need for local civil rights protections. While the request may be made based on a presumption that this is simply a non-issue, opponents may unknowingly strike at the Achilles heel of many efforts to address LGBT issues–the difficulty of establishing documentation of a problem in a marginalized, stigmatized community. The issue was no different in this local community.

Because resources for grassroots efforts are often limited, considerations about what will provide the greatest return for the input are critical. When the issue is one that is highly political and emotionally charged, empirical evidence based on sound research provides a basis for more objective arguments. A random sample survey of community residents, conducted by a local research firm, provided such data for KFA-Bluegrass. The survey addressed questions of community support for civil rights protection based on sexual orientation in areas of employment, public accommodations, and housing. Findings of the survey indicated that over three-quarters of the 400 respondents (200 men and 200 women) believed that it should be unlawful to discriminate in these areas based on sexual orientation. A press conference provided an opportunity to share findings of the survey with the public, while also providing easily presentable material for television and print media (Mulvihill, June 25, 1999).

Coalition Building: Building Bridges

Like many grassroots efforts in contemporary social movements, the Kentucky Fairness Alliance's approach involves the pursuit of a broad social justice agenda. This fundamental view of social justice as an issue of fairness-to-all supports the importance of coalition building among a myriad of social justice-oriented organizations and groups (Rawls, 1999). Building these bridges among groups and organizations in the Lexington community was a key factor in the ultimate success of the brief campaign for the passage of the Fairness Ordinance. Three arenas–the religious community, the business community, and other social justice organizations–were particularly important to the achieving the goals of KFA.

Religious Community

There are few places where the issue of LGBT rights is more widely and vehemently debated than among members of the religious community. Like all debates waged on religious grounds, the arguments are more philosophical than factual, but also difficult to refute. Ultimately, the answer rests not in providing evidence of being right, but rather ensuring that the response is fair to all, regardless of religious beliefs and affiliations. For members of the religious community, the bridge to LGBT civil rights generally relates to beliefs of about social justice. Because the arguments of social justice and many religious messages are compatible, soliciting support from the religious community is often a matter of educating leaders on the common ground that rests between the two.

In a community in the Bible-belt, ignoring the possibility of religious opposition is not an option. For the Fairness Ordinance to be successful, religious concerns not only had to be addressed, they had to be a focus of the effort. In many ways, the successful passage of the ordinance had much to do with the central focus of religious concerns in a debate of civil rights. Rather than seeking to reconcile the religious debate over what was "right," KFA-Bluegrass used the centrality of religious concerns as an opportunity to show that the religious community was far from unified on the issue. Ultimately, 13 community religious leaders provided letters of support for the ordinance. Three of those individuals, including the president of a local seminary, testified in support of the Fairness Ordinance.

Business Community

The Fairness Ordinance addressed three areas–employment, housing, and public accommodations. Should efforts to pass the ordinance be successful, each of these areas had significant implications for members of the business community. Letters of support for the ordinance were solicited from large and small business leaders in the community.

The focus of many of these letters was on the economic impact of nondiscriminatory policies on individual businesses and the community as a whole. Highlighted in the letters was the company's own position on nondiscriminatory hiring practices as evidenced by company policy. In addition to letters of support, information on company policies relating to sexual orientation was collected and included in packets distributed to city council members and the media.

Social Justice Organizations

Social change through coalition building among interest groups characterizes much of what has occurred in contemporary social movements. In the local community a number of organizations devoted to social justice issues operate with limited resources and volunteer power–not unlike KFA. For any of these organizations, tackling the significant task of lobbying for the passage of a piece of local legislation would be difficult. Early in the process, however, members of KFA began to draw on the shared goals of social justice and social change that existed in other local and state organizations.

The process began with the identification of all community organizations that had expressed a shared mission of addressing social justice issues. Many members of KFA had existing links to the organizations through employment, membership, or other relationships. The process of coalition building began with outreach from KFA to those organizations. This outreach served a number of purposes. First, KFA provided educational materials on the ordinance and its potential impact on the community. The organizations shared this information with their members and made decisions on whether or not to speak out officially in support of passage of the Fairness Ordinance. This process of community education also increased the number of individuals who could speak knowledgeably about what the ordinance would actually do. However, the goal was not to increase the number of official spokespeople for the ordinance, but to reduce the gravity of misinformation as opponents put forward propaganda on the potential impact of the ordinance on community life.

Coalition building with members of the religious, business, and social justice communities is clearly goal-oriented. It is not, however, a time-limited process. While energy and resources were focused on the immediate task of successfully moving the Fairness Ordinance forward, these linkages also provided the foundation for future social justice-oriented efforts. Even as the Fairness Campaign was under way, members of KFA were called upon to assist other social justice organizations in their own efforts to increase visibility of issues relating to hate crimes, sexual assault, AIDS, and the death penalty.

Lobbying

Initial lobbying efforts began quietly. Knowing that an emotionally charged debate would eventually occur around the ordinance, proponents began by quietly approaching city council members and community leaders to discuss the possibility of pursuing local civil rights protection for LGBT people. With limited resources to wage the campaign for the passage of the ordinance, it was important to avoid a protracted debate. Instead, proponents developed a strategy that concentrated lobbying efforts in an approximately four-week period. This strategy reduced the strain on limited resources and also put opponents at disadvantage.

Ultimately, the passage of the Fairness Ordinance rested on the decisions made by 15 city council members and the mayor. Lobbying focused on their responsibilities as elected officials and their future desires to continue in public office. Thus, a significant factor in the lobbying effort related to the civic-mindedness of ordinance supporters. The process began with contact between KFA representatives and each local council member. In each case, two KFA members who were also constituents of the councilperson offered to meet personally to provide information and answer any questions or concerns. If the councilperson was resistant to such a meeting, KFA members asked if they could at least provide some information for the councilperson to read. While there was no guarantee that the councilperson would read the materials provided, in each case the councilperson agreed to either a meeting or review of materials.

Rallying constituents to contact their area representatives was a tactic heavily used by both supporters and opponents of the Fairness Ordinance. The key to being heard was in both the volume of contact and the nature of the message. For supporters of the ordinance it was important to keep the focus on the issue of civil rights and fairness. This consistent message of social justice sat in stark contrast to the numerous calls city council members received from opponents who argued against the ordinance on religious grounds, sometimes casting their opposition in the form of both political and personal threats. The gravity of the lobbying efforts was quite evident in the council chambers as some council members spoke with sometimes angry, sometimes strained, voices about the threatening phone calls they had received. In two cases, the council members indicated that the vehement reaction of some opponents of the ordinance helped to solidify their support by making evident the need for such protection in the community.

KFA could not control how supporters of the ordinance might choose to frame their own position when calling council members. Efforts to encourage KFA members to be fair-minded in their requests to council members, however, were made through phone tree contacts.

MAKING A CASE IN THE PUBLIC FORUM

When the time comes to make the case for LGBT civil rights, there is no substitute for preparedness. KFA members came to the city council having anticipated nearly every question. Questions of economic impact, religious freedom, private business concerns, community support, and myths versus fact were all carefully addressed in individual folders which were distributed to each member of the council and the media in advance of the ordinance hearing. Supportive speakers were carefully picked to ensure that all areas of concern were covered. Business leaders, researchers, religious leaders, social justice leaders, and individuals with personal stories of discrimination stepped forward one at a time to provide another piece of the argument for LGBT civil rights, frequently reminding their audience that the question on the agenda was one of fairness.

What to Expect from the Other Side

The oppositional arguments to the specifics of the proposed ordinance tended to fall into three categories: religious freedom, protection of the small business owner, and protection of youth. In anticipation of these arguments, the ordinance included caveats which allowed churches to continue to hire based on compatibility between employee and church beliefs; exempted small business owners with fewer than 20 employees; and excluded schools from the jurisdiction of the policy. Once these stipulations were acknowledged, much of the opposition's argument rested on attempts to frame the ordinance as morally wrong or as "special rights" for LGBT people.

The issue of special rights is not new to social justice work among LGBT people and their supporters. Part of this framing rests on the argument that being lesbian, gay, or bisexual is a choice, and we should not legislate to protect people from the potential negative consequences of their choices. While the debate on the origins of sexual orientation continues in the world of academia and research, many individuals on both sides of the argument have come to conclusions that resonate with a large segment of the population. As such, the argument that LGBT people are born, not a product of individual choice, is often forwarded in response to oppositional views that see such civil rights protection as inappropriate. On the other side of that argument is the recognition that religious freedom–an area of social life that clearly falls in the realm of personal choice–is protected by existing civil rights legislation.

The other oppositional stronghold, and certainly the more volatile of the two, is the issue of morality. For many opponents of civil rights protection for LGBT people, the fundamental argument rests on interpretations of religious texts and the belief that homosexuality is at a minimum, a sin, if not an abomination. Little ground would be gained by arguing that holding such views was simply wrong. Instead, the KFA's tactic was to allow proponents of such a view a voice, and then to counter with a different perspective from the religious community. The approach did two things. First it provided a sharp contrast to the often hostile message that came from members of the opposition. Supporters often took exception to the suggestion that God would want anyone to be treated unjustly, regardless of their sexual orientation. The message of fairness and social justice permeated the supportive response of the religious community, as noted in this letter from a local minister (W.B. Kincaid III, personal communication, June 28, 1999):

> Those who would make this a debate over homosexuality miss the point badly. I am a minister who serves a congregation where gays and lesbians participate fully in our life together. Yet, the point of this ordinance is not to debate homosexuality, but to guarantee that our community life closely approximates the ideal of equality and freedom of all citizens. I do believe this is a moral issue, but the moral issue at stake is that of fairness.

A VICTORY–BUT NOT THE END: STRATEGIES FOR MAINTAINING COMMUNITY SUPPORT AND INVOLVEMENT

One of the most difficult tasks for any contemporary social movement organization is maintaining involvement and focus in the absence of the pursuit of a concrete objective. For KFA the ordinance effort provided a time-limited, unifying focal point for social justice-minded members of the local community. Once the Fairness Ordinance was signed into local law, the organization, LGBT community, and larger community no longer had that focal point, and the potential for the disintegration of the foundation built during the ordinance campaign was high. For future activism efforts, as well as the protection of newly achieved successes, maintaining a sense of focus on the larger picture of social justice was a necessity. Staying true to the organizational mission was a key part of this process.

Once the Fairness Ordinance was passed, the next important step was to make sure that members of the community were aware of the parameters of the ordinance, and the appropriate recourse should their civil rights be violated. While the media can play an important role in this process, explicit details of a local ordinance, rarely lend themselves to good media coverage.

Community Education, Outreach, and Visibility

Community education serves a number of important purposes. First, the impact of protective legislation is felt only to the degree that members of the community are aware of its existence. For employers and business owners it is important to provide the necessary information to avoid unknowingly violating an individual's civil rights. For many individuals, diversity training is an important part of the process of moving beyond discriminatory practices. Social justice-oriented organizations can assist in this process by providing access to information on inclusion and factual information on LGBT issues and lives.

KFA-Bluegrass addressed this responsibility in a number of ways. First, early in the ordinance campaign process a volunteer established a Website for the organization (www.bluegrassfairness.org). The Website provided up-to-date information on the status of the ordinance, information on its passage and scope, and links to a variety of LGBT-friendly sites. The site also included a link to the local Human Rights Commission, the entity responsible for responding to discrimination reports related to the ordinance (www.lfuchr.org). Second, recognizing the need for outreach beyond the Internet, KFA regularly places outreach materials in a number of local businesses and has information tables at community events.

Partnership in Communitywide Social Justice Efforts

As noted previously, coalition building with other social justice-oriented groups and individuals was key to the successful passage of the ordinance. These partnerships began prior to the passage of the ordinance on a number of fronts. One of the most visible was the successful election of an openly gay, KFA member to the local Human Rights Commission. His presence on the Commission certainly served to forward the discussion of the proposed ordinance, but it also had an additional, equally relevant impact. It made clear the desire and commitment of members of the LGBT community to serve the local community as a whole.

In addition to involvement with the Commission, members of KFA continue their active support and involvement in a variety of social justice-oriented organizations and groups throughout the community. This support has taken a myriad of forms. Participation on organizational boards of directors, speaking for shared causes, shared involvement in problem solving efforts to address other community problems, and memberships in organizations and groups thus provided much-needed financial and human resources for continued social justice work.

The growth in social capital necessary to continue to address LGBT-related social justice issues has been clear. For the first time, in the summer following the passage of the ordinance, politicians seeking (re)election actively pursued the LGBT vote–willingly completing community education voter surveys and attending LGBT events.

Celebration and Reflection

Social activists are, almost by definition, production-oriented. As committed volunteers, many activists pack social justice activities into already full lives. Further, as history makes clear, social justice work is an ongoing process that seeks to improve people's lives, with few delusions that there will be some end in sight. Those involved in the effort to pass the Fairness Ordinance knew the significance of the victory for the community, but they also saw it as a building block to the next step in the process of achieving protection for all of the citizens of the state. That vision is important for the continuation of social justice work and active involvement, but it may also lead social activists to miss the opportunity to celebrate the successes they achieve along the way. A community celebration hosted by KFA, provided an opportunity for everyone to reflect on the significance of the achievement.

The significance of the achievements of the Kentucky Fairness Alliance was also recognized by the National Gay and Lesbian Task Force (NGLTF) at their annual awards banquet in 2000. KFA and its director each received Creating Change Awards from NGLTF (see www.ngltf.org). Sharing this acknowledgment with the rest of the LGBT and social justice community played an important role in reminding supporters of what had been accomplished–and what must continue to be pursued.

CONCLUSION

A number of factors contribute to successful social justice work. For the KFA-Bluegrass Fairness Campaign, contemporary social movement strategies attending to the importance of timing, community education, media engagement, coalition building, and lobbying were instrumental in securing the passage of a comprehensive civil rights ordinance in the community. An exploration of the literature makes it clear that these strategies have become an important part of grassroots social justice work. Most of this literature, however, focuses on the activities of organizations and groups within large metropolitan communities. This case study provides an examination of how smaller communities may achieve the goals of social justice through strategic planning and coalition building.

REFERENCES

Adam, B. D. (1995). *The rise of a gay and lesbian movement (Social movements past and present Series)*. (Rev. ed.). New York: Twayne Publishers.
Cruikshank, M. (1992). *The gay and lesbian liberation movement*. New York: Routledge.
Fisher, R. (2001). Social action community organization: Proliferation, persistence, roots, and prospects. In J. Rothman, J. L. Erlich, & J. E. Tropman (Eds.), *Strategies for community intervention* (6th ed.) (pp. 350-363). Itasca, IL: F. E. Peacock Publishers.
Gitlin, T. (1980). *The whole world is watching: Mass media in the making and unmaking of the New Left*. Berkeley, CA: University of California Press.
Hick, S. F., & McNutt, J. G. (Eds.). (2002). Advocacy, activism and the Internet: Community organization and social policy. Chicago: Lyceum Books, Inc.
Kahn, S. (1982). *Organizing: A guide for grassroots leaders*. New York: McGraw-Hill.

Kentucky Fairness Alliance (n.d.). Our Mission Statement. Retrieved October 11, 2002, from <www.kentuckyfairness.org>.

Klandermans, B. (1992). The social construction of protest and multiorganizational fields. In A. D. Morris & C. M. Mueller (Eds.), *Frontiers in social movement theory* (pp. 77-103). New Haven, CT: Yale University Press.

McCarthy, J. D. (1994). Activists, authorities, and media framing of drunk driving. In E. Larana, H. Johnston, & J. R. Gusfield (Eds.), *New social movements: From ideology to identity* (pp. 133-167). Philadelphia: Temple University Press.

Mulvihill, G. (1999, June 25). Poll: Discrimination against gays opposed by Lexingtonians. *Lexington Herald-Leader*, p. B1.

Mulvihill, G. (1999, July 9). Gay bias law is adopted 12-3. *Lexington Herald-Leader*, p. A1.

Ostrander, K. (1999, August 15). Lexington's gay ordinance. *Louisville Courier-Journal*, p. D-4.

Otis, M. D., & Skinner, W. F. (1996). The prevalence of victimization and its effect on mental well-being among lesbian and gay people. *Journal of Homosexuality, 30*(3), 93-117.

Rawls, J. (1999). *A theory of justice* (Rev. ed.). Cambridge, MA: Belknap Press.

Saleebey, D. (Ed.). (1997). *The strengths perspective in social work practice* (2nd ed.). New York: Longman.

Schwartz, M., & Paul, S. (1992). Resource mobilization versus the mobilization of people: Why consensus movements cannot be instruments of social change. In A. D. Morris & C. M. Mueller (Eds.), *Frontiers in social movement theory* (pp. 205-223). New Haven, CT: Yale University Press.

Standup and be counted. (1990, March). *GLSO News*, 1.

Taylor, V., & Raeburn, N. C. (1995). Identity politics as high-risk activism: Career consequences for lesbian, gay and bisexual sociologists. *Social Problems, 42*, 252-273.

U. S. Census Bureau. (2000). American FactFinder–2000 Census. Retrieved November 28, 2001, from <www.factfinder.census.gov/servlet/BasicFactsServlet>.

Vago, S. (1989). *Social change* (2nd ed.). Englewood Cliffs, NJ: Prentice Hall.

Werum, R., & Winders, B. (2001). Who's "in" and who's "out": State fragmentation and the struggle over gay rights, 1974-1999. *Social Problems, 48*(3), 386-410.

Coalition Building and Electoral Organizing in the Passage of Anti-Discrimination Laws: The Case of Connecticut

John Bonelli
Louise Simmons

SUMMARY. The passage of a civil rights law with protections for individuals based on sexual orientation in Connecticut in 1991 was the culmination of over a decade of activism. Gay rights activists achieved success with the help of many progressive allies. This article traces the development of gay rights organizations and their participation in several important political coalitions locally in Hartford and statewide in Connecticut that helped achieve support for GLBT issues and the civil rights law in particular. The authors argue that a narrow, isolationist focus does not achieve long-term victories for gay rights, but rather that victories

---

John Bonelli, MSW, is Director of Policy and Community Organizing, Connecticut Positive Action Coalition, and Adjunct Professor, University of Connecticut School of Social Work, .

Louise Simmons, PhD, is Associate Professor, University of Connecticut School of Social Work, 1798 Asylum Avenue, West Hartford, CT 06117.

Author note: We dedicate this article to all of the courageous and visionary activists who have participated in these struggles and who provide the inspiration for these stories. We especially recognize those individuals who we have lost to AIDS.

[Haworth co-indexing entry note]: "Coalition Building and Electoral Organizing in the Passage of Anti-Discrimination Laws: The Case of Connecticut." Bonelli, John, and Louise Simmons. Co-published simultaneously in *Journal of Gay & Lesbian Social Services* (Harrington Park Press, an imprint of The Haworth Press, Inc.) Vol. 16, No. 3/4, 2004, pp. 35-53; and: *Gay and Lesbian Rights Organizing: Community-Based Strategies* (ed: Yolanda C. Padilla) Harrington Park Press, an imprint of The Haworth Press, Inc., 2004, pp. 35-53. Single or multiple copies of this article are available for a fee from The Haworth Document Delivery Service [1-800-HAWORTH, 9:00 a.m. - 5:00 p.m. (EST). E-mail address: docdelivery@haworthpress.com].

Journal of Gay & Lesbian Social Services, Vol. 16(3/4) 2004
http://www.haworthpress.com/store/product.asp?sku=J041
© 2004 by The Haworth Press, Inc. All rights reserved.
10.1300/J041v16n03_03

are best achieved by developing strong relationships with progressive allies. *[Article copies available for a fee from The Haworth Document Delivery Service: 1-800-HAWORTH. E-mail address: <docdelivery@haworthpress.com> Website: <http://www.HaworthPress.com> © 2004 by The Haworth Press, Inc. All rights reserved.]*

KEYWORDS. Gay rights, coalitions, political activism, political organizing, Connecticut, Hartford, gay rights legislation

The passage of a civil rights law protecting Connecticut citizens on the basis of sexual orientation and its signature into law in 1991 by then-Governor Lowell Weicker marked the culmination of 17 years of a multifaceted struggle. This victory for the gay community was built upon a dynamic series of relationships among individuals and organizations, coalitions and adversaries on a multitude of issues, over many years. While analysis of political struggles of the gay, lesbian, bisexual, and transgender (GLBT, or "gay") community is frequently subsumed under the mantle of "identity politics" and thereby assumed to be narrowly focused on singular issues associated with GLBT identity (Bailey, 1999; Rosenthal, 2000), the Connecticut experience reveals a different pattern. Rather than being placed in a position of choosing between gay identity and issues, or sublimating their issues to support other liberal and progressive allies or causes that were "gay-friendly," Connecticut gay rights activists were able to effectively do both, thus defying the burdensome dichotomy. The following account will analyze this process and highlight the most lasting effects of these political efforts.

Although this account highlights the role of coalition building and electoral organizing in achieving legislative success, the social movement that developed in favor of the gay rights legislation employed a broad range of strategies and tactics in its quest to secure protections for gay men, lesbians, and bisexuals. These included lobbying, direct action, community building, leadership development and civil disobedience, as well as coalition building and electoral organizing. We focus here on the choice by progressive gay rights activists in Connecticut during the 1980s and 1990s to forge alliances that would strengthen their power by active participation in two electoral political coalitions: People for Change and the Legislative Electoral Action Program. They achieved visibility through involvement in several specific electoral campaigns: the People for Change campaigns of 1987, 1989, and 1991, the Democrats for Change Democratic Town Committee race of 1988, and Juan Figueroa's successful campaign for the Connecticut General Assembly in 1988.

In candor, the authors must acknowledge our active participation in all of these political efforts. We are not disinterested writers observing from a distance. We sat through the meetings, helped draft the platforms, mobilized the volunteers, and were leaders who added our voices to the chorus for social and economic justice in Hartford and in the state of Connecticut. Thus, this history is our history. Together, we also illustrate one of the major points of this article, the "symbiosis" of the gay rights movement and the larger progressive movement. First author Bonelli is a leading gay rights activist in Connecticut and served as Hartford's first openly gay candidate for citywide public office on the 1989 People for Change slate for the Hartford City Council. Second author Simmons is a progressive activist and professor who ran for Hartford City Council and was elected in 1991 on the People for Change slate. Each supported the other's candidacy, and we continue to work together on many important community issues, as well as in teaching collaborations. We believe that documenting these historical experiences is both challenging and necessary to extract lessons from our actions and share our successes with a wider audience. Too often organizers allow their experiences to be relegated solely to oral history or "war stories" of successful campaigns, and we hope the Connecticut story is instructive.

EARLY DAYS IN THE GAY AND LESBIAN RIGHTS MOVEMENT

In the mid 1980s, the locus of civil rights activity for the gay community was the Connecticut Coalition for Lesbian and Gay Civil Rights (hereinafter referred to as the Coalition), essentially a network that maintained a minimal governing structure through a steering committee. It began in 1983 when leading lesbian activists convened a strategy meeting with others to discuss the plight of lesbians and gay men in Connecticut. Out of this meeting the Coalition was born and two years later, on May 29, 1985, election of officers took place (Frances & Warren, 1992). The Coalition developed and sustained organizational momentum toward the ultimate goal of passage of a gay civil rights law. While numerous activists waxed and waned in their involvement in this statewide formation, the steering committee remained determined. In this context author Bonelli became involved in statewide gay political organizing in Connecticut. The Coalition believed that there was a need for community organization on the town and city level and established local chapters to amass sufficient power to achieve legislative success.

Even preceding the formation of the Coalition in 1983, gay and lesbian political activity had been taking place in Hartford. The city government in Hartford enacted a city ordinance as far back as the 1970s to protect gays from discrimination in employment. A local Greater Hartford Lesbian and Gay Task Force existed for several years before 1983, and much of the gay and lesbian political organizing in Connecticut prior to 1985 was centered in Hartford. Thus, some space existed in the political environment in Hartford for GLBT organizing to take hold.

Hartford Organizing and People for Change

Connecticut's high per capita incomes and super-wealthy communities are in stark contrast to the state's poor central cities. Hartford is a city with vast disparities in downtown corporate wealth and massive neighborhood poverty. Consistently among the top ten poorest cities in the U.S. in the last three Censuses, it is a city with a troubled school system taken over by the state, a problematic and eroding tax base, major urban health problems such as high rates of infant mortality, teen pregnancy, and HIV/AIDS, and most other modern urban dilemmas. Yet it has the dynamism of a truly multicultural environment, with a large Puerto Rican and Latino population, a significant West Indian community and a large, long-standing African American community. Part of Hartford's vibrancy includes its GLBT community, and numerous gays and lesbians of color have been among the activist base in the city.

One crucial development for the GLBT community in Hartford was the inclusion of gay activists in the formation of a local third party, People for Change (PFC), which emerged in Hartford in 1987 and existed until 1994. Gay activists were a critical part of the network that developed and maintained this electoral coalition:

> People for Change constituted itself as a combination third party and community coalition. The group emerged from a battle for "linkage" waged by community organizations in which they pressed for some form of tax on downtown development to benefit the neighborhoods, and from dissatisfaction by labor unions over the council's inaction on the lengthy strike at Colt Firearms. Several forces joined in the coalition effort, including the Puerto Rican Political Action Committee and women's and gay rights organizations. (Simmons, 1994, pp. 14-15)

Sensitivity to gay issues by the heterosexual allies within PFC–all involved in various struggles for economic and social change–was essential for the success of their work alongside gay and lesbian activists. Friendships and working relationships among gays and heterosexuals within PFC had been built through an activist network known as Homefront that functioned in Hartford from 1977 until 1987, one important foundation for PFC. Although small in numbers, Homefront brought together a racially and ethnically diverse group of activists working on labor, housing, neighborhood improvements, anti-racism, and other progressive issues, and it enthusiastically embraced the gay rights movement. Through the efforts of Homefront coordinator Steve Thornton (now a labor activist), author Bonelli became involved with PFC.

The larger social context in which the various coalitions developed also was critical to gay inclusion in the PFC coalition. During the Reagan era, many local and national social movements joined forces to resist the administration's reactionary policies. The first Jesse Jackson campaign for President in 1984 and the creation of the Rainbow Coalition set the stage for the inclusion of a broad range of gay issues into an inclusive progressive agenda. Anti-gay violence was increasing both nationally and locally: In Connecticut, the murder of a local closeted gay man, Richard Riehl, at his home by two teenagers, inspired new gay and lesbian leaders to speak out in Connecticut.

Additionally, the emerging AIDS crisis that was disproportionately affecting gay men, and federal government inaction on that crisis dramatized the oppression of homosexuals. Despite mass deaths, President Reagan's refusal to acknowledge the AIDS crisis until five years into the epidemic epitomized the stigmatization of gays and the influence of homophobia and heterosexism. AIDS began to raise public understanding of oppression of homosexuals and presented progressive allies with a tangible issue–government funding for AIDS services and HIV prevention efforts–as a rallying point. Advocating for government funding was familiar ground for progressive allies, in contrast to the more sexually based political gay issues. Thus, the formulation and articulation of the issues agenda for gay and lesbian political organizing–advancing civil rights, fighting hate crimes and seeking funding for HIV/AIDS services–appeared legitimate, just, and winnable to many progressive allies.

Within this context, the chairperson of the People for Change coalition invited Coalition activists from the gay community to participate. The early planning meetings included neighborhood, civil rights, labor, and women's rights activists, as well as leaders from the Puerto Rican and African American communities. Initially, the discussions revolved around making the Hartford City Council accountable for past actions or inaction, particularly around their betrayal of community groups in not passing a linkage policy. Numerous PFC activists had been involved in the linkage coalition and began to fashion a platform of municipal issues that could be a tool for judging candidates in the upcoming 1987 Hartford City Council election. Coalition activists participated in the platform committee. As the platform development meetings continued, these activists decided that a more specific gay agenda needed to be included. Initially, the platform reaffirmed basic protections for gays and lesbians in employment. Later, a more thorough gay, lesbian, and bisexual agenda was proposed and, despite some resistance, the platform committee agreed to adopt and recommend to the larger PFC membership an enhanced agenda. The following provisions were included:

1. The City of Hartford will establish a comprehensive AIDS education program for all city adults and youth.
2. The City Council will actively enforce the Affirmative Action Plan and Civil Rights ordinances in all of the city's departments and contracts.
3. The Police Department will include a "crimes of bias" category, which includes crimes of bias against gays and lesbians.
4. The City Council will pass a comprehensive civil rights ordinance which will include sexual preference protection.
5. The City Council will establish a Permanent Commission on the Status of Lesbians, Gays and Bisexuals.
6. The City Council will pass an ordinance outlawing discrimination against people with AIDS, ARC, or who test HIV positive.
7. The City Council will propose comprehensive nondiscrimination Articles in all their agreements with city employees.
8. The City Council will ensure establishment of an AIDS treatment program.
9. The City Council will instruct the City lobbyists to support state and federal Legislation (gay rights bill), which is consistent with this platform and its goals (*People for Change Platform*, 1987).

Eventually, PFC leadership focused on a strategy to run three candidates in the November election, taking advantage of a state law that reserved three of Hartford's nine at-large city council seats for minority parties or individual petitioning candidates. (No party may run slates of more than two-thirds of the seats on at-large public bodies, and no boards or commissions may have more than two-thirds of their seats occupied by one party.) The idea gained support and the group assembled a candidate selection committee on which gay and lesbian activists served. While laboring to develop a stronger pro-gay PFC platform, author Bonelli, then a graduate student at the University of Connecticut School of Social Work and a gay rights leader, decided to seek the nomination of PFC for the City Council. All candidates who were interviewed for the slate were asked if they would continue supporting PFC even if they were not nominated to the PFC slate.

Three candidates, Marie Kirkley-Bey, Eugenio Caro, and Bill Hagan were selected for the PFC City Council slate. Although not selected for the slate, Bonelli's affirmative response to the question of unconditional support for the slate, coupled with his subsequent graduate social work field placement with PFC, enabled the gay, lesbian, and bisexual community to gain increased respect within PFC and the broader Hartford activist community. In turn, Bonelli's internship allowed PFC to have crucial human resources and provided the gay community with an organizer who sought to increase their participation in the overall campaign. Gay volunteers served in all capacities within the campaign, including phone banking, door-to-door canvassing, fundraising, get-out-the-vote tasks, and numerous other responsibilities.

The 1987 PFC City Council campaign provided the gay and lesbian community with a foray into local electoral political organizing. Gays gained access to and helped create a new political party, participated in the campaign, and exerted power through the developing strength of the community's volunteer and donor base. PFC candidates had access to a formerly untapped constituency that was responsive to political leaders who challenged homophobic and heterosexist institutions and embraced gay equality. However, unlike the Puerto Rican and African American heterosexual communities that could identify clearly established voting blocs within targeted neighborhoods, the gay community in Hartford and the region was dispersed. While cities such as San Francisco and New York possess clearly defined gay neighborhoods, Hartford gay organizers approached their community through the existing networks supporting a statewide gay rights law. Organizing tactics included (a) outreach and public education, including outreach at gay and lesbian bars, PFC visibility at gay pride rallies and anti-hate crimes rallies, and presentations at gay and lesbian community organizational meetings, (b) use of established mailing lists of gay organizations, (c) media strategies, including articles and ads in the gay press and gay-specific campaign literature, and (d) voter registration drives.

A new era dawned for the Hartford gay community on election night in 1987, when PFC won two seats on the Hartford City Council as Eugenio Caro and Marie Kirkley-Bey were elected. The pride that gay, lesbian, and bisexual activists felt was unmistakable when the community and its leaders were acknowledged for their hard work in achieving victory. The gay community emerged as a force in local politics.

PFC success in the gay community could be attributed to numerous factors, six of which are identifiable. First, the Hartford Democratic Party's lack of direct, active inclusion and recruitment of the GLBT community left an opportunity for a political party which spoke to its concerns to gain the community's support. Second, GLBT leaders in Hartford possessed a progressive, pro-labor vision and paved the way for progressive activists to approach the gay community for inclusion in its broad agenda for change. Third, the PFC leadership was receptive to gay issues and included gay activists. Fourth, the Hartford GLBT leadership increasingly grasped the significance of electoral organizing and coalition building to gain support for gay rights issues, particularly the state anti-discrimination bill. Fifth, the social environment in Hartford, as in many other places, was one in which gays and lesbians experienced intense homophobia and heterosexism and, within such an atmosphere, GLBT community members thirsted for a legitimate political force that openly embraced its causes and issues. PFC opened the doors for the gay community's inclusion in local and statewide electoral organizing efforts. Finally, the successful organizing efforts undertaken by the GLBT community in support of PFC demonstrated the efficacy of this community as a political force.

Democrats for Change and the Juan Figueroa Campaign

Subsequent to the PFC victory in 1987, the Puerto Rican Political Action Committee (PRPAC) (see Cruz, 1998), an organization that united a broad range of Puerto Rican community activists, began laying the groundwork for the election of Hartford's first Puerto Rican state representative, Juan Figueroa. PRPAC's strategy was to build on the PFC victory by establishing a stronger voice within the Democratic Party. Eugenio Caro's election, after he had been passed over by the Democratic Party, sent a message to the Democratic establishment that Puerto Rican incorporation into the party apparatus had to become a priority for the party's own viability in Hartford. So the PRPAC, with support from PFC, created Democrats for Change (DFC). PFC leadership had decided to pursue both "inside" and "outside" strategies–the third party route simultaneously with the creation of greater opportunities for progressives within the Democratic Party.

The first steps in electing Juan Figueroa involved the 3rd District Town Committee in Hartford, the entity which hands out party endorsements. DFC put forward candidates for the Democratic Town Committee in what was then the 3rd General Assembly District. Replacing the sitting town committee members would be required to successfully nominate Figueroa. He had to challenge an incumbent State Representative, Arthur Brouillet. If nominated by the 3rd District Town Committee, Figueroa would be the endorsed candidate and Brouillet would have to challenge in a primary.

PFC, working through DFC, supported the Puerto Rican community's quest to gain badly needed representation in the state legislature. Although Brouillet, a white teacher union activist, had a liberal voting record in the General Assembly, Figueroa was representative of the large Puerto Rican and Latino population in the 3rd District, and he was becoming a leading progressive activist in his own right. Figueroa was one of PFC's "own," and the organization shifted into full gear to support his candidacy.

The candidate selection process was fraught with controversy due to the gay community's pursuit of a seat on the DFC slate. An "out" lesbian activist, Carol Gale, also the chairperson of the annual Hartford Gay Pride celebration, sought the nomination for the Town Committee slate from the DFC selection committee to become a voice for gay and lesbian concerns within the Democratic Party Town Committee structure.

In order for the DFC slate to be elected to the 3rd District Democratic Town Committee, it would have to win a caucus-style local election. All Democrats in the district were eligible to attend the caucus and vote for candidates for the 3rd District Town Committee. A local political activist, then a closeted gay man and now an openly gay state representative, organized a competing slate for the Town Committee. His slate included several of the same individuals on the DFC slate but excluded Carol Gale. It won the 3rd District caucus vote. Gale's candidacy had tested PFC's ability to support gay issues, and her defeat sparked intense internal PFC dialogue about its strength and cohesion. Since the PFC's purpose was both to advocate a progressive urban agenda and to empower disenfranchised constituencies, her defeat carried symbolic and strategic implications. While PFC was not directly at fault for this defeat, gay and lesbian activists pressed the organization to endorse various pro-gay provisions. The most direct concession was that PFC and DFC would support only an "out" gay or lesbian to fill any vacancies on the 3rd District Town Committee.

All of the remaining DFC-backed candidates were elected to the Town Committee. Gay and lesbian community activists had decided to raise funds for only the four Puerto Rican slate members who had been backed by DFC, an action designed to send an unambiguous message to the other slate members that actions against Gale would be punished and that they had to prove their support for gay issues. Several members of the Democratic Town Committee race committed to support gay and lesbian issues and concerns, as did PFC. Yet when a vacancy later surfaced on the town committee, it required an aggressive multi-month organizing strategy to get key members to support the appointment of Gale. Finally, she was appointed to fill the vacancy, served out her term, and was reelected.

The experience points out the necessity of tenacity and commitment to affect political institutions at the grassroots level. Many voters are totally unaware of the inner machinations of the Democratic or Republican Party establishments. Democratic Town Committee structures have tremendous power in terms of the endorsements and can be vehicles for injecting gay and lesbian issues into the party platform and the candidate interview process. The struggle in Hartford's 3rd Assembly District provided dozens of gay activists and other voters an essential education in electoral party organizing.

After winning the Democratic Town Committee race, DFC, PFC, and the PRPAC set their sights on electing Juan Figueroa as Hartford's first Puerto Rican state representative. The campaign also provided the Coalition a chance to show its strength by helping elect a pro-gay state representative to the General Assembly and an opportunity to build stronger alliances with the Puerto Rican community. It had been a long-standing desire for progressive gays to build a multicultural gay rights movement and work in coalition with progressive allies of color.

Gay and lesbian support helped build Juan Figueroa's campaign infrastructure. Bonelli was hired as volunteer coordinator and focused on mobilizing both the gay community and key PFC volunteers. Figueroa's campaign also helped increase Latino gay participation in political issues. Yet, although numerous GLBT Latino/a activists participated in the campaign and voted for Juan Figueroa, they did not do so in an open, "out" fashion. One Latina activist stated, "We [Latino/as] have to go back and live in the Puerto Rican community. White gays can leave. We want to maintain relationships with our families." Despite these issues, Juan Figueroa was elected in 1988 with strong and visible gay support. He publicly recognized the participation of the gay community in his campaign. He brought his commitment to gay civil rights issues to his tenure in the Legislature, an important step in increasing the ranks of pro-gay elected officials in the state House and Senate to finally pass nondiscrimination legislation. Figueroa's victory signaled another step in the maturation of Connecticut's gay rights movement.

The Lesbian and Gay Rights Coalition Political Action Committee and the Legislative Electoral Action Program

On January 28, 1988, the Coalition formally established the Lesbian and Gay Rights Coalition Political Action Committee (LGPAC). The LGPAC was encouraged to join the Legislative Electoral Action Program (LEAP), a statewide coalition of progressive political action committees that included the United Auto Workers, New England Health Care Employees-District 1199-SEIU, Connecticut State Federation of Teachers, the Connecticut Citizen Action Group, National Organization for Women, and the Puerto Rican Political Action Committee. LEAP had formed in 1980 in response to the ascendancy of the right, with the goals of electing progressives to the state legislature and passing progressive legislation. Until 2001, LEAP functioned as an alternative operation for the progressive and left elements both inside and outside the Democratic Party. It fostered leadership development, trained campaign staff, and doled out support based on candidates' positions on progressive issues. LEAP was a strong counterforce to the moderate and conservative elements within the Democratic Party and a home for those who felt disenfranchised from the entrenched party leadership.

LEAP encouraged and assisted in the formation of the LGPAC. Its invitation to LGPAC to affiliate was additional validation of the gay community's evolving political power, as well as a positive proactive step for LEAP. Each advance made by the gay community and those acts of inclusion initiated by progressive heterosexuals were increasingly significant and meaningful. They were blows against institutionalized heterosexism and engendered tremendous pride and self-confidence in members of the gay community.

If a central component of organizing is relationship building, LEAP proved to be a critical vehicle for networking among progressives and for dispelling myths and strengthening ties for gay and lesbian political activists. Through LGPAC joining LEAP, gay issues became more integrated into the overall agenda of the progressive movement, and the gay and lesbian community could secure support for a range of significant issues from candidates seeking LEAP's endorsement. Gay and lesbian activists sat on the LEAP Executive Committee and were encouraged to participate in all LEAP activities. LEAP sponsored an annual fundraising dinner in which progressive activists from across Connecticut came together. Gay and lesbian activists joined in these festivities and were awarded special recognition for their organizing and issue victories.

Although there had been no overall community plan to engage in strategically advantageous coalitions, gay and lesbian activists' ideological perspectives motivated them to participate in progressive coalitions both in Hartford and statewide during the late 1980s and early 1990s. The gay community's leaders understood the importance of coalition building and took advantage of the opportunities to participate in PFC and LEAP. Through the coalitions, they gained visibility for the gay community and made progress toward the ultimate goal of passage of a statewide nondiscrimination law.

While it increased the number of pro-gay allies in the legislative arena, the gay and lesbian community's coalition and electoral involvement also bolstered the progressive movement locally and statewide, and created new allies for gay rights. One example of unlikely support for gay issues came from the International Association of Machinists (IAM). An IAM official who was also a leader in LEAP encouraged the Coalition to reach out to his union to solicit their endorsement of the state gay rights bill. Without the relationship building that had occurred within LEAP, he would not have been likely to advocate within his union for the endorsement of this bill.

Because many Connecticut unions have cultivated enduring and effective relationships with elected officials, the Coalition sought union support of the gay rights bill with the hope that labor would actively lobby legislators on behalf of the bill. In the process, many unions, specifically their leadership, were willing to take the political risk of supporting the gay civil rights bill. The Coalition also began to frame the struggle as a workers' rights issue that would benefit their memberships. Several unions eventually signed on in support of the legislation, including the United Auto Workers, Connecticut State Federation of Teachers, New England Health Care Employees-District 1199-SEIU, the IAM, and the Service Employees International Union State Council.

Through gay community participation in LEAP and PFC, labor gained the gay community's support for unions' struggles. For example, the Coalition endorsed a strike by the United Auto Workers at Colt Firearms and encouraged its members to participate in strike-support fundraisers. This was a regionally significant strike for the labor movement. It began in 1986, lasted for over four years, and involved over 800 workers at Colt plants in Hartford and West Hartford, Connecticut (Lendler, 1997; Simmons, 1994). Coalition leaders participated in large strike-support rallies and spoke at these events. Prior to the Coalition's participation in LEAP and PFC, gay activists' support for the strike would have hardly been expected, but under the circumstances it was relatively easy to cultivate.

1989: Out and Running

The next logical and principled step in the quest for gay and lesbian rights was to run an openly gay or lesbian candidate for Hartford City Council. It was clear to gay and lesbian activists within PFC and the Coalition that if the community wanted to elect from its ranks, then it would have to launch an aggressive organizing effort that maximized the fundraising and volunteer mobilization talents of its members. Ultimately, John Bonelli (first author) was selected for the PFC City Council slate in 1989 along with Eugenio Caro and Sandra Little. This time, Bonelli's candidacy was pursued with greater sophistication and insight into electoral politics afforded by all of the activism he and other gay and lesbian activists had undertaken.

Bonelli's nomination was not automatic simply because he had been a PFC activist. In the months leading up to the official endorsement, Bonelli established an exploratory committee that worked to position him for nomination. The Bonelli campaign raised $12,000 as a show of community support and capacity even before receiving the endorsement. Since PFC had expended tremendous resources between 1987 and 1989 in electing two people to Hartford City Council, unseating a Democratic Town Committee slate, and electing Juan Figueroa as a state representative, candidates who would be on its slate needed to bring resources to bear–both financial and human.

Previous PFC efforts helped empower two significantly disenfranchised communities in Hartford, both, however, with significant, identifiable voter bases–Puerto Ricans and African Americans. In selecting a gay candidate, PFC would be more deeply fulfilling its mission, but it also needed to consider the candidate's resource base, the ethnic and historic roots of the individual, and any other significant factors. Bonelli was a strong and credible addition to the slate: He was born and raised in Hartford's South End, a predominately Italian and Irish neighborhood. He had visibility due to his activism within the gay community and former roles within a local Catholic church and as a student at Trinity College, both also in the South End. His family had roots within the city, and his Italian heritage was an additional asset. Through aggressive outreach in the South End, he could seek votes from a base largely untapped by PFC. He also had appeal in the West End of Hartford, a constituency which included many liberal whites and a growing gay and lesbian community. His candidacy was taken seriously in the larger Hartford community and by the media:

> Bonelli's candidacy illustrates the enormous strides taken by Hartford's gay and lesbian community over the past year and a half, metamorphosing from a scattered, low-profile group of people, to a vocal, organized, issue-oriented coalition. Bonelli attributes the change to the national issues of AIDS and homophobic violence, as well as local incidents such as the murder of gay Wethersfield resident Richard Riehl. (Riva, 1989)

Bonelli won PFC's nomination and mounted a serious, spirited campaign that galvanized gay and lesbian activists throughout the area, as well as PFC activists and supporters. LEAP's professional campaign organizers counseled him to focus on citywide issues that reached a broader audience than the gay community. To be taken seriously, he had to be conversant with a range of municipal government issues such as taxation, education, urban development, and other matters. He could draw on his lifelong knowledge and commitment to the city as he also raised concerns of gays and lesbians.

Although he received the nomination and ran a tireless campaign, Bonelli lost the election. He came in tenth in a race for nine seats, with 141 votes less than his running mate Eugenio Caro. This left one Republican, Roger Ladd, on the Council.

Despite Bonelli's loss, the campaign elevated the issue of gays running for office and served as a catalyst for further attention to gay and lesbian civil rights issues. The campaign forced the political establishment to take the gay community seriously and dramatically illustrated the organizing capabilities of this community. Bonelli's campaign also demonstrated that voters would support an openly gay candidate. Voters of all racial and ethnic backgrounds voted for Bonelli for Hartford City Council as part of the racially and culturally diverse PFC slate of 1989.

As Hartford is the capital of Connecticut and one of its largest cities, political activities and strategies undertaken there are watched closely throughout the state. The substantial press coverage of Bonelli's run for office validated the gay and lesbian community as an authentic and distinct voting bloc and community. Electoral political activists observed a new force making its mark in this arena. The campaign set the stage for future openly gay and lesbian candidates to pursue office and get elected.

1991:
Mayor Carrie Saxon Perry and the Triumph (and Eventual Fall) of Progressives

After two terms of serving as the minority voice on the Hartford City Council, PFC was open to new strategies that would broaden its power and ability to advance progressive policies. In 1987, Carrie Saxon Perry was Hartford's first African American female to be elected mayor and had previously served as a state legislator. Hartford's Council-Manager form of government (the subject of several charter revision referenda) limits the role of the mayor. She did not have a vote on Council and thus could primarily use her office as a bully pulpit. In order to assert her leadership and increase her power, Mayor Perry decided to challenge incumbent Democrats by mounting a slate in a Democratic primary. PFC decided to coalesce with Perry in her efforts. The strategy involved Perry's slate of six Democrats winning a September primary and then, with the support of the Mayor and her forces, finally being able to elect all three PFC candidates to Hartford City Council in hopes of functioning as a progressive governing coalition.

The coalition established to unseat the incumbent Democrats included labor, PFC, African American leaders, the Puerto Rican Political Action Committee, and South End leaders. Perry's enormous popularity and the breadth of the coalition led to victory in 1991. PFC was finally able to unseat the last Republican councilperson and elect its entire slate: Eugenio Caro, Sandra Little, and Louise Simmons (second author).

Once again, GLBT participation in the campaign was significant. A newly formed Hartford Pride PAC interviewed the slate of Democratic candidates. Their responses and the significant support for Mayor Perry within the gay and lesbian community motivated many activists to volunteer and contribute. Bonelli was hired to assist with organizing for the Democrats and PFC. Gays, Lesbians and Bisexuals for Democrats for Leadership (the name of Perry's primary slate) was formed. PFC's proven track record in its support of gay and lesbian issues and the inclusion of Simmons on its 1991 slate also garnered significant gay and lesbian support. Simmons was among the founders of PFC, had a long history of progressive activism, and had won the trust and confidence of the gay and lesbian community.

The 1991-1993 City Council term turned out to be a tumultuous one (see Simmons, 1996a, 1996b). After six months in office, the coalition of PFC and Democrats fractured. Two of the three PFC councilmembers and two Democrats aligned with Mayor Perry in a "minority" bloc. One PFC councilmember and four Democrats forged a "majority" voting bloc. Despite the intense conflict, a variety of actions by the City Council benefited the gay and lesbian community. Among these were the establishment of a city commission on gay and lesbian issues; a process of registration for gay and lesbian unions; progress on domestic partnership policies (certain limited benefits, but not full insurance coverage); expansion of city involvement in AIDS programs, including the inauguration of a needle exchange program; and other programs. Moreover, gays and lesbians were regular participants in city hall activities, and their participation was sought for many municipal activities.

The unfortunate postscript in this is that in 1993, PFC ran a slate of three and Perry sought reelection with a slate of Democrats. However, the electoral scene was more complicated than ever. A four-way Democratic mayoral primary took place, including slates led by incumbent councilmembers and one by Mayor Perry. After the electoral dust settled in November, Perry and several of her council slate had lost. A petitioning Democrat for Mayor, Mike Peters, and a hodge-podge of Democrats and Republicans who had constituted themselves as a slate won and took office. Among newcomers who ran for City Council with Perry was Susan Hyde who ran as an out lesbian. Also on the Perry slate was Evelyn Mantilla, who lost in the primary but later ran for and won a State House of Representatives seat in Hartford. During her first term, she came out as bisexual and has championed GLBT rights in the state legislature (where she remains) throughout her legislative career.

Peters, his five City Council allies, and four candidates who had run with Perry, including Susan Hyde, took office. The four "Perry Democrats" were outnumbered and endured a frustrating term. Hyde resigned part-way through the term and was replaced by an individual who joined with the five "Republi-crats," as they were called, in a new era of urban conservatism (Simmons, 1998). Gay and lesbian issues took a marked back seat on the City Council's agenda.

Connecticut Becomes the Third State to Pass Gay Civil Rights Legislation

As the gay and lesbian community pursued an agenda that encompassed support of a broader spectrum of progressive issues, progressive organizations reciprocally began to include gay rights in their agendas. It was important that gay and lesbian leaders did not view their issues as isolated from comparable issues of discrimination and oppression. Their ideology embraced both issues of identity politics and economic justice, including the struggle for workers' rights, for abortion rights, and against racism. All opportunities to ally with progressive organizing efforts were cultivated by leadership within the Coalition. However, these initiatives were not met with universal support within the organization. Regional and class divisions surfaced as the Coalition attempted to support a statewide progressive income tax and the endorsement of Jesse Jackson for President in 1988. However, internal political differences during this period did not hamper the Coalition leadership from fully allying with progressive allies.

The clarity with which the Coalition moved forward in order to position the gay rights movement within a broader progressive movement proved to be a successful organizing model. Carrying out this philosophical perspective required maintaining a majority vote on the Coalition steering committee. This was accomplished through chapter representatives and issue task forces whose leadership was aligned with the progressive vision.

Progressive allies invited Coalition representatives to major organizing strategy sessions for labor and community activists sponsored by Region 9A of the United Auto Workers (UAW), held at the UAW conference and recreation center on Black Lake in northern Michigan. These retreats were opportunities for increased relationship building among labor leaders, rank-and-file, and progressive activists, including gays and lesbians. Although the participation of gay activists was limited in the first retreat, subsequent gatherings saw greater gay visibility. Through both activism within the retreat and increased sensitivity of the UAW leadership to gay civil rights concerns, gay issues became included in the overall planning. The larger implications of including gays in these retreats were significant. Unions who were involved became more receptive to gay issues. For example, unions in Connecticut (notably SEIU unions) have advocated for domestic partner benefits for members.

All of the activities outlined above in which the Coalition was involved resulted in greater visibility for civil rights struggles of the GLBT community. This translated into support for the passage of statewide civil rights legislation that was introduced in Connecticut's legislature in 1991, as it had been for more than a dozen previous years. The organizing effort by the Coalition was extremely broad and involved several important developments. An important element was the education of LEAP-endorsed and elected officials on this issue. Second, the Coalition established local chapters throughout the state and hired a leading progressive lobbyist to monitor the progress of the legislation and advise the entire organizing effort. Finally, a coordinated campaign of direct action and civil disobedience was carried out by community members and allies targeting the governor and legislators, including planned arrests at the state capitol and the defying of a ban on carrying signs and banners inside the capitol building by the unfurling of a banner from the gallery of the Legislature.

Also contributing to the success was the support of several groups. Two important leaders publicly came out as part of the campaign and expressed their support: a then-state representative, Joseph Grabarz, who later served for several years as Director of the Connecticut Civil Liberties Union, and a feminist leader, Leslie Brett, then chairperson of the State Commission on Human Rights and Opportunities and Executive Director of the Connecticut Women's Education and Legal Fund. In addition, a Religious Task Force was created that mobilized supportive spiritual leaders, and representatives of the Catholic Church, who had earlier opposed the legislation, lent their support. Finally, a broad coalition of supportive labor, religious, and community groups was formed to participate in the campaign.

Finally, after years of organizing, planning, strategizing, and protesting on the part of the gay community, the Connecticut Legislature passed the bill which protected heterosexuals, bisexuals, and homosexuals on the basis of sexual orientation. The basic protections barred discrimination in housing, employment, credit, state services, and accommodations. Governor Lowell Weicker signed the bill into law in 1991 and the Coalition achieved its central goal. A new era of respect for the gay, lesbian, and bisexual communities had begun, and the vast network of individuals and organizations that supported basic civil rights protection for the gay community celebrated the newly established rights for sexual minorities within Connecticut.

The struggle for passage of a basic gay and lesbian civil rights law was the single most unifying issue addressed by the Coalition. In order to unite the GLBT community, various activists agreed to support an agenda and actions that they would not ordinarily be expected to support. Those whose class interests conflicted with a broader progressive agenda remained active in the Coalition until victory on the statewide civil rights bill. The latent regional and class divisions that lay beneath the surface, but remained dormant during the struggle for the legislation, emerged more strongly in subsequent years when the gay community lacked a single unifying concern. Participation in the Coalition waned immediately after passage, but later revived in response to regressive federal legislation and efforts by the Coalition to broaden its agenda and organizational base.

Subsequently, the Coalition organized for passage of, and won, domestic partner benefits for state employees and second parent adoption rights for nonbiological parents, and has continually fought off attempts to pass Defense of Marriage legislation. The Coalition has worked on these issues in tandem with Love Makes a Family, a powerful statewide coalition that it helped found in 1999. Love Makes a Family has maintained a strong active role in advancing legislative issues supporting gay families, including the struggle to secure either marriage or civil union rights for the gay community in Connecticut. It has a broad base of support throughout the state and maintains volunteer involvement and local organizing networks within each of the Congressional districts.

ANALYSIS AND CONCLUSION

As this article outlines, the struggle for gay civil rights in Connecticut has involved all the central elements of community organization, particularly coalition building and electoral organizing. Important allies have been cultivated and their support has been essential to the significant victories and inclusion of gay rights issues in broader progressive movements within the state. Through this combination of tireless efforts of courageous members of the gay community willing to risk their livelihoods and lives to come out and the advocacy by progressive allies, basic rights for individuals on the basis of sexual orientation have been expanded in Connecticut.

Examples from the late 1980s and early 1990s of People for Change, the Legislative Education Action Program and the Connecticut Coalition for Lesbian and Gay Civil Rights–each of which attempted to create broad coalitions for economic and social change–remain important models to be explored by other cities and communities. As vehicles for progressive change, coalitions help to clarify who the allies are in the larger struggle for economic and sexual freedom. Moreover, contemporary gay and lesbian causes could benefit from a reinvigoration of coalition politics and, conversely, the progressive movement must include the struggle for the rights of sexual minorities.

While this article attempts to highlight the successes of such coalitions and electoral strategies, the authors are well aware of the problems, limitations and mistakes inherent in such strategies. Electoral politics takes enormous patience, and legislative advocacy is replete with partial victories, as well as setbacks. The petty deal-making and the tedious campaign work require vigilance, perseverance, and an ability to see beyond these sometimes annoying necessities of politics toward the larger goals of equity. In Connecticut, gay and lesbian political activists have developed a great deal of sophistication after years of experience.

The inclination on the part of numerous gay rights organizations to portray themselves and the movement in terms of single issues, concerned with a narrow vision of identity politics, has grave implications for the entire effort of advancing gay, lesbian, bisexual, and transgender rights. Ultimately, such a narrow vision excludes the significant issues facing working class, poor, and unemployed members of the gay and lesbian, bisexual and transgender communities. A movement that does not embrace a broader vision which includes an economic analysis and highlights the staggering numbers of homeless, uninsured, and hungry gay men, lesbians, bisexual, and transgender individuals does a disservice to efforts to change the culture and broader society. Although slick marketing efforts and public relations schemes highlight the financial wealth of certain segments of the gay community, the vast majority who are in the working class remain invisible and ignored. Gay leaders must remember that large segments of their constituency *are* poor or working class, and their needs are not different from those of other poor or working class people. Thus, issues addressed by coalitions that cross class, race, and ethnic lines are also important to members of the gay community. Organizing strategies must encompass this reality to identify the breadth of GLBT concerns.

There are widespread attempts within the gay rights movement to isolate gay issues, buttressed by arguments that single-issue strategies lead to success. Yet isolationist strategies and identity politics alone simply cannot achieve victory for the gay rights movement. Until gay rights organizations incorporate broader social justice and economic analysis into their ideological perspectives, victories will be limited. Hartford's experience confirms that long-term victories for gay rights are best achieved by developing strong relationships with progressive allies. The reciprocal support that develops in such strategies strengthens and enhances the broader progressive movement, while the gay rights movement in particular obtains much-needed support toward its important goals.

REFERENCES

Bailey, R. (1999). *Gay politics, urban politics: Identity and economics in the urban setting.* New York: Columbia University Press.

Cruz, J. (1998). *Identity & power: Puerto Rican politics and the challenge of ethnicity.* Philadelphia: Temple University Press.

Frances, D., & Warren, J. (1992). *A history: The Connecticut Coalition for Lesbian and Gay Civil Rights: 1983-1991.* Unpublished manuscript.

Lendler, M. (1997). *Crisis and political beliefs: The case of the Colt Firearms strike.* New Haven: Yale University Press.

People for Change Platform. (1987). Leaflet.

Riva, L. (1989, July 19). Knocking on new doors. *Hartford Advocate*, pp. 1, 4.

Rosenthal, D. (2000). Gay and lesbian incorporation into four urban regimes in upstate New York. In R. Keiser and K. Underwood (Eds.), *Minority politics in the millennium* (pp. 227-255). New York: Garland Publishing.

Simmons, L. (1994). *Organizing in hard times: Labor and neighborhoods in Hartford.* Philadelphia: Temple University Press.

Simmons, L. (1996a). The battle for city hall: What is it we fight over. *New England Journal of Public Policy, 12,* 97-116.

Simmons, L. (1996b). Dilemmas of progressives in government: Playing Solomon in an age of austerity. *Economic Development Quarterly, 10,* 159-171.

Simmons, L. (1998). A new urban conservatism: The case of Hartford, Connecticut. *Journal of Urban Affairs, 20,* 175-198.

Organizing to Amend Antidiscrimination Statutes in Maryland

Daphne L. McClellan
Geoffrey L. Greif

SUMMARY. Federal law and statutes in most of the 50 states prohibit discrimination in housing, employment, and public accommodations on the basis of race, creed, sex, and national origin. However, only 12 states and the District of Columbia have statutes which include prohibitions of discrimination based on sexual orientation. Maryland became the twelfth state with such a provision when the State Legislature passed the Antidiscrimination Act of 2001. The road to passage of this legislation was long and winding, beginning in 1976. This article describes one of the organizations involved in the effort, Free State Justice, and the strategies that led to eventual legislative success; the article also discusses

---

Daphne L. McClellan, PhD, MSW, LSW, is Assistant Professor, Department of Social Work, University of Maryland Baltimore County, 1000 Hilltop Circle, Baltimore, MD 21229 (E-mail: dmcclellan@umbc.edu).

Geoffrey L. Greif, DSW, LCSW-C, is Associate Dean and Professor, University of Maryland, School of Social Work, 525 W. Redwood Street, Baltimore, MD 21201 (E-mail: ggreif@ssw.umaryland.edu).

Shannon Avery and Cathy Brennan, former Free State Justice board members and co-founders of the Committee for Legislative and Political Action, Gay, Lesbian, Bisexual and Transgender Community Center of Baltimore and Central Maryland, contributed to this article.

[Haworth co-indexing entry note]: "Organizing to Amend Antidiscrimination Statutes in Maryland." McClellan, Daphne L., and Geoffrey L. Greif. Co-published simultaneously in *Journal of Gay & Lesbian Social Services* (Harrington Park Press, an imprint of The Haworth Press, Inc.) Vol. 16, No. 3/4, 2004, pp. 55-68; and: *Gay and Lesbian Rights Organizing: Community-Based Strategies* (ed: Yolanda C. Padilla) Harrington Park Press, an imprint of The Haworth Press, Inc., 2004, pp. 55-68. Single or multiple copies of this article are available for a fee from The Haworth Document Delivery Service [1-800-HAWORTH, 9:00 a.m. - 5:00 p.m. (EST). E-mail address: docdelivery@haworthpress.com].

how the dynamics and processes involved in initiating such efforts can be generalized to other settings. *[Article copies available for a fee from The Haworth Document Delivery Service: 1-800-HAWORTH. E-mail address: <docdelivery@haworthpress.com> Website: <http://www.HaworthPress.com> © 2004 by The Haworth Press, Inc. All rights reserved.]*

KEYWORDS. Sexual orientation discrimination, gays, lesbians, bisexuals, sexual orientation legislation

> Seventeen years ago I lost my job as a partner in a law firm in Bethesda when my other law partner found out that I was gay. We had been associated with each other for nearly ten years at that time. The shock and hurt, which resulted, lasted for years and heavily impacted my family. (Testimony # 95)

The preceding quote and other italicized quotes throughout this article came from testimony collected by the Special Commission to Study Sexual-Orientation Discrimination in Maryland. The purpose of the Special Commission was to investigate discrimination in housing, employment, and public accommodations based on one's sexual orientation and develop recommendations for the governor. Though the incidents were recounted to the Commission in the fall of 2000, discrimination against gay and lesbian people in Maryland is not a new phenomenon. The first nondiscrimination legislation of this type was introduced to the Maryland General Assembly in 1976. In 1989 a group of gay residents in Montgomery County approached their delegate, Sheila Hixson, and asked her to sponsor an amendment to the state's antidiscrimination statutes to add sexual orientation to the protected categories of race, sex, creed, and ethnicity (S. Hixson, personal communication, November 27, 2001).

Outside of Maryland, similar legislation was introduced at all levels of government. The Equality Act was first put before Congress in 1974 by Bella Abzug (Feldblum, 2000). In spite of 28 years of efforts, a federal civil rights bill that includes sexual orientation has not yet passed. The present bill before Congress is the Employment Non-Discrimination Act (ENDA). First introduced in 1994, it is narrowly defined, and would prohibit private employers from discriminating on the basis of sexual orientation. Employment discrimination is often the most blatant and wearing. According to Rivera (1991),

> The one legal issue that presses on the daily existence of almost all gay citizens is employment discrimination. Gay employees wonder whether, in order to pursue a career and have a stable livelihood they must be closeted and live in constant fear of being found out. (p. 88)

Though there has not yet been success at the federal level, gay activists have experienced some success at the state and local levels. Select municipal governments and 12 states now have laws prohibiting discrimination in employment, housing, and/or public accommodations. Each achievement has had its own individual story; this is the story of the hard won success in Maryland.

In order to accurately reflect the history of the issue and the strategies used for the passage of the Maryland Antidiscrimination Act, numerous interviews were conducted. The data presented are compiled from interviews and published news stories, as well as the author's direct involvement. Individuals interviewed were actively involved in the legislative effort, including several members of Free State Justice, legislative staff, the primary House sponsor of the bill, Delegate Sheila Hixson, and an attorney with the American Civil Liberties Union (ACLU).

THE POLITICAL PROCESS

> A group of about eight young men, dressed in dark clothes, shouting obscenities and a few choice words such as "dykes" ran full speed at us . . . pellets/bullets pounded my car as one of my friends, Lisa, cried out that she had been shot. . . . The first response we received from the police officer we found to help us was, "Well, what would pretty girls like you be doing coming out of a lesbo bar?" The officer refused to pursue our assailants or file a police report despite our repeated requests for one to be filed. (Testimony # 91)

> I worked as a car sales consultant in Calvert County from 1985-1997 at two separate local car dealerships. . . . Behind the customers' backs, the salespeople–and even the managers and one owner–regularly called these customers (those they assumed to be homosexual) all sorts of offensive names, including fags, queers, faggots and AIDS carriers. One of the owners instructed me to "blow them off the lot," which means to do a bad job of greeting and serving them so that they will not come into the showroom. (Testimony # 81)

Finding a Sponsor and Rallying Support

After being approached by her constituents regarding the need for antidiscrimination legislation, Montgomery County Delegate Sheila Hixson was very willing to accommodate the request. Having received a master's degree in social work from the University of Michigan, she was committed to social justice and civil rights issues. She also represented a heavily Democratic district and was not concerned with being voted out of office due to her support for the legislation. The Antidiscrimination Act had first been introduced into the General Assembly in 1976-1978 and then revived in 1992. Hixson picked up the legislation and introduced and supported it beginning in 1993 and each subsequent session until its passage in 2001. Her original bill not only provided for the protection of gay, lesbian, and bisexual people but also specifically addressed the needs of the transgendered community. Although for years it attracted the ire of anti-gay groups and individuals and drew little support from the general population, Hixson persisted, believing that education and awareness would eventually win the day.

In 1990, a small group of gay activists formed the Baltimore Justice Campaign, an organization dedicated to fighting anti-gay measures in Baltimore. Several years later, after meeting with success in the city of Baltimore, the group expanded and created a statewide organization focused on supporting the Anti-Discrimination Act. The new group named itself Free State Justice (FSJ) but remained small.

At its inception, FSJ was composed of six active members and a database of approximately 200 people. The group formed a board of directors, wrote by-laws, and hired a lobbyist. Over the years, the organization struggled for survival. At last, in 1998 a meeting was held to determine whether to continue. Not wanting to quit, the remnants of the board decided to recommit themselves to the effort. One of the two female co-chairs agreed to become the first paid executive director. Always a board-driven organization, the other co-chair agreed to remain chair of the board and committed herself to building that body. Newly energized, the group continued grassroots organizing and educating legislators as the budget and database of the group grew.

Earlier, in 1994, Parris Glendening was elected governor of Maryland, something that later proved to be a victory for the gay and lesbian population. Governor Glendening had a gay brother who died of AIDS. His brother had spent his career in the military and had been closeted about his sexual orientation for fear of adversely affecting his career. His brother's experience made the governor acutely aware of the discrimination that gay and lesbian people face and made the issue personal. In 1998, after the governor had decisively won reelection, the revitalized FSJ organization approached him about supporting the Anti-Discrimination bill. In 1999, the governor included the Anti-Discrimination Act in the administration's legislative package, putting the power of his office behind the bill.

By then, a small coalition of GLBT-supportive groups had become actively involved. This included the Gay, Lesbian, Bisexual and Transgender Community Center of Baltimore and Central Maryland (GLCCB), Parents, Families and Friends of Lesbians and Gays (PFLAG), the Maryland Chapter of the National Association of Social Workers (MD-NASW) and the ACLU. The Maryland Legislative Council of Social Workers adopted the bill in 1999, 2000, and 2001 as one of its priorities, lobbying for the bill and rallying support among its constituent organizations. In addition, two members of FSJ began GLCCB's Committee for Legislative and Political Action which became a key participant in the legislative effort. Members of these groups lobbied the legislature and testified in favor of the legislation in 1998, 1999, 2000, and 2001.

Despite organized opposition from the business community and some religious groups, in 1999 the bill passed out of Maryland's House Judiciary Committee. Subsequently it passed on the floor of the House of Delegates. It was a tremendous victory after many years of effort, but one drawback was that the House Judiciary Committee voted to exclude transgendered people from mention in the legislation. Though FSJ and the Hixson had been actively supportive of including transgendered people in the legislation, they decided to continue to support the bill after transgendered people were excluded. They had received some data suggesting transgendered people would be covered under wording regarding gender. They also hoped that this population could be specifically added at some future date.

The bill did not fare as well in the Maryland Senate. The Senate Judicial Proceedings Committee, the committee comparable to the House Judiciary Committee, was heavily weighted in opposition to the bill. The issue received a hearing but never came up for a vote and died in committee.

Undaunted, the GLBT community reveled in the success it had achieved up to this point. As the eventual passage of the legislation seemed increasingly likely, more people became involved. The FSJ database grew from its early 200 to more than 8,000 entries. One long-time member of FSJ remarked, "Everybody likes a winner. We were such a small group for a long time" (C. Taylor, personal communication, November 1, 2001). Many groups had also become involved and testified at the hearings, organized their members, or contributed money. These groups included unions such as the Maryland State Teachers Association, Association of Federal, State, County, and Municipal Employees, and the AFL-CIO. The NAACP was also helpful, as were various business, religious, and civic leaders. At the national level FSJ received a great deal of support from the Human Rights Campaign, which provided three organizers and assisted in raising $20,000 to pay a lobbyist in 2001. The National Gay and Lesbian Task Force, the National Center for Lesbian Rights, Dignity USA, and People for the American Way all supported the work in various ways.

Unfortunately, the transgendered community split over the amended act, which ignored their existence. Some felt that they had been betrayed and sacrificed for the survival of the bill and refused to support the amended version. Others in the community remained involved and continued to fight for their inclusion in the final product. GLCCB followed a strategy of lobbying the Human

Developing a Strategy

Relations Commission to cover transgendered people under already-existing gender protections.

> In 1985, a large financial services company headquartered in Cumberland, Maryland, hired me. My task was to start from scratch a full-service investment brokerage firm. This I did, and I ran that subsidiary company very successfully as its President for approximately four years. Professionally it was a good career move and a challenging job that I enjoyed. On January 10, 1989, I was called into the office of the Chairman of the Board of the parent company and fired, effective immediately. I was told that my gay lifestyle was neither acceptable nor compatible with the company and the community. This, in spite of the subsidiary's success, and my personal involvement in numerous civic, social, and charitable activities. (Testimony # 41)

One group that became galvanized as a result of the 1999 success was composed of some professional lobbyists in Annapolis who happened to be gay. These men and women were professionally active on behalf of a number of different organizations, but they also had a personal interest in the passage of the Antidiscrimination Act. A couple of these lobbyists had been involved with Free State Justice and its legislative committee for some time. After the 1999 Maryland legislative session, they solicited the involvement of some of their professional colleagues who agreed to offer their services to the cause and join the legislative committee. The board and legislative committee worked together to develop a three-part strategy to present to the governor.

With 47 members of the Maryland Senate, it would require 24 votes to pass the legislation; eighteen Senators were already cosponsors of the bill. The critical first step of the strategy in 2000 was the formation of what came to be called the Constituent Action Network. The group decided to identify a volunteer campaign manager in each of the 47 voting districts. These campaign managers would work at the grassroots level to make sure that each member of the Senate received personal visits, phone calls, and letters from their constituents in favor of passage of the bill. The second aspect of the strategy identified eleven Senators considered either "must-have" votes or "possible" votes. Though the Constituent Action Network was able to secure campaign managers in only 28 of the 47 districts, they did obtain campaign managers for all 11 of the districts with the senators identified as crucial to the passage of the bill. The third aspect of the strategy was to introduce some additional gay-themed bills that would probably be assigned to committees other than the Judicial Proceedings Committee. The idea behind this strategy was to assure that if the

Antidiscrimination bill was once again held up in committee, another bill might get through to the Senate floor and could be amended with the Antidiscrimination bill's language.

Two problems occurred with the strategy. First, the governor was not interested in pressing the issue so soon after the bill's previous defeat in the Senate. His main goal in 2000 was gun control, and he was spending his political capital on that issue. Second, even though five gay-themed bills were introduced in the 2000 legislative session, the Senate leadership sent all of the bills to the Judicial Proceedings Committee. In one devastating day, all five bills were heard in committee and none made it out to the Senate floor. On the other hand, the strategy did make inroads with some undecided legislators. The commitment of the lobbyists and the groundswell of support in the GLBT community set the stage for the renewed effort in 2001.

The success of the gun control legislation sponsored by the governor was also instructional. After the 1999 legislative session, in order to convince legislators that there was public support for the gun control bill, the governor had appointed a special commission after which he held hearings around the state to assess the will of the citizens. The hearings were useful to passage of the bill because they established the political viability of the issue. Based on the success of the gun control legislation, the original strategy was revised and it was recommended that a special commission be established to investigate discrimination in employment, public accommodations, and housing based on sexual orientation. The governor received this recommendation in the summer but waited until October to appoint the special commission. As chairperson, he appointed a member of the University of Maryland Social Work faculty, Geoffrey Greif (the second author).

An attempt was made to ensure that membership on the commission was diverse and represented people opposed to the legislation as well as those who supported it. However, as hard as the governor tried, he was unable to find a business or religious representative opposed to the legislation who was willing to serve on the commission. During the fall of 2000, hearings were held in five different locations around the state. Seventy-seven percent of those testifying were in favor of a statewide antidiscrimination ordinance and 23 percent were opposed. The hearings were successful in demonstrating the need for such an ordinance, as many of those testifying recounted their personal experiences as victims of anti-gay discrimination. Free State Justice had hoped for some specific outcomes of the hearings. They had hoped that the commission would recommend passage of an antidiscrimination bill that included transgendered people. They also hoped that the commission would recommend that a budgetary component be attached to the bill for education. Attaching a budgetary component to the bill would have forced it into a different legislative committee for consideration and would have rendered it "referendum-proof," since bills with a budgetary component cannot be taken to a referendum of the voters. Ultimately, however, the commission wrote an interim report that recommended the governor reintroduce the bill that had been passed by the House of Delegates in 1999.

PASSAGE OF THE BILL AND CONTINUED RESISTANCE

> The landlord stated that he knew who those people were and "what kind they were" and he didn't want them staying in anything that he owned because he didn't want it on his conscience that he was renting to that kind.... (Testimony #22)

> I am a public school teacher in Maryland in a county that does not provide protection against gay or lesbian discrimination. You see, I could lose my teaching job in Maryland, not for lack of teaching credentials (which are in excellent standing) but for who I am. (Testimony # 116)

In the 2001 legislative session, the governor once again placed the Antidiscrimination Act in his legislative package, pledging his considerable resources. The focus of the advocacy groups continued to be on educating the members of the Senate and grassroots organizing in each district. However, instead of concentrating on 11 senators, the field had been narrowed to one specific member of the Senate Judicial Proceedings Committee. Between the 1999 session and the 2001 session, one member of the committee who was opposed to the bill had been replaced with a cosponsor of the bill. The governor had indicated that if another vote could be found on the committee, he felt certain the committee chairperson could also be persuaded to vote in favor of the bill.

The focus turned to a Democratic senator, a member of the Judicial Proceedings Committee. A paid campaign manager made sure that the senator had visits by at least one constituent every week to discuss support for the senate bill and that he heard from many others by letter, phone, and e-mail. In addition, at least one supporter of the bill attended and made him/herself known at all of the senator's public appearances. This had the effect of interesting other citizens who happened to be at the meetings and garnering additional unsolicited support. Even though the state Chamber of Commerce did not take a supportive position, the senator's local county Chamber of Commerce came out in clear support of the bill. In the end, the targeted senator chose to support the legislation. He stated that he had received more support for the bill than any in his experience as a legislator. Finally, though, the determining factor was personal. He said he made his decision to support the bill after considering what sort of world he would want if his child or grandchild were gay. The chair of the committee then decided to support the bill also.

In April the Senate Judicial Proceedings Committee passed the bill to the floor of the Senate which subsequently approved the bill by a vote of nearly two to one. On May 15th, 2001, Governor Glendening signed the bill into law.

But victory was still not assured. Maryland law states that if citizens want to challenge a law passed by the Legislature, they have 60 days to obtain signatures equivalent to three percent of the electorate that voted in the last gubernatorial election. A Maryland resident opposed to gay civil rights had been organizing others who shared his convictions. He began a petition drive immediately after the bill was signed by the governor, contending that it was "a bad law which ultimately protects illegal and immoral behavior." In 30 days he had enough signatures to continue, and within the required 60 days he and his supporters (who named themselves TakeBackMaryland; see www.takebackmaryland.org) had gathered 47,539 signatures, 1,411 more than the number legally required. The election board certified the validity of the signatures and the issue was slated to appear on the ballot in November 2002. As a result, the rights guaranteed in the Anti-Discrimination Act could not be implemented as scheduled on October 1, 2001.

Free State Justice and its many allied coalition members (most notably the GLCCB) prepared for the fight. They decided to work under the assumption that the anti-gay rhetoric leading up to the election would be highly inflammatory. Even though 60 percent of Maryland voters polled had supported gay and lesbian civil rights, there was no guarantee that more supporters than opponents would actually go to the polls on election day. GLBT leaders around the state anticipated a very difficult road ahead and formed a new organization, the For Fairness Campaign, to combat the referendum drive. Several organizations comprised the steering committee for the effort and pledged a minimum $50,000 to the campaign. The organizations included the Human Rights Campaign, the ACLU, the GLCCB, PFLAG, FSJ, the Maryland State Teachers Association, the Legislative Black Caucus, and the League of Women Voters. This degree of diversity and commitment on the steering committee sent a strong message to both sides of the issue.

The strategy for defending the law was twofold: prepare for the political campaign by educating the public to defeat the referendum, and at the same time fight the results of the petition drive in court. To prepare for the political campaign, FSJ and many of the other GLBT advocacy organizations started fundraising. They knew that the task ahead was formidable and would require a great deal of financial resources. They set a preliminary goal of raising five million dollars and planned to use part of their funds to hire an experienced campaign director/lobbyist.

A Washington, D.C., law firm took on the court battle with the assistance of the ACLU. The plaintiffs were FSJ, GLCCB, and individuals from almost every jurisdiction in the state. The defendant was the state election board and, eventually, TakeBackMaryland. The plaintiffs' strategy was to question the validity of the signatures collected. In fact, gays from across the state had been contacting FSJ and the GLCCB reporting that they had signed the petition because it had been presented to them under false pretenses. They wanted to know what to do to have their names removed.

The law in Maryland is very specific regarding petition drives for referenda. Some of the requirements clearly stated in Maryland law are that: (1) all the signatures on an individual petition must be of residents from the same county, (2) the complete text of the referendum must be printed on the back of each page of the petition, and (3) each signature on the petition must be actually witnessed by the petition gatherer at the time it is made. The petitions gathered by TakeBackMaryland failed to meet the letter of the law on each of these grounds. There were signatures on the same petition of citizens from more than one county. On many petitions the text of the referendum had been stapled to the back of the form, leaving in question whether that had been done before or after the signatures had been gathered. Some of the dates on the petitions did not correspond with the dates of the petition drive. But most damaging was the fact that when the plaintiffs started deposing the petition gatherers, they found that often the petition gatherers had not actually witnessed each individual signing the petition, though they had signed their names attesting that they had.

A special master, appointed by the circuit court judge, filed a preliminary report that thousands of the signatures contained factual errors. After considering exceptions to his report, he filed a summary of his findings on October 31 (Fox, 2001). On Wednesday, November 21, TakeBackMaryland withdrew its challenge, conceding that it had not obtained the required number of legal signatures. The presiding judge signed the order and the Anti-Discrimination Act went into effect at 3:00 p.m on November 21, 2001. Under Maryland law, the act is safe and no attempt can be made to take it to referendum again.

ANALYSIS OF THE DYNAMICS AND PROCESSES INVOLVED

Much GLBT activism around the country has been initiated around perceived discrimination issues. In fact, this is the area where much of the American public is supportive of the GLBT community (Alexander, 2002, p. 2). However, invisibility is a significant problem faced by individuals or groups who support antidiscrimination legislation. This fact is emphasized by Vaid (1995):

> Politicians and the general public often greet claims of discrimination with disbelief: gay rights advocates are asked to "prove" that such prejudice exists. But because most gayness remains closeted and stigmatized, widespread data on employment, housing, and other types of discrimination are difficult to obtain. For one, gay people who experience such treatment do not always report it, because they know they lack recourse or because they fear further stigmatization if they disclose their sexual orientation. For another, researchers studying discrimination have not asked the gay question and have therefore uncovered little data. Finally, legislative hearings on antigay and antilesbian discrimination are rare. (p. 9)

Swan (1997) not only agrees that visibility is important but also asserts that the GLBT community is becoming much more visible to attain their objectives:

> The emphasis of the GLBT community has changed from an initial assault upon discriminatory practices into a much higher profile and much more ambitious set of policy objectives.... Community members are beginning to "come out" in many people's own business, church, and community organizations. This is a threatening change to many people, and has resulted in the development of a very powerful "backlash." (p. xxii)

Other groups experiencing discrimination have blazed the trail. Small groups of individuals acknowledging common problems they experience come together and form an organization or contact an elected official who they perceive to be friendly to their concerns. However, in the context of the struggle for human rights in the United States, the first overture is rarely successful. After accepting the Nobel Peace Prize in 1964, Dr. Martin Luther King, Jr., had the opportunity to meet with President Lyndon Johnson. King broached the subject of a voter rights bill with the president during two different meetings but the president did not see the need. Though access at the highest governmental level was important, what brought about the needed change and resulted in the Voting Rights Act were the local activists throughout the South, especially in Alabama. They organized, built a grassroots movement and took their demands to the public and to the media through planned actions and marches (Gordon, Guinier, Quintero, & Vaid, 2001). They risked their jobs and their lives to tell their stories. Drawing on the lessons from the Civil Rights movement of the 1960s, gay and lesbian people are fighting for their rights–again risking their jobs and in some cases their lives and often feeling a backlash of violence (D'Emilio, Turner, & Vaid, 2000). This is what happened in the Maryland case in 1989.

The GLBT community is paying attention, learning from other issues, and banking that knowledge from national organizations such as the Human Rights Campaign can be shared throughout the country. Although few states have held legislative hearings on GLBT discrimination (Vaid, 1995), Maryland was successful in bringing anti-gay discrimination to the legislative floor. Though the situation in every state is different, the lessons learned or confirmed in Maryland can be applied to other states and other related issues.

LESSONS LEARNED

The eventual passage of the Antidiscrimination Act reflects a model referred to as the group theory model, which Haynes and Mickelson (1997) describe:

> Individuals with shared interests commonly group together to strengthen support for their demands.... Often the group is viewed as a vehicle for transmitting ideas and demands from individuals to the government. In this model, politics is seen as a struggle among groups to influence policy-making. Changes in the relative power of the group vis-à-vis another are expected to determine changes in public policy. The relative influence of a group is related to its size, the resources at its command, its leadership, and its access to decision makers. (pp. 59-60)

The success of the Maryland Antidiscrimination Act reflects all of the elements mentioned above. The size of the group grew from a handful of people to a mailing list of 8,000 supporters. The resources at its command grew considerably. Most of the resources were in terms of people who stepped forward and offered their services, people in other organizations willing to work in coalition, and people willing to write one letter, make one phone call, or visit one legislator. Money was also an important resource and the financial donations to the effort grew considerably over the years. However, once again, people stepped forward, offered their time and talent, and their commitment to seeing the process through. Finally, the access to the decision makers changed the balance. Between 1978 and 2001, the support of the decision makers grew from a handful to a two-thirds majority in both houses and a governor not only willing to sign, but willing to champion the bill. Obviously, none of this happened overnight. And, as helpful as the governor was, his support alone did not make this happen. Ultimately, the one thing that worked was action by volunteer supporters.

After seeing the bill that she had sponsored nine times finally pass, Delegate Hixson was asked what she saw as making the difference in the end. She responded that it was the fact that her colleagues had met and heard from real people. Gay people in their districts had taken the time to call, write letters, and visit in person. Many legislators had never met a gay person before, or at least not someone who said, "I am gay." Within the GLBT community, the importance of "coming out" is often discussed. This is what the annual Coming Out Day in October is all about. An effective way to change a stereotype is for the holder of that stereotype to be confronted by a contradiction. Living, breathing contradictions to stereotypes of gay men, lesbians, bisexual, and transgendered people are everywhere. During the campaign in Maryland, hundreds of these "contradictions to stereotypes" were convinced to come forward, to "come out" to their elected officials, and to tell about their lives. As a result, when the vote was taken in the committee meetings, on the floor of the House of Delegates and on the floor of the Senate, most of the people voting knew someone who would be directly affected by their vote, and who had personally asked them to vote in favor of the legislation.

The governor was predisposed to sign the bill because an individual close to him, his brother, had come out about who he was. No matter how closeted his brother had to be to maintain his military career, members of his family knew about his sexual identity. And one, eventually elected governor, was profoundly affected by that knowledge.

The lesson learned from the passage of the Anti-Discrimination Act is not revolutionary for social workers–it might be called "Community Organizing 101"–but it is a lesson which needs to be reinforced by naming it and by claiming the successes that it produces. In the case of organizing in the GLBT community, an individual can make a tremendous difference. An individual willing to be out about who he or she is can do even more. And finally, a number of individuals working together, for as long as it takes, and with a common purpose, can accomplish almost anything. This is the lesson our profession needs to learn repeatedly, a lesson exemplified by the GLBT community of Maryland and the passage of the Anti-Discrimination Act of 2001.

REFERENCES

Alexander, S. E. D. (2002). *Romer v. Evans* and the Amendment 2 controversy: The rhetoric and reality of sexual orientation discrimination in America. *Texas Forum on Civil Liberties and Civil Rights, 6*, 261-302. Retrieved July 26, 2002, from Lexis-Nexis database.

D'Emilio, J., Turner, W. B., & Vaid, U. (Eds.). (2000). *Creating change: Sexuality, public policy, and civil rights*. New York: St. Martin's Press.

Feldblum, C. R. (2000). The federal gay rights bill: From Bella to ENDA. In J. D'Emilio, W. B. Turner, & U. Vaid (Eds.), *Creating change: Sexuality, public policy, and civil rights* (pp. 149-187). New York: St. Martin's Press.

Fox, K. (2001, November 6). Pro-gay initiative wins send positive sign to Md. *The Washington Blade.*

Gordon, J., Guinier, L., Quintero, S., & Vaid, U. (2001). Looking forward: Forging the path, building the movement. *New York University School of Law Review of Law and Social Change: Vol 127. Building a multiracial social justice movement.* Retrieved July 26, 2002, from Lexis-Nexis database.

Haynes, K. S., & Mickelson, J. S. (1997). *Affecting change: Social workers in the political arena.* White Plains, NY: Longman.

Rivera, R. R. (1991). Sexual orientation and the law. In J. C. Gonsiorek & J. D. Weinrich (Eds.), *Homosexuality: Research implications for public policy* (pp. 81-100). Newbury Park, CA: Sage.

Swan, W. K. (Ed.). (1997). *Gay/lesbian/bisexual/transgender public policy issues: A citizen's and administrator's guide to the new cultural struggle.* Binghamton, NY: Haworth.

Vaid, U. (1995). *Virtual equality: The mainstreaming of gay and lesbian liberation.* New York: Random House.

VISIONS OF COMMUNITY FOR GLBT YOUTH

Resisting Fragmentation, Living Whole: Four Female Transgender Students of Color Speak About School

Nova Gutierrez

SUMMARY. This paper presents interviews with four male-to-female transgender students of color under the age of 21 at an alternative school in the Northeast. The interviews expose the need to advocate for education that acknowledges and addresses the ways that race, sexuality, class, ethnicity, and gender together inform life experience and identity, especially within the context of educational institutions. These interviews point to the need to include an activist-oriented curriculum in schools, a curriculum relevant to the lives of gay, lesbian, and transgender students of color. *[Article copies available for a fee from The Haworth Document Delivery Service: 1-800-HAWORTH. E-mail address: <docdelivery@haworthpress.com> Website: <http://www.HaworthPress.com> © 2004 by The Haworth Press, Inc. All rights reserved.]*

KEYWORDS. Transgender, race, sexuality, Latino, black

Although race, class, and gender each are recognized and serve as the basis for curriculum and other services (clubs, counseling, mentoring) in many urban schools, particularly progressive, alternative, or charter schools, sexuality is not. However, GLBT schools, like any of the other *segregated* schools, are not by virtue of their existence progressive, radical, or challenging to systemic norms. Although GLBT schools address sexuality, they often fail to effectively address issues of race, class, and gender. For students whose survival, in life and in school, depends on how they navigate their complex and completely integrated identities, a better school is one that provides a space for community-building, role models, historical grounding, and opportunity for active and involved project-based learning; challenges their critical thinking; and raises consciousness and self-awareness.

This paper presents interviews with four male-to-female transgender students of color under the age of 21 at an alternative school for lesbian, gay, bisexual, and transgender youth in the Northeast. The student population of the school is predominantly gay male, with a small number of lesbians. Most of the students are transgender in dress or behavior, but only a small number of them *live as the other gender* or are on hormone therapy. Racially, nearly all of the students are black and Latino, most with backgrounds in the Caribbean. At least one student is an English as a Second Language student; a few are classified as learning disabled. Many of the students are living on their own, and work in addition to attending school. A few have been homeless at some point in their lives.

The interviews expose the need to advocate for education that acknowledges and addresses the ways that race, sexuality, class, ethnicity, and gender together inform life experience and identity, especially within the context of educational institutions. These interviews point to an additional need to include an activist-oriented curriculum in schools and to include diverse faculty and staff representative of the student population.

I taped interviews in the fall of 2000 with four students who are identified by their alternative school as transgender, but who identify themselves in a variety of terms. I chose to interview transgender students specifically because, according to some of the teachers, the transgender students appeared to be the ones struggling the most to be successful in this school. Some were hustling, and many had begun getting illegal silicone injections to look more like *real* females. Some were angry and volatile; others chronically absent or late. Some were drug users while some were living and working completely on their own in addition to attending school. At least three were doing well in their classes in terms of grades.

At the time of these interviews, there were no transgender employees at the school, so there were no adult mentors who intimately understood what these students were going through on a daily basis. I chose to interview these students so they could speak about their particular experiences in their former schools as well as their experiences at this alternative school. It is crucial to honestly examine alternative schools for GLBT students that are labeled progressive in order to assess whether the education happening in these schools is truly liberatory for all student populations. Within the gay and lesbian community, the subjective voices of transgender people are often marginalized or ignored (Currah & Minter, 2000). Although they have been the objects of study, their life experiences and ideas as subjects are conspicuously absent (Beemyn & Eliason, 1996). Therefore, the assessment and interpretation of their own school and social experiences as transgender students of color should reveal much about how power operates in their lives and how they resist in a variety of settings, both progressive and traditional.

I interviewed each of the four students–Shari, Cassandra, Debbie, and Marisol–for about an hour and a half in cafes near the school. They were interviewed individually and as a group, in order to have the opportunity to also be in conservation with each other. They seemed very eager to share. Cassandra had recently been expelled from the alternative school, but continued to visit the after-school program. Shari was enrolled in the GED program, while Debbie and Marisol were students in the school. All were students of color and identified as black, Latino, or both. Although the school identified them as transgender (male-to-female), all four of students criticized the use of the word. Shari commented,

> I never used it [the word] because I never liked it. It sounded like a science project. . . . Oh, you're transgender, Shari. Not transgender, Shari. But, like, oh you, we have this transgender [this or that]. . . . They [the

school] always refer to you as being transgender ... I understand the word and why people use it. That ... a lot of times people need labels to better understand things. ...

Cassandra described her feelings about the label more in depth:

> Honestly I've never heard of the word transgender until I went to [the alternative school]. I've heard of a transsexual and a drag queen. But I never heard of a transgender or a femme queen.... Before I went there I always considered myself a woman. To this day I still consider myself a woman. I don't consider myself transgendered, you know. I feel like me. We're women. We're not transgendered. We're who we are. That word transgender. It really does irk me. But I can't say anything about it.
>
> Like after school, the [program] they have there, I'm gonna use the word they use, the transgender people, when they come in, when you stand there and they take your name and your age and sex, they'll put female, but when you walk away, they slash it and they'll put transgender, TG, and a lot of females and males that are transgender, they get very offended by it. I got offended by it too. But they explained why they do it, like, so I kind of paid it.
>
> The reason why they do that is so that they could get funding for the building, so they could know how many transgender people are coming. How many gay people. But for that I mean they could just put something else. Transgender makes it sound like I'm a transformer or something, or a toy that could change into something to another, okay, like, Cassandra, change. Transform. Like a cartoon or something. It's a label that shouldn't be used. I think if someone's gonna portray themselves as a woman they should be considered as a woman.

Each one of the girls felt a strong desire to operate outside of the label *transgender*, though in their interviews, they recognized the ways that they had been treated differently in the gay, lesbian, and straight communities because they are transgender. Debbie, in particular, spoke about how other people perceive transgenders as wanting to be "legitimate" in the eyes of society. Debbie's analysis of her own identity in relationship to her girlfriend, who identifies as a woman and is lesbian, illustrates a nuanced understanding of the relational nature of identity:

> I don't like the fact that you have to be labeled as a transgender, I feel that transgender shouldn't even be a word at all.... Another thing I don't like about that, that if you're transgender, the reason you're transgender is to get with the opposite sex, with the same sex, it's to be approved by the society, whatever. I don't think that's true.... People feel comfortable dressing and being the person they want to be.

> You know, because I date a girl, people think that's not right, because, you're a male trying to be a female, because that's one of the reasons you're trying to be a female. You know I don't think of it that way. I think of myself as a female that likes females. A female that likes males and females, just a female at the moment. I don't think of myself as a female with transgender experience.
>
> If she [my girlfriend] considered herself a male, then I would consider myself to be straight at the moment, [if] I consider myself a female, and she considers herself a male. But, since she considers herself as a female, I consider myself as a lesbian.

When asked about their experiences in the traditional schools they attended before this alternative school, each of the girls spoke about how race and class in addition to their sexuality affected them. Cassandra recalled:

> Elementary school was ok. I was trying to figure out my sexuality then. But nobody really bothered me then. My trouble getting spooked, as Marisol puts it, was during junior high, but guys still wanted me anyway. That was in [another state]. Also, it was very nice. I graduated with honors, um, the students were a****; the teachers, forget it, they were jerks. I had really rough teachers that really, really didn't understand children....
>
> In junior high school, when I decided I wanted to be a girl, my teachers gave me a hard time because I was growing nubs for some reason. I don't know why. They were like, oh, we can't call you a different name. And we have to call you *he* and this, that, and the third. And it really hurt me, because, you know, I'm trying to be something else and they're bringing reality into my face and it really bothered me a lot.

Marisol, more explicitly, speaks about her family's economic situation and how it affected which schools she attended. When these students spoke about the different aspects of their racial, class, sexual, and gender identities, they did so effortlessly. Just as they expressed their aversion to the label transgender because it does not capture how they perceive themselves, they spoke of their identities in holistic, completely integrated terms. The identities they speak of depend rather on the contexts of their experiences.

> *Marisol*: [At my elementary school] I made good friends... I hung out with the boys, I hung out with the girls. I didn't know I was gay. Then one day I just told my mother I wanted to move with my father. And... [when] I went to... [a new] school,... all these people was thinking I was a girl. Like, what's your name, what's your name? So I fell into the role, "My name is Cindy." So I fooled the whole damn school into thinking my name was Cindy.

I was dating my classmates. The teachers were nice to me, I don't know what the hell they said behind my back.... So, I went to junior high school. Child, that was the worst experience of my life.... I got my a** beat from the time I got there to the time I left, child.... It was really severe. Girls used to follow me home and throw rocks to me, like I'm some witch. Like I'm gonna cast some spell on their a**. But anyways, I just felt bad. Nobody cared about me.

Like by eighth grade, I just got more bold. Whatever happens happens. So I was just like, whatever. I just started fighting them and then they started to respect me. That's how I saw it. If I had to defend myself by any means necessary, then that's what I had to do to protect myself.... And then I got a nasty ... attitude. Cuz I just picked it up off the streets....

When Marisol talks about moving back with her mother, she recalls not fitting into her new high school, in particular because of the racial composition of the school:

Three years ago, I was in a high school [in the northside of the city] and it was cute. At first it was rocky, cuz of the straight boys calling me names or whatever, but then I started to meet gay people there and I started to build friendships.... Everybody was hanging out with me and they got used to it, and they paid it no more. I was hanging out with the [girls], I was hanging out with the boys. It felt nice there.

But then I kept messing up on my grades, so they moved me back upstate with my mother so I could live with her. So I was up there like a couple of months, and I was going to this school, and I knew right when I walked in, I did not fit in. Because the students were just so white, it was a white school, and it was like so damn preppy. White students would give you dirty looks. And I got harassed I would say like an average of twenty times, in like four months.

The students were like, it's not that they didn't understand what I was, it was just that they wanted to be mean for no reason. So they was like calling me names. So I felt real bad and I would tell the teachers, and they played it like it was nothing. And I was like, if I fight, do I get suspended and kicked out? I mean what?

So one day me and my mother had a fight, whatever, and I just ran away. I couldn't take it no more. I ran back to the city.... I was going from house to house, with my aunts and my mother's friends ... it was hurtful.... I hadn't been in school to close to like a year and a half. One day I was just talking to Sarah [a counselor] and I told her I wanted to join [the alternative school]. And she was like, okay, I'll see what I can do. Since you are like a member here, since you been here for a long time, you'll be highly recommended by all of the staff here.

This is my first year. It's been decent.

Again, all of the students I interviewed had learned to fight to defend themselves. Cassandra had a black belt in karate. The traditional schools they had all attended before the alternative school had forced them to perfect tough attitudes and sassy mouths as well as fighting skills. Shari had attended a traditional high school in the northside of the city and ran around with a clique of girls who would get into fights along with her, often defending her against harassers. She eventually got expelled for fighting a girl in her school. They all seemed to want a place where they "wouldn't have to use their skills," as Cassandra phrased it.

In so many of the schools, it wasn't only harassment from students that was a hindrance. Teachers, principals, and even security guards posed threats. Debbie recalled the incident that got her expelled from her high school. One of the security guards had called her a "faggot" and pushed her, so Debbie grabbed the guard's stick and slapped her with it. Debbie was suspended, but the guard was not.

When Cassandra began to really explore her sexuality in high school, she was living with her cousin's family, who eventually kicked her out. She moved in with her grandmother and continued to experiment with wearing women's clothing and her coming-out process, for which she was attacked by her uncle, who also went to jail for "busting her eye open." The incident that resulted in her expulsion from her former high school involved Cassandra breaking another student's nose on the lunchroom table after he had harassed and hit her. But she says she didn't really want to come to the alternative school. In fact, Cassandra was expelled from the school a month before our interview.

> I really never wanted to come [here]. How can I say this? It wasn't by choice that I got selected to that school. I was placed there because of my sexuality. And I feel that was very disrespectful on the Board of Education's behalf. Because I really didn't want to go to that school. I was accepted in 1997 and I didn't want to go. I explained that to them and they just put me there anyway. . . .
>
> I had already joined the after-school program and I saw how kids were, how shady [aggressive] they were, and I wasn't shady then, and I didn't know how to throw shade, I was very quiet. I just didn't like that area. . . . Being in my other school for so long, it made me more aggressive and it made me more fighting because I had skills that I never really wanted to use, you know, and I had to use them. After I used them so many times, I felt like I was big and bad because nobody beat me . . . so that's how my attitude, that's how my stronger attitude came along, and to this day my attitude is still, *No one can beat me.*

Most of the students simply seemed to be demanding respect for their identities–their *whole* identities, not just fragments. They wanted to be acknowledged, listened to, and accepted as whatever gender or persona they chose to put forward. Debbie recalled:

> And then I applied to [the alternative school] and I really didn't get chosen, but the Board of Ed sent me there. And I was like, well, I'm gonna go there anyway, because I wanted to start my transformation from a boy to a girl. So when I'm done with my transformation I want to go back to a straight school, to a regular school, where they treat you more fairly than how they do in [the alternative school].
>
> Well, if they know that I'm a boy they wouldn't treat me fairly, but if they think I am what I appear to be, then they will treat me fairly, but everything else, like . . . I came [to the alternative school] as a boy, but then I started dressing like a girl. They'll give me all "he's" and push my birth name. And all the other transgenders that came in as transgender, they'll respect them and call them the name they want to be called and they won't do that for me, and I feel that that isn't right.

Given their experiences, the students had very clear ideas about the kind of schools they envisioned as ideal. Their experiences in a place like the alternative school described here show that creating a school around a particular, singular identity might not be the solution. Progressive schools serving these populations must come up with other strategies for education and not rely on traditional systems in nontraditional settings. In a physical sense, adequate facilities and resources are needed to be able to meet the needs of large populations, but also, a diverse faculty and staff, representative of the student population, is needed to provide mentors and role models.

Curriculum must be engaging and activity-centered, with explicit links made between content and real, lived experience. Students who have been disenfranchised and who are on the outside of the political structure of society must receive an education that will help them learn how to organize and build communities that will be able to struggle for justice. Students need safe spaces where they can build trust, talk with each other, talk with caring and empathetic adults, process and theorize about their daily experiences, and use those discussions in classroom activities that are structured to help them actively build new social and academic spaces.

Many of these issues came up when I asked students to describe the schools they envisioned as well as their future aspirations:

> *Shari*: There's not really much I want to do that I don't think I can. Maybe there's something I haven't thought of that might be hard for me to do, but everything's hard. Nothing is impossible.

Debbie: I want a school where everyone is equal, is accepted. It wouldn't be another [school like this]. It would just be equal . . . [everybody] all in one school. I don't think any of that should be segregated at all. And one class I would really want to be in there is gender studies, because a lot of people don't really know much about gender. They just know what's on the television, you know, the media. . . . I read that it's not just what's between your legs, it's what's inside your mind. So, it's like, that's one thing I would have. So that everyone will have an understanding of the gay life. The transgender life. So there will be more of an understanding and there will be more of an acceptance in the community, in the world.

Cassandra spoke about the difficulty of living as a "transgender" and remarked on how society is not accepting of her, either legally or socially. The students recognized the injustice of society, that the rights of citizenship, like marriage, are denied them:

It's really hard for transgenders more than regular gay men who walk off as men. It's harder for transgenders to be accepted by society because of the way they dress and present themselves to be. . . . For us to walk out of our house it takes a lot of guts, to walk out of our houses like this, cuz I mean, we're trying to be women, and some guys could tell that we're not, and they be like, oh you . . . fag, that's a man or whatever, it's really hard sometimes. Sometimes guys want to bash you. . . .

There's a lot of things in this society that just aren't right. You can't even get married in this society. Gay people can't even get married. And I think that's wrong. Like you can get married, but not legally. . . . I congratulate a lot of transgenders, even females who look like guys, we give them a very big applause because it takes a lot of guts to walk out of your house like that knowing that society will not accept them more than regular gay people.

Marisol spoke at great length about her vision, which was one that summed up the spirit of an inclusive education quite well:

If I was to make a school, child, you know I would have a school for every sexual orientation, whether gay, straight, lesbian, bisexual, questioning, and transgender youth. I would have a class like Debbie said, gender studies. The reason I would have that class is cuz I feel even though people will know about gay and lesbian and transgender youth and adults, I think they know about it, but they don't fully understand it.

There's some of us out there who actually want to make a difference. I feel that people just don't understand that. They just have a one-track mind. They really don't even really care to understand. Like my grandparents. So I wish there was a school back then that actually taught them about that stuff. It wouldn't be so narrow minded when I speak to them now about it cuz they don' t understand what I'm saying. They try to interpret what I'm saying. But I don't think they fully understand. . . .

I would have a school like that. I want everybody to feel comfortable with one another. The straight people could just walk by the gay people and be like, "hey wassup" . . . give them five . . . not be like, that's a fag, watch out for your a** . . . all that other stuff, that's stupid, that's ignorant. . . . I've dealt with that s*** for a long time and I really think it's stupid.

I actually really wanted to become a singer and an actor. A female singer or actor. I see that as, I don't think I would be accepted like that. So really, I want to work more in gay activism and stuff like that. Cuz I want to pave the way for people who have the dreams that I have to like, become a singer or an actor, to don't get judged by it. I want to pave the way to make a difference. . . . it's like people who are actually making a difference, I don't feel like they're reaching out to people like they should, they don't try as hard as they should. . . . I mean it's cute that we have a couple of laws about sexual orientation and things like that and you can't be judged about how you dress or how you act on a job. But there's so much more stuff that people seem to forget.

I just really want to make a difference I just feel that before I die I just want to touch a lot of people and let them know that gay people are not what people interpret us to be . . . we really have minds. We're really strong people. We have ideas. We don't think about all the things that people think we do. I really want to prove to people that we can also make a difference. . . .

FINAL THOUGHTS

More research is needed: more oral histories, personal narratives, focus groups, ethnographies. The voices of gay, lesbian, and transgender students of color must be part of academic theorizing, especially where education is concerned. Race, class, gender, sexuality, ethnicity, and nation must all be simultaneously addressed in any research about the culture of any school. There need to be spaces within educational institutions and academic literature where students can communicate freely. Ideally, those spaces should be in every classroom. Curriculum ought to be relevant to their lives. Young people need to see adults taking stands, posing critical questions, encouraging dialogue, self-critiquing. That is the first step in building a community of activists within schools. Young people need adults on their side who are willing to model activism and encourage it.

REFERENCES

Beemyn, B., & Eliason, M. (Eds.). (1996). *Queer studies: A lesbian, gay, bisexual, and transgender anthology.* New York: New York University Press.

Currah, P., & Minter, S. (2000). *Transgender equality: A handbook for activists and policymakers.* New York: The Policy Institute of the National Gay and Lesbian Task Force.

Building Community for Toronto's Lesbian, Gay, Bisexual, Transsexual and Transgender Youth

Bev Lepischak

SUMMARY. This paper describes the development of Supporting Our Youth, an innovative grassroots program that builds community for lesbian, gay, bisexual, transsexual and transgender youth in Toronto. Hundreds of adults and youth have worked together to develop a broad range of arts, cultural, recreational, and employment training activities, as well as a very popular mentoring and housing program. Initiated in 1997, Supporting Our Youth has been developed according to underlying principles of community development and community building which value broad participation, diverse skills, partnerships, coalition building, and grassroots ownership and direction. As a model, it is transferable to other queer and trans communities, as well as to other marginalized populations. *[Article copies available for a fee from The Haworth Document Delivery Service: 1-800-HAWORTH. E-mail address: <docdelivery@haworthpress.com> Website: <http://www.HaworthPress.com> © 2004 by The Haworth Press, Inc. All rights reserved.]*

Bev Lepischak, MSW, is a Program Coordinator in the Pride & Prejudice program at Central Toronto Youth Services, and Project Supervisor for Supporting Our Youth.

Correspondence may be addressed to: Central Toronto Youth Services, 65 Wellesley Street East, #300, Toronto, Ontario, M4Y 1G7 (E-mail: bev_lepischak@ctys.org).

[Haworth co-indexing entry note]: "Building Community for Toronto's Lesbian, Gay, Bisexual, Transsexual and Transgender Youth." Lepischak, Bev. Co-published simultaneously in *Journal of Gay & Lesbian Social Services* (Harrington Park Press, an imprint of The Haworth Press, Inc.) Vol. 16, No. 3/4, 2004, pp. 81-98; and: *Gay and Lesbian Rights Organizing: Community-Based Strategies* (ed: Yolanda C. Padilla) Harrington Park Press, an imprint of The Haworth Press, Inc., 2004, pp. 81-98. Single or multiple copies of this article are available for a fee from The Haworth Document Delivery Service [1-800-HAWORTH, 9:00 a.m. - 5:00 p.m. (EST). E-mail address: docdelivery@haworthpress.com].

KEYWORDS. Lesbian, gay, bisexual, transsexual, transgender, youth, community building

Recent decades have witnessed the exponential growth of large, visible lesbian and gay communities in Canada. Unfortunately, they are largely adult-focused. Youth are coming out or transitioning at younger ages, but most supports available to them are service oriented; few age-appropriate, positive community supports exist. Supporting Our Youth builds community for youth. Established in 1998 in response to massive funding cuts to services in Toronto, it has evolved into a unique, multifaceted initiative that attracts support from youth, adults, community organizations, media, and funders. Based on the belief that youth and adults mutually benefit by working together, it successfully challenges the stereotype of lesbians and gay men as essentially predatory. As a model of community building, it is adaptable to other queer communities as well as other disenfranchised populations.

SUPPORTING OUR YOUTH (SOY):
AN OVERVIEW

In just four years, Supporting Our Youth (www.soytoronto.org) has established itself as a unique, creative response to the needs of lesbian, gay, bisexual, transsexual and transgender youth in Toronto. It has achieved name recognition in Toronto's diverse lesbian, gay, bisexual, transsexual, and transgender communities. Hundreds of adults and youth are active in developing a broad range of arts, cultural, recreational, and skill-building activities, and thousands participate in SOY's community events. Community media regularly provide positive coverage of SOY activities, and even mainstream media feature particular events from time to time.

SOY began operating in 1998, following a broad, community-based needs assessment and feasibility study. Essentially a volunteer project with staff support, SOY operates a broad range of community activities for queer and trans youth. Fruit Loopz, a cabaret that highlights the creative talents of queer and trans youth, regularly draws large crowds of youth and adults alike. The Rainbow Book Club and Pink Ink Literary Café provide opportunities for youth to explore their sexual and gender identity through literature and poetry, as well as contact with queer and trans authors. Community forums honor queer and trans heroes, and encourage debate about the changing face of queer activism. The Bill 7 Award, commemorating the inclusion of protection for lesbians and gay men in Ontario's Human Rights Code, provides scholarships to needy postsecondary students whose connection to their families has been severed because of homophobia. Creative arts and expression allow newcomer and immigrant youth to explore their sexual orientation or gender identity in the context of their life experiences. Annual summer programs in theater and visual arts provide youth with employment training and skill building, as well as opportunities to dialogue with queer and trans artists, actors, and activists who reflect the community's history.

Besides providing age-appropriate community activities, these initiatives enable youth to develop relationships with adults who are mentors and positive role models. The Mentoring and Housing Program adapts mainstream mentoring models to the particular needs of queer and trans youth who are often isolated and disconnected from their families. Youth are matched with adult mentors on a one-to-one basis, or placed in the homes of adult mentors. A supper club/drop-in enables street-involved youth, who may have difficulty committing to a regular one-to-one relationship, to share a meal and conversation, and celebrate cultural holidays with adults whose sexual and gender identities reflect their own. Finally, being matched with a mentor enables some homeless youth to access permanent subsidized, nonprofit housing.

Historically, youth have had difficulty finding a place in Toronto's huge Pride Week celebrations that are among the largest in North America. To fill this gap, SOY operates a number of youth-oriented Pride Week activities. Fruit Loopz @ Pride, a day-long arts and cultural festival featuring youth performers and artists, draws large crowds of all ages. The Youth Contingent provides opportunities for youth from all over Ontario and the American Northeast, and their allies, to find a place in the excitement of the parade, and meet their peers. After coming to Pride 2001, a New York youth wrote:

> Hey Fruit Loopz kidz–I'm from Syracuse, NY, USA and came down with kids from Antioch College. I just wanted to say how AMAZING what you set up is! It is *so* important that we as queer youth support each other and *demand* the support we deserve from older queers, and make Pride inclusive of all queers. Thanks so much for the inspiring show of power! All the people I came down with have been talking about how amazing you all are! Yours in struggle, J.

These initiatives operate in the context of an organization whose structure and roles are fairly informal, and have continued to evolve over time. SOY is overseen by a Community Advisory Committee consisting of queer and trans volunteers with significant expertise in organizational and program development but no formal power or responsibility. SOY is officially sponsored by Central Toronto Youth Services (CTYS), a mainstream children's mental health center located in the heart of the lesbian and gay community. SOY operates out of cramped space provided free of charge by CTYS which also provides administrative support, and "nonprofit" sponsorship, giving SOY credibility and access to foundation grants and tax deductible donations.

Despite its informal and somewhat confusing structure, SOY has succeeded in attracting the support of mainstream funders and the community. The Ontario Trillium Foundation committed basic operating funds for a total of seven years, enabling SOY to access project funds from a broad range of foundations and corporate donors. Community organizations and businesses have organized fundraising events on behalf of SOY, and donor support for the project has expanded. The operating budget quadrupled in the first three years. In just four years, SOY has strategically positioned itself in Toronto's lesbian, gay, bisexual, transsexual, and transgender communities, and altered the landscape for youth from those communities in the process.

SOY is not simply the result of a successful funding application. Rather, it is an outcome of a long struggle for liberation, protection, and equal rights for lesbians and gay men in Canada; the rapid development of a large, visible lesbian and gay community in Toronto; and the evolution of alternative support for queer and trans youth in the face of declining government support for social services. This paper describes the development and operation of this unique and dynamic model, based on underlying principles of community building which value broad participation, diverse skills, partnerships and coalition building, and grassroots ownership and direction. It will begin by briefly describing the social and political context for lesbian, gay, bisexual, transsexual, transgender, and queer Canadians at the end of the twentieth century. It is within this context that a large, visible community has become established in Toronto with the capacity to take up the task of building community for queer and trans youth, and the strength to challenge prevailing predatory stereotypes. SOY's unique characteristics have enabled it to expand rapidly, diversify its programs with limited resources, and attract substantial community support.

The article is based on a review of detailed documentary records maintained by SOY and on extensive involvement in the organization on the part of the author. This involvement included participating in activities leading to the establishment of SOY and currently serving as project supervisor. In this article, the term "youth" is used to refer collectively to lesbian, gay, bisexual, transsexual, and transgender youth. When reference is made to a subgroup of these youth (lesbian, gay, and bisexual youth, for example), they are explicitly named. The term "queer and trans youth" is also used to refer to lesbian, gay, bisexual, transsexual, and transgender youth.

LESBIANS AND GAY MEN IN THE CANADIAN CONTEXT

During recent decades, lesbians and gay men in Canada have achieved significant visibility and unprecedented gains in legal protections and equity rights. Consenting homosexual sex acts undertaken in private have not been criminalized anywhere in Canada since 1969. Protections in areas of employment, housing, and access to services are entrenched in the human rights codes of most provinces and the Canadian Human Rights Code. Lesbian and gay relationships are accorded the same responsibilities and rights as heterosexual common-law couples, except the right to marry. (An Ontario Court decision of July 12, 2002, found this restriction to be discriminatory and ordered all relevant laws changed, but the decision may be appealed.) Discrimination in the Royal Canadian Mounted Police and the Canadian military has been prohibited. Age of consent laws for anal sex were ruled discriminatory. Finally, the definition of "conjugal partner" in Canada's new Immigration Act allows lesbians and gay men to sponsor same sex partners, including those who are HIV-positive.

Large, visible, diverse communities now exist in most urban centers, and increasingly, smaller urban and rural areas also host lesbian and gay groups and organizations. Three openly lesbian or gay Members of Parliament hold seats in the Parliament of Canada, and numerous others in provincial legislatures. The mayor of Winnipeg, a city in the middle of the Canadian prairies, was recently elected as an openly gay man. Increasingly, politicians of all leanings with substantial lesbian and gay constituencies clamor to demonstrate their support, and corporations target lesbians and gay men, whom they consider an affluent consumer market. For years, Toronto has hosted huge Pride celebrations that rival those of New York and San Francisco.

These changes by no means reflect the eradication of discrimination against lesbians and gay men in the broader Canadian culture. Struggles with the police over the control of lesbian and gay spaces such as bathhouses and bars continue (Kinsmen, 1996; Valverde, 2000). Fearing prejudice and recrimination, some lesbians and gay men remain closeted, especially outside large urban centers. Most schools remain unsafe for queer youth, and few recognize their needs for support, or have any relevant curricula. Some religious groups and political parties continue vehemently to oppose equality rights for lesbians and gay men, and violence is still prevalent. In some provinces, lesbians and gay men are not yet permitted to adopt children, and print and video materials destined for lesbian and gay bookstores are confiscated disproportionately by customs officers. Unlike lesbians and gay men, transgender and transsexual people have neither protections nor rights based on gender identity (Namaste, 2000; Ontario Human Rights Commission, 1999). Despite this, there has been a growing tolerance of lesbians and gay men in Canadian society, and expanding support for according them basic rights and protections.

These changes in the political and social landscape have resulted from four decades of grassroots organizing, political lobbying, and community building by lesbians and gay men. In some ways, the Canadian lesbian and gay experience has mirrored developments in the United States (Epstein, 1999; Faderman, 1991), although on a smaller scale (Canada's population is much smaller), and usually occurring a few years later (Kinsmen, 1996; Nicol, 2002; Ross, 1995). In other ways, there are significant differences. Given geographic proximity and decades of encroachment of American culture in Canada, the differences are not easily explained.

Adam (1999) suggests a number of different factors. Canada has relatively fewer religious fundamentalists who consistently oppose equality rights for lesbians and gay men; a stronger, broader union tradition that historically has promoted human rights; and a "lengthy social demographic tradition... which has come to power from time to time" (Adam, 1999, p. 17). It also "lacks the imperial and militaristic traditions of the United States... which bind national identity with homophobic panic" (Adam, 1999, p. 17). Perhaps the most significant differences are related to the nature of the Canadian state itself. Three factors are relevant here.

Firstly, Canada is based on two "founding nations"–English Protestants and French Catholics–with radically different cultures and histories. Although, like the United States, Canada contains within it reactionary forces that have always pressed for a national culture and moral regulation, the national deadlock between English and French has prevented a "successful hegemonization of traditional white, Anglo-Saxon, Protestant culture" (Adam, 1999, p. 18).

> The long historical stalemate between francophone and anglophone cultures, federal multiculturalism, and the weak federal state has resulted in a Canadian "character" of endless compromise, tolerance and politeness. The result has been a fractured elite hegemony that might otherwise have been more repressive toward many minorities, including lesbians and gay men. (Adam, 1999, p. 22)

Secondly, Canada consists of ten provinces and two territories with substantial powers, and has a history of ongoing struggles between federal and provincial governments over jurisdiction in many matters. However, the federal government has sole jurisdiction over a broad range of criminal matters. In 1969, when the Canadian government changed the Criminal Code to decriminalize homosexual sex acts, the law applied to all Canadians, unlike in the United States where individual states have jurisdiction over the criminalization of sodomy (Epstein, 1999). Canadian lesbians and gay men were spared the relentless struggle of their American counterparts who are forced to challenge sodomy laws on a state-by-state basis.

Finally, the effect of Charter-based decisions on lesbians and gay men has been profound (Kinsmen, 1996; Smith, 1999). Embedded in the 1982 Canadian Charter of Rights and Freedoms is recognition of the rights of minority groups and recourse to judicial intervention where political will is lacking. The Charter has been interpreted to include "sexual orientation as a prohibited ground of discrimination in federal jurisdiction" (Smith, 1999, p. 83). During the last 15 years, the Supreme Court of Canada has ruled on more than two dozen Charter-based equality challenges involving sexual orientation, and almost all have resulted in findings favoring equality rights for lesbians and gay men. Furthermore, most rulings have had the power to change discriminatory laws across Canada.

As a result of substantial gains during recent decades, Canadian lesbians and gay men are more comfortable being out in large numbers, creating visible communities, and taking on new challenges. Feeling more confident and less afraid for their personal safety and security, they have been more willing to turn their attention to more disenfranchised groups within the community, such as queer and trans youth.

QUEER AND TRANS YOUTH: A SOCIAL SERVICE RESPONSE

An outcome of increased visibility is that youth become aware of struggles with sexual orientation and gender identity at ever-younger ages. Unfortunately, this occurs at a time in their lives when they are often still attending school and are financially and emotionally dependent on biological families, making them extremely vulnerable to the heterosexist assumptions and homophobic prejudice and discrimination that continue to exist in Canadian society. The challenge of dealing with stigma, along with the usual adolescent developmental tasks, can be incredibly difficult for many. Issues are further magnified for youth who must also cope with discrimination based on race or culture.

Feeling rejected, isolated, and alienated from their families and communities, many, especially those from rural areas, migrate to large urban centers like Toronto in search of security and community. Unfortunately, given the high costs of living, low housing vacancy rates, high rates of youth unemployment, and eroded social supports, many end up leading a marginalized existence or become street involved. Despite the existence of large visible adult communities in urban centers, most youth struggle to find a place in those communities. Adults are often reluctant to engage with them, except in sexualized interactions. Historically, age-appropriate social and recreational activities for queer and trans youth have been minimal, since most have been adult oriented, and the response to the needs and issues of these youth has been limited to a social service response.

During the 1970s and 1980s, mainstream health and social service organizations established a range of shelters and group homes, and mental health counseling and employment programs to meet the needs of marginalized and street-involved youth. Although queer and trans youth were among those served, their particular needs and issues were rarely addressed. Shelters were often unsafe, especially for youth who did not conform to gender stereotypes (O'Brien, Travers, & Bell, 1993). Substance abuse services ignored underlying issues of sexual orientation or gender identity, and religious-based services refused to address the particular needs of queer and trans youth (Simpson, 1994). Specialized services that openly addressed their needs were rare. Lesbians and gay men employed by these services were concerned about the lack of quality services; however, many themselves were not out at work or met with resistance when they advocated for accessible, relevant services. Existing peer support groups at universities or in the community could not address many of the needs of queer and trans youth. A volunteer-run lesbian and gay counseling program, fearing legal recrimination, restricted its services to adults 21 years of age or older.

In response to this service gap, health and social service workers formed the Coalition for Services for Lesbian and Gay Youth in 1991. Primarily lesbians and gay men, Coalition members came together to advocate for the development of specialized services for lesbian, gay, and bisexual youth within existing services. By the mid 1990s, a number of professionally facilitated coming out groups had been established across Toronto. Openly lesbian and gay counselors were available, a gay-positive youth substance abuse program was operating, and a transitional school program had been established for youth encountering discrimination in the regular school system. In addition, many health and social service organizations had begun training their staff to work more effectively with this population.

Although lacking a formal structure and a clear mandate, the Coalition developed a sizeable membership and credibility in issues related to lesbian, gay, and bisexual youth. By the latter part of the 1990s, it was able to access government and foundation funding to organize two conferences on issues related to lesbian, gay, and bisexual youth. Attended by hundreds of youth and adults from across Ontario, a clear message emerged: As well as relevant services, youth needed age-appropriate social and recreational activities, and a place in the largely adult-oriented lesbian and gay communities.

QUEER AND TRANS YOUTH: A COMMUNITY-BUILDING RESPONSE

Growing awareness of the need for community-based activities and supports for lesbian, gay, and bisexual youth coincided with political changes that diminished the likelihood of expanded social services to meet their needs. In 1995, Ontario's neo-Conservative government made major cuts to health, social services, public housing, education, and other relevant programs, along with substantial eligibility restrictions for social assistance and dramatically reduced levels of support. These had a profound impact on the lives of queer and trans youth and the services they used. Broad efforts to mobilize resistance across affected groups produced few tangible results. A community-based response that did not rely on government support seemed a more viable option.

In 1997, the Coalition undertook a broad community consultation to identify the particular needs of lesbian, gay, and bisexual youth, and gauge support for a community-based response that brought together adults and youth. Feedback indicated unanimous support for a grassroots community response focused on arts, cultural, and recreational activities; employment and skill-building initiatives; and access to safe, affordable housing and positive adult mentors.

Despite the general optimism, potential challenges were clearly identified. There were concerns about motivating adults, whose own lives were fairly comfortable, to direct their energy and resources to support youth initiatives:

> There is a middle-class, closed "me me me" nature of my community, a lack of awareness of the issues. There is a disconnection within the community . . . generally we forget about the struggles that we had as adolescents, especially in the white, middle class. . . . (Lesbian Co-ordinator of a Queer Youth Outreach Program, 1997)

Competition for limited community resources was a concern, as the AIDS epidemic had consumed considerable human and financial resources for more than a decade.

> AIDS has depleted our community . . . there isn't the level of leadership and expertise in the older generations as there should be. Men have died or their energies are going into organizations around AIDS. Money-wise, we have to go beyond this community. . . . There is only so much the businesses within our community can do . . . (they) have been squeezed by AIDS. (Gay AIDS Activist, 1997)

Concerns were raised that any initiative would fail to reach the most marginalized youth in the community, including youth of color, street-involved youth, and trans youth.

> [New immigrants] need access to lesbigay organizations or groups that offer appropriate services where language, social, and cultural norms may be different from the "mainstream" community. It's very challenging to truly reflect and incorporate diversity. (Gay Immigration Lawyer, 1997)

> Adult gays are all happy to donate money to [mainstream queer youth groups] because those kids are nice kids ... that we recognize, that don't make us feel uncomfortable. No one's gonna help out the 16-year-olds working as transsexual prostitutes, because they don't look like us, and they don't have access to the right language and approach, and all that. (Lesbian Journalist, 1997)

And repeatedly, the issue of the prevailing stereotype of lesbians and gay men as predators was highlighted, along with concerns that adults would distance themselves from any involvement, for fear of being labeled pedophiles:

> There is this fear of recruiting, for lack of a better word ... We can say on a certain level that we don't believe that or don't buy into that. I think, though, somewhere, on some subconscious level we've bought into these homophobic messages so we just distance ourselves from younger people. (Gay AIDS Activist, 1997)

Based on the results of the Coalition's needs assessment, an application was made to the Ontario Trillium Foundation for operating funds. Much to the surprise of many, a three-year project was approved, and SOY began operating in 1998. Building on the knowledge and enthusiasm of the participants in the needs assessment, a few activities were quickly developed, giving SOY much needed visibility and leading to rapidly expanding community support for the project, in terms of both human and fiscal resources. Coverage in both mainstream and community media was frequent and generally positive. In light of the project's visibility and broad-based support, several mainstream foundations agreed to fund specific initiatives. Within a short period of time, SOY had established itself as a credible and relevant response to the need for community for lesbian, gay, and bisexual youth.

Feedback from volunteers, staff, and community partners indicated a general agreement that SOY was strategically positioned to play a major role in community building for queer youth in the future. There was strong support for continuing SOY's activities, with particular attention to the needs of those youth who were most marginalized: street-involved youth, transgender and transsexual youth, and youth of color. Subsequently, Trillium extended operating funds, with the provision that SOY focus on becoming sustainable within four years.

A FRAMEWORK FOR COMMUNITY BUILDING WITH QUEER AND TRANS YOUTH

Although developed at least in part in response to service cuts, SOY does not attempt to meet the needs of queer and trans youth for professional counseling and group work, crisis intervention, and other traditional services. Rather, it aims to complement services by creating community-based alternatives for youth seeking peer supports or contact with positive adult role models.

Two different sets of factors contribute to SOY's success. One is the current Canadian context, briefly described earlier, which is more tolerant of lesbians and gay men, and provides a measure of safety and security that enables them to focus on building a diverse and caring community for all its members. The second is the commitment to underlying principles of broad participation, diverse skills, partnerships, coalition building, and grassroots ownership and direction–principles which were integral to SOY's initiation and ongoing development. These principles represent SOY's greatest strengths but also present it with significant challenges for the future.

The vision for SOY emerged from within the community, and was developed only after a broad community consultation that identified specific needs, established general directions, and laid the foundation for strong community support. There were no illusions about the challenges facing the project; despite this, there emerged a collective sense of responsibility to address the issues of youth, and consensus about the way it should be undertaken.

> Not to be too hard on the community, we have so few resources and those resources have gone into care and helping people who were dying. But I think there's a switch now. I perceive a real growing interest in the community, not to abandon care but to also look at other issues. Can we start to support youth? I think there's a real openness now, I really do. (Gay Minister of Metropolitan Community Church, 1997)

> There has got to be mutual responsibility, responsibility (on the part of youth) to ask for what they need and for me to take some responsibility to provide it. This is the only way to build community. (Lesbian Broadcaster, 1997)

Developing a Volunteer Base

As a volunteer organization with minimal staff, SOY is deeply rooted in Toronto's queer and trans communities, creating a strong sense of community ownership and direction. Since its inception, several hundred adult and youth volunteers have participated in SOY's work. Volunteers are involved in every aspect of the organization, including visioning, developing, and implementing initiatives and activities, and evaluating them.

Adults volunteer for a variety of personal reasons. Many mentors, for example, are involved either because they had the support of a positive adult during their coming-out or transitioning process and could not have survived without it, or because they struggled without any support and want to ensure that this is not the case for youth today. Whatever the specific reason, the unifying theme among adult volunteers is a desire to "give back to the community." Youth also volunteer for a variety of personal reasons, such as an interest in performing or a desire to meet peers, but also more generally because they want to be part of a community.

Both adult and youth volunteers also share a desire to have contact with people who span the generations. Youth are often alienated from their families or rejected by them, and have no meaningful adult contact. Many adults have very little contact with youth, as they are less likely than heterosexuals to have had children, and the predatory stereotype has caused them to shy away from any contact with youth. Both value opportunities for meaningful, mutually beneficial contact across generations. Fortunately, participation is not time limited; as youth become older, they can remain as adult volunteers and use their experiences to support those younger than themselves.

Volunteers bring tremendous energy, expertise, and creativity to every level of SOY. Toronto's lesbian and gay community has a long history of "doing for ourselves," and many have honed their skills and talents in political activism or AIDS work. However, SOY is strongly committed to nurturing volunteers with limited knowledge, skills or experience, enabling them to develop confidence and expand their involvement.

> One of SOY's greatest strengths is its appreciation of volunteers. I have never felt more appreciated in my life. Volunteers are given personal power to make things work. Even though it's called Supporting Our Youth, adults also reap many benefits from being involved in this project. (Lesbian Adult Volunteer, 1999)

SOY has always been mindful of both the challenges posed by the predatory stereotype, and by potentially exploitative situations that might occur. It has intentionally promoted a culture that clearly defines the parameters of appropriate relationships between adults and youth, and demands mutual respect. The mentoring program has actually developed formal policies that define appropriate adult-youth relationships, and established a thorough screening, orientation, training, and follow-up process to ensure adherence to those policies. Adult and youth volunteers endorse the way SOY addresses these issues; it protects them from external criticism and suspicion, and provides a framework for establishing close, meaningful adult-youth relationships.

SOY staff reflect the diversity of Toronto's lesbian, gay, bisexual, transsexual or transgender communities, and have a commitment to queer and trans youth. Most have well-established roots in the community, and bring experience and networks that promote SOY's goals. They demonstrate a deep commitment to the organization, and feel privileged to have the opportunity to work with their own communities. Staff perform both complex and extremely mundane tasks, often working long hours. Given the organization's lack of adequate stable funding, they are never assured of job security.

The role of paid staff is conceptually simple but practically complex. Staff are responsible for enabling adult and youth volunteers to carry out the work of building community together. Practically, it involves leading and following at the same time. Staff spend a tremendous amount of time recruiting and nurturing volunteers, supporting them in developing and implementing activities, and providing administrative support to initiatives and the day-to-day running of the organization. At another level, staff are ultimately responsible for overseeing all of the organization's activities, acquiring the funds necessary for their operation, planning for the future of the organization, and maintaining its credibility with both funders and the community. As members of the same community who share a vision and commitment, the relationship between staff and volunteers has always been extremely respectful and supportive.

Implementing New Initiatives

SOY has a broad mandate to develop initiatives and activities in areas such as arts, cultural, and recreational activities and employment and skill building, and to increase youth access to adult mentoring and safe housing. However, the organization has a great deal of flexibility in deciding what the specific activities of the project will be at any time. Ideas for activities or initiatives generally come from volunteers or partner organizations. If the proposals generally fit the framework of community building, and sufficient funds are available or can be acquired, the development of the idea depends primarily on volunteer interest.

Over the years, SOY has undertaken a broad range of initiatives because of strong volunteer and community support. Some are mentioned at the beginning of this article, but others are also noteworthy. Trans_Fusion Crew, for example, is a support group for trans youth and their allies that organized a gala event honoring local trans activists, artists and community builders, and published a zine for trans youth. The Black Queer Youth initiative provides a regular meeting space for queer youth who identify with the Black diaspora to meet their peers, explore queer Black history and community, and organize activities that celebrate queer Black identity. Queer South Asian volunteers spent three years producing and distributing a video that is a valuable resource for South Asian families with queer or trans members. Volunteers concerned with urban environmental issues organized a public forum and roof-top garden tours, and undertook the unpleasant task of recycling garbage during Toronto Pride. Chats at the Gallery provides monthly opportunities for youth to meet local activists from previous decades and learn about the community's struggles for liberation and equality. The nature of activities evolves over time, and activities that do not attract sufficient interest are often dropped in favor of ones that do. This flexibility, and lack of vested interest in any given activity, has helped to keep SOY relevant and responsive, and has reinforced the sense of community ownership and direction.

Over the years, SOY has developed initiatives in partnership with dozens of community groups and organizations. Partners have included queer and trans youth groups, health and social service organizations, arts and cultural organizations in the adult community, environmental organizations, and heterosexual allies, among others. Partnerships allow organizations to pool limited resources for the benefit of all concerned, learn from each other, reach broader audiences, and avoid duplication or competition. Some partnerships have significantly enhanced the development of activities, while others have been more difficult and frustrating.

One of SOY's other major strengths is its ability to continuously recruit new adult and youth volunteers, and draw community participants to its activities. Since its inception, the organization has made outreach and promotion a priority, and has worked to ensure that its efforts are sufficiently varied to reach diverse groups of people. It has used a wide range of media, including a Website and listservs; paid advertising and feature stories; brochures and newsletters; and flyers, posters, and display boards. In this way, SOY has been successful in promoting its activities and attracting increasing numbers of volunteers and participants. Ultimately, however, word of mouth is one of the most important ways of reaching new volunteers and participants.

In addition to access to recreational activities and supportive relationships, queer and trans youth have benefited from SOY in many other ways. Many have acquired organizing and technical skills, as well as increased confidence in their abilities. Some youth who first performed their creative works at SOY events have gone on to develop careers as actors, performers, or musical artists, and others have become writers or successful Web designers. Internships and volunteer experiences have provided many youth with the work histories and references necessary for obtaining paid employment. In the mentoring program, where adults and youth are matched on a one-to-one basis, mentors have assisted youth to return to school; secure and maintain employment; or acquire stable housing, furniture, or household items. In short, they have offered the information and support the vast majority of Canadian youth receive from their families and communities, and take for granted.

Facing Challenges

Despite its enormous success, SOY faces significant challenges. These center around incorporating diversity, managing growth, funding initiatives and activities on a day-to-day basis, and ensuring sustainability in the long term.

Like many large urban North American centers, Toronto's population includes significant numbers of immigrants or newcomers, and where previously, the majority of immigrants came from European countries, more recent immigrants come from places around the globe. They bring with them religious, cultural, and racial backgrounds that are extremely diverse, and attitudes toward homosexuality and gender nonconformity that may be radically different from those of dominant western cultures. Many must also deal with racial and cultural discrimination in Canadian society, and within the queer and trans communities as well.

Youth who are immigrants or newcomers or identify as people of color have always been involved in SOY's various programs, and the organization has had some success in attracting adult volunteers and mentors who reflect this diversity. In recognition of the particular challenges for youth who are immigrants, newcomers, or people of color, however, SOY has developed initiatives specifically geared toward their needs. That said, being truly inclusive continues to be one of the organization's biggest challenges.

Although these rapidly expanding programs and activities create a great deal of excitement and satisfaction for staff and volunteers, they also place significant pressures on the organization. While the staff component has increased slightly over the years, and staff have become more skilled and efficient at juggling multiple tasks, the pressures on them have also increased significantly. Financial and space restrictions make it difficult to expand the staff complement further, since most new funding that is acquired (especially foundation funding) is targeted primarily at program costs and not organizational infrastructure costs. Efforts to enhance staff capacity through student and intern placements help alleviate some pressures, but also increase workloads due to the need for significant training, supervision, and evaluation. Volunteers with sufficient time and skill have occasionally shouldered significant responsibilities, but the risk of burn-out for both staff and volunteers is real.

Space restrictions also limit potential growth. Currently, SOY is housed, free of charge, in two small offices at CTYS and utilizes the agency's group and meeting space for most of its activities. Although meetings can be held in other locations, there is no possibility of expanding the organization's offices at the current location. Financially, the organization is not in a position to rent larger office space elsewhere at this time.

Acquiring funding to support the infrastructure and programming costs is another major challenge. Without doubt, the organization has been successful in expanding its revenue base over the years. Unfortunately, the conditions of funding from government programs and foundations means that monies can be used only in specific and prescribed ways. Furthermore, demands related to acquiring this funding, such as writing funding applications, reporting to funders, organizing fundraising events, and managing a donor base, limit time available for program-related activities.

The role played by CTYS in enabling SOY to develop and flourish cannot be underestimated. Because of the amenities it has provided, the bulk of the funds acquired by SOY could be used to develop programs rather than support infrastructure costs. At the same time, CTYS has been content to let the organization manage and run itself. This has allowed the community to take major responsibility for the direction of SOY, ensuring its relevance and ownership by the community, and ultimately contributing to its success. On the other hand, as a children's mental health center, CTYS has always regarded the delivery of clinical services to youth and families as its primary role. SOY's focus on community building and prevention is not incompatible with the agency's goals; however, the methods used to achieve those goals are radically different. Barring unforeseen circumstances, SOY will continue this arrangement with CTYS in the short term. In the long term, however, driven by the restrictions of the current situation, potential competing interests, and a strong desire to maintain community direction and ownership, SOY plans to work toward eventually becoming an independent organization.

This goal will present the biggest challenge yet. Locating the funds to offset the supports provided by CTYS will be a monumental task, especially in a fiscal climate where ongoing funding is virtually unavailable and never guaranteed. In addition, developing a structure for the organization that meets corporate legal requirements, but continues to embrace and value underlying principles of flexibility, broad participation, and community ownership and direction will be significant balancing act.

CONCLUSION

SOY's success, as a model for community building for queer and trans youth through the active involvement of adult communities and heterosexual allies, is unprecedented in Canada, perhaps even North America. Historically, one of the measures of success for most funders is the degree to which a community building project such as SOY is applicable or transferable to other communities or groups. White, former Executive Director of Ontario's Trillium Foundation, writes:

> For many years, the effectiveness of a funded initiative was related to its capacity to be "replicated." But we have come to see that a cookie cutter approach to community programs doesn't just not work, it is counter to the concept of building capacity. Communities, like individuals, learn by doing. Sometimes they may appear to be reinventing the wheel, but more often than not, given access to ideas, encouragement to create, resources to try things, and time to reflect, wonderful things happen. The ability to adapt and to innovate encourages getting "underneath" things. It means not accepting assumptions holus-bolus, but asking questions . . . making surprising, unexpected connections. (White, 1997, p. 9)

SOY came out of Toronto's lesbian, gay, bisexual, transsexual, and transgender communities, and serves those communities. The specific activities and capacities that have been developed are relevant to the needs and interests of those communities. Without a doubt, these were significant factors in its success.

The basic principles of SOY, however, are transferable to other queer and trans communities, as well as to other groups that are marginalized or oppressed. They include a shared community understanding of needs; significant and diverse community involvement in visioning and direction setting; ownership by those involved in carrying out the work; as much attention to process as to outcome; and sufficient financial and other resources to undertake the work.

Communities that are less cohesive, have fewer financial and human resources, and are collectively less experienced in advocacy and community organizing, may require more time to develop a common vision. As well, expectations regarding the number and complexity of activities may need to be reduced. However, the rewards of this approach reaped by individual participants and organizations make it more empowering than externally imposed problem-solving interventions. Supporting Our Youth has been successful principally because it is based on a community building approach.

REFERENCES

Adam, B. D. (1999). Moral regulation and the disintegrating Canadian state. In B. Adam, J. W. Duyvendak, & A. Krouwel (Eds.), *The global emergence of gay and lesbian politics: National imprints of a worldwide movement* (pp. 12-29). Philadelphia: Temple University Press.

Epstein, S. (1999). Gay and lesbian movements in the United States: Dilemmas of identity, diversity, and political strategy. In B. Adam, J. W. Duyvendak, & A.

Krouwel (Eds.), *The global emergence of gay and lesbian politics: National imprints of a worldwide movement* (pp. 30-90). Philadelphia: Temple University Press.

Faderman, L. (1991). *Odd girls and twilight lovers: A history of lesbian life in twentieth-century America.* New York: Penguin Books.

Kinsmen, G. (1996). *The regulation of desire: Homophobia and hetero sexualities.* Montreal: Black Rose Books.

Namaste, V. K. (2000). *Invisible lives: The erasure of transsexual and transgendered people.* Chicago: University of Chicago Press.

Nicol, N. (Producer and Director). (2002). *Stand together: A history of the lesbian & gay rights movement in Ontario from 1967 to 1987* [Film]. (Available from Intervention Video, 91 Bude Street, Toronto, Ontario, M6C 1X7).

O'Brien, C. A., Travers, R., & Bell, L. (1993). *No safe bed: Lesbian, gay and bisexual youth in residential services.* Toronto: Central Toronto Youth Services.

Ontario Human Rights Commission (1999). *Towards a Commission policy on gender identity.* Queen's Printer for Ontario.

Ross, B. L. (1995). *The house that Jill built: A lesbian nation in formation.* Toronto: University of Toronto Press.

Simpson, B. (1994). *Making substance abuse and other services accessible to lesbian, gay and bisexual youth.* Toronto: Central Toronto Youth Services.

Smith, M. (1999). *Lesbian and gay rights in Canada: Social movements and equality seeking.* Toronto: University of Toronto Press.

Valverde, M. (2000, November 30). Policing morality: How did we get here in the first place? *Xtra! Magazine*, 26-27.

White, J. (1997). *Building caring communities: Five capacities that build communities, and ten things funders can do to support them.* Unpublished manuscript.

Building Community-Based Alliances Between GLBTQQA Youth and Adults in Rural Settings

Carol A. Snively

SUMMARY. This article discusses the need for community-based, gay-straight, youth-adult alliances in rural settings and provides a beginning framework for how to create this type of organization. It describes an emerging local community-based alliance of gay, lesbian, bisexual, transgender, queer, questioning, and youth and adult allies. Unlike school-based gay-straight alliances, this group, known as Prism, is open to youth from several schools in a college town and nearby rural communities. *[Article copies available for a fee from The Haworth Document Delivery Service: 1-800-HAWORTH. E-mail address: <docdelivery@haworthpress.com> Website: <http://www.HaworthPress.com> © 2004 by The Haworth Press, Inc. All rights reserved.]*

Carol A. Snively, PhD, is Assistant Professor, University of Missouri-Columbia, School of Social Work, 702 Clark Hall, Columbia, MO 65203 (E-mail: snivelyc@missouri.edu).

The author wishes to acknowledge that many diverse persons have contributed to Prism's strong presence in mid-Missouri. This article reflects the perspective of one adult advisory board member. Special thanks to Justin Dijak and Nikole Potulsky for their contributions to the first draft of this paper.

[Haworth co-indexing entry note]: "Building Community-Based Alliances Between GLBTQQA Youth and Adults in Rural Settings." Snively, Carol A. Co-published simultaneously in *Journal of Gay & Lesbian Social Services* (Harrington Park Press, an imprint of The Haworth Press, Inc.) Vol. 16, No. 3/4, 2004, pp. 99-112; and: *Gay and Lesbian Rights Organizing: Community-Based Strategies* (ed: Yolanda C. Padilla) Harrington Park Press, an imprint of The Haworth Press, Inc., 2004, pp. 99-112. Single or multiple copies of this article are available for a fee from The Haworth Document Delivery Service [1-800-HAWORTH, 9:00 a.m. - 5:00 p.m. (EST). E-mail address: docdelivery@haworthpress.com].

KEYWORDS. Youth, community, gay-straight alliance, rural, adults

This article introduces a model for organizing gay and straight youth and adults in rural settings. The purpose of such an effort is to create safe and affirming communities for sexual and gender diversity. The first section provides background information on the experiences and needs of gay, lesbian, bisexual, transgender, queer, questioning, and ally (GLBTQQA) youth, with special attention given to research on GLBT persons living in rural areas. The next section explores how recent efforts to organize youth through school-based, gay-straight alliances can be adapted to meet the specific needs of rural youth. The article then describes an emerging local community-based, adult-youth, gay-straight alliance with a nonprofit, volunteer, and youth-focused organizational structure serving a midwestern college town and several nearby rural communities. In addition to establishing a broad social network of support for GLBTQQA youth, the organization, known as Prism, also facilitates educational activities and workshops to create a more inclusive community environment. In this manner, Prism addresses many of the needs of GLBTQQA youth who reside in rural settings.

GLBTQ YOUTH

Gay youth, youth believed to be gay, and their allies have long been targets of prejudicial and discriminatory attitudes, behaviors, and policies. Recent reports have highlighted the widespread, self-reported victimization of gay, lesbian, bisexual, transgender, and queer persons (GLBTQ), especially youth, through hate crimes, institutional oppression, social discrimination, and personal prejudice (Henry J. Kaiser Family Foundation, 2001; Human Rights Watch, 2001). While the general climate for GLBTQ persons appears to be improving (Henry J. Kaiser Family Foundation, 2001), exclusion of, discrimination against, and violence (verbal and physical) toward GLBTQ youth occur on a daily basis at schools and/or in homes (Hunter et al., 1998; Savin-Williams, 1994). Schools continue to be particularly unsafe for many GLBTQ youth. According to the Gay, Lesbian and Straight Education Network's School Climate Survey (2001a) of 904 youths from 48 states and the District of Columbia, 41.9 percent of GLBTQ youth had experienced physical violence because of their sexual orientation, up from 27 percent in 1999. The current prevalence and severity of violence toward GLBTQ youth is cause for alarm because it has implications for their immediate and long-term health and well-being (D'Augelli & Dark, 1994; Gustavsson & MacEachron, 1998).

Although most GLBTQ youth (84.6 percent of males and 71.7 percent of females) are expected to be well adjusted (Savin-Williams, 1994), the protracted stress of growing up in a homophobic/heterosexist society can bring about behavioral and mental health-related problems. Certain experiences, such as social isolation and alienation (Robinson, 1991; Savin-Williams, 1994), depression, substance abuse, and suicidal behavior (D'Augelli & Hershberger, 1993; Rein, 1999; Russell & Joyner, 2001; Safren & Heimberg, 1999; Saulnier, 1998) are commonly experienced by GLBTQ youth and are also known as risk factors for self-harm among the general population (McWhirter et al., 1998). Even when GLBTQ youth seek professional help, there is no guarantee for their safety. Professional help has been cited as one of the risk factors for suicidal behavior of gay youth (Van Wormer, Wells, & Boes, 2000). This is due in part to poorly provided and nonaffirming services involving attempts by the therapist to alter or dismiss the youth's same-sex romantic and sexual feelings and/or gender identity. GLBTQ youth who live in rural areas may be particularly affected by the aforementioned issues (Moses & Buckner, 1982; Smith, 1997).

THE GAY EXPERIENCE OF RURAL COMMUNITIES

The rural environment offers different challenges than those faced by GLBTQ persons in urban settings (Smith, 1997). A small, homogenous population creates a barrier to open expressions of diversity and often exerts pressure to conform to community standards (Ginsberg, 1998). Because sexual diversity is typically not recognized and accepted in rural settings, persons who do not express their sexuality or gender in traditionally accepted ways are often made to feel like outsiders until they either show that they can "fit in" or leave the community (Boulden, 2001). GLBTQ persons sometimes adapt by presenting themselves as heterosexual or asexual, or by keeping secret the extent to which their social networks include GLBTQ persons. These "closeted" GLBTQ adults tend not to associate publicly with those who are known to be gay, lesbian, or bisexual so as to avoid the perception that they themselves are gay (for example, hiding the car two blocks away when having dinner at the home of a gay friend so that others are not aware of their association) (Boulden, 2001). These barriers to open socialization between GLBTQ persons foster social isolation (McCarthy, 2000; Smith, 1997). While some GLBTQ adults stay in rural areas and hide their sexuality, others move to urban settings so that they may more openly express their sexual and/or gender identities (Boulden, 2001; Lindhorst, 1997; Smith, 1997).

Research has documented that persons with conservative values (in terms of religion and gender roles), who have minimal social interaction with

GLBTQ persons and who are generally unsupportive of diversity (i.e., exhibit racism and sexism), tend to be homophobic (Herek, 1984; Hunter et al., 1998). The social isolation of rural areas and the lack of visibility of GLBT people within these communities make rural areas particularly vulnerable to homophobic attitudes. As a result, rural environments are often less hospitable and, potentially, more dangerous for GLBT persons of all ages.

As Boulden (2001) explains, the pressure to conform combined with a rural value of freedom has been referred to as a "don't ask, don't tell" philosophy toward GLBTQ persons, where "if someone believes you are gay, they do not directly ask you about it and if you are gay, you do not offer to directly share that information" (p. 65). Living in such a community requires vigilance regarding how one expresses one's identity and feelings toward others in order to avoid social isolation and victimization.

GLBTQ persons oftentimes migrate from rural to urban areas to feel safer, to gain a sense of community with persons similar to themselves, and to experience greater acceptance of diversity (Lindhorst, 1997; Smith, 1997). Although some openly GLB persons are now returning to rural areas (Smith & Mancoske, 1997), the numbers appear to be small. At the same time, there is not much empirical data on how these individuals manage their sexual and gender identities in their new communities (see Boulden, 2001; Cody & Welch, 1997).

Compared with urban settings, rural communities typically have less diverse populations (Ginsberg, 1998) and more concentrated homophobia/heterosexism (Hunter et al., 1998; Reinhardt, 1994). These factors, in addition to the past trend of migration by GLBTQ adults between rural and urban areas, make it difficult to organize strong gay communities of support beyond the insulated small groups of friends typically found in rural settings (Boulden, 2001). These weak ties among GLBT persons may result in a greater dependence by individuals on formal services for support.

SUPPORTIVE SERVICES FOR RURAL GLBTQ PERSONS

When GLBTQ persons seek formal support, what do they find? Rural social and mental health services tend to offer few specialized services for diverse populations. In addition, rural social workers tend to reflect the values of the communities in which they live and are often more homophobic than are their urban peers (Berkman & Zinberg, 1997; Foster, 1997). Thus, GLBTQ persons in need of services often do not access those that are available. When they do, these services may lack cultural competence and have a service focus on treatment rather than community organization.

A climate of fear, along with pressure to conform and the out-migration of GLBTQ adults, restores a perception of homogeneity in the rural community, increases isolation for those who either choose not to or are unable to leave, and makes it difficult for GLBTQ persons to organize a supportive community. Since there are few formal services available for GLBTQ persons, individuals must rely on their own resources in adapting to rural life. GLBTQ persons of all ages would benefit from assistance in removing the sociocultural barriers they face.

Literature on the subject of social services for gay persons in rural areas has emphasized the need for service providers to act as advocates and community organizers instead of providing more traditional mental health services (Smith, 1997). Such advice is particularly applicable to those working with GLBT youth who experience prejudice, discrimination, and violence in their schools, homes, and community settings and yet seem to be expected to respond by getting treatment for their reaction to oppression. Focusing on individual solutions to sociocultural problems pathologizes, and to some extent revictimizes, the GLBT youth. It implies that they must create change within themselves in order to cope with, and adapt to, dangerous and unhealthy environments. Because youth often cannot leave rural areas, change of their home communities must be pursued. Yet, youth often have limited power and resources to effect true community change. Alliances between youth and adults have the potential of creating a bridge between those without and those with better access to power and the resources needed for such an effort.

CHANGING THE CONTEXT OF RURAL SETTINGS FOR GLBT YOUTH

Homogeneity and concentrated homophobia in rural areas, minimal access to openly gay adults and supportive services, and the threat of violence can create an environment that is not conducive to healthy overall development by rural youth, including sexual identity development. As individuals attempt to reconcile their personal identities with the values and behaviors of their families and communities, they risk developing behavioral and mental health-related problems (Anhalt & Morris, 1998; Rein, 1999).

Because there are few adult GLB persons available for GLB youth in rural settings, teens have little opportunity to receive guidance or affirmation from gay role models regarding their maturational process as gay, lesbian, or bisexual persons (Sears, 1991). To decrease their social isolation, GLBT youth may visit high-risk environments to seek out other gay persons with whom to interact. For example, public highway rest stops and gay bars are sometimes the most accessible places for gay socialization in rural settings (D'Augelli & Hart, 1987).

In the case of ethnocultural minority groups, adult role models (familial and otherwise) play an important part in healthy youth development by acting as buffers to oppression (Levitt, Guacci-Franco, & Levitt, 1993). Is this true for sexual minority persons? And if so, would a strategy of strengthening social bonds and expanding social networks with nonfamilial adults offer youth some protection from the daily experiences of homophobia/heterosexism? If so, adults who openly express their identity as GLBT persons could act as role models and mentors to GLBT youth. However, the small numbers of openly GLBT adults in rural communities reduces the likelihood that such adults would be part of a rural GLBT youth's informal social network. Efforts to bring together persons across smaller communities and create strong, supportive social networks could be components of an important strategy to prevent mental health-related problems. Since there is no research on the topic, we must look to emerging community programs for information about how community organization and mentorship strategies may enhance the social networks of GLBT youth.

Despite the many negative experiences previously noted and minimal adult support, some GLBTQ youth have organized nonclinical support groups and have actively worked to create change in the communities, schools, and families where oppression is experienced (Gay, Lesbian and Straight Education Network, 2001b). These groups have become known as gay-straight alliances (GSAs). Until recently, their efforts were often met with overt hostility and a refusal to treat GSAs in the same manner as other extracurricular school groups. Student leaders continue to articulate a need for more resources and support. Similar efforts outside schools often include community adults as alliance members.

Strategies aimed at reducing risks through a unified community vision, enhancing youth development, and strengthening protective factors are more likely to succeed than those addressing specific problem behaviors of any one population (Barton, Watkins, & Jarjoura, 1997). For these reasons, comprehensive community initiatives that focus on collaborative partnerships are needed to promote the well-being of youth, families, and communities. Some community practitioners and residents have recognized the value of partnering with youth to create innovative strategies (Barton, Watkins, & Jarjoura, 2001; Finn & Checkoway, 1998).

The next section briefly reviews the literature on supportive networks that are developing in schools and communities. It is followed by a description of a gay-straight, community-based alliance (Prism) that combines youth and adult resources to address GLBT youth needs that are specific to rural settings.

While Prism is a young, still-developing organization, a description of its structure and activities is provided to stimulate discussion about how to adapt current school-based GSA models to fit the needs of persons from rural settings.

BUILDING ALLIANCES ACROSS DIFFERENCES: GAY-STRAIGHT, ADULT-YOUTH

As described by the Gay, Lesbian and Straight Education Network (GLSEN) (2001b), a gay-straight alliance (GSA) is typically a school-based, student-led, and organized group for all youth, regardless of members' sexual orientation or gender identity/expression. Adults, who are GLBT or allies, often act as the GSA's faculty advisors. The mission of a GSA is to provide a safe, welcoming, and accepting school environment for students who are GLBT or are perceived as GLBT, those who are questioning their identities, children of GLBT families, and straight students. Steps taken to accomplish this mission meet a larger objective of creating safer, inclusive school environments for all students. A GSA typically provides education, support, and refuge to GLBT students, and a safe and affirming place to be during the school day. The need for such a place has been made clear in the previously discussed documented incidents of harassment and by the fact that few states or public school districts protect students from harassment based on sexual orientation. Some GSAs organize coalitions to address issues affecting all students, including harassment, discrimination, and bias based on sexual orientation, gender identity, and expression. Although the literature about gay-straight alliances is not yet well developed, anecdotal evidence from the Gay, Lesbian and Straight Education Network underscores the benefits of both school and community alliances for youth participants.

In the past two years, the number of gay-straight student clubs in secondary schools registered with GLSEN has risen from 600 to 1,000. GLSEN estimates that 1 in every 15 U.S. high schools has a GSA and that 20,000 students are directly involved in GSA activities each year (Gay, Lesbian and Straight Education Network, 2001b). While the numbers of gay-straight alliances (GSA) are growing daily, the number of support groups for GLBT youth is still low when measured against the total number of GLBT youth across the nation (Gay, Lesbian and Straight Education Network, 2001b; Morrow, 1993).

School-based GSAs play a very specific and important role for youth during the school day; however, there are limits on what such a group can provide. For example, school groups restrict the amount of adult community involvement in that only teachers and administrators can typically participate in school activities with youth. In addition, school-based GSAs force educators to play leadership roles that may put them at risk if their school districts do not include GLBT persons in their nondiscrimination policies. Even if faculty advisors are not GLBT, their support of the group may place them in a vulnerable position if fellow teachers and administrators are not supportive of GSAs or are homophobic. Lastly, there may not be enough resources among the teachers and administrators to adequately support a school-based GSA (i.e., accurate knowledge, time, financial resources, willingness of teachers to serve as faculty advisors).

Alliance participation may protect participants from the impact of verbal and physical violence, alienation, and other forms of oppression (Blumfeld, 1994; Platt, 2001) and may be helpful in environments other than schools. Interdisciplinary research on community involvement supports the need for *both* school and community alliances. Findings have demonstrated that adolescents' sense of community appears to differ by setting–community versus school. While school settings tend to have a greater overall influence, communities can't be discounted and may provide different supports for youth (Pretty, Andrewes, & Collett, 1990). Interestingly, school and community networks of youth often remain separate; thus, efforts to establish support in schools for GLBT youth do not always carry over to communities to assist youth after school hours. Therefore, until a seamless system of support is achieved, both school and community alliances are needed in rural settings in order to ensure the safety and the healthy development of GLBT youth.

COMMUNITY-BASED ALLIANCES

Community-based gay-straight alliances do exist but are not discussed in much detail throughout the literature on gay and lesbian youth. Instead, information about their services is more accessible through an Internet search. Like school-based GSAs, community-based GSAs generally seem to be organized for all youth and dedicated to providing a safe, welcoming, and accepting community space. Participants include youth who identify themselves as GLBT, those who are perceived as GLBT, youth who are questioning their identities, children of GLBT families, and straight youth who want to be allies of their GLBT friends and family members. A group of local adults, members of which may or may not be GLBT, typically act as an advisory board. Community-based gay-straight alliances meet in the evenings and on weekends. They seem to provide many of the same types of social and educational activities as school-based GSAs. The number of meetings and level of structure in the activities varies by the resources and interests of the group. Some groups meet in a designated community space for GLBT persons, such as a drop-in or community center. Others offer toll-free crisis and support lines. And some participate in community change activities, such as providing community education (workshops, newsletters, and films), giving media interviews (with local TV and radio stations and newspapers about issues having an impact on the lives of GLBT youth), lobbying for changes in school board, community, and state policies, and publicly protesting a lack of recognition of diversity issues and discrimination against minority groups.

There are many benefits to community-based GSAs, both for the individuals involved and for their communities. Participation in a community-based GSA provides individuals with greater anonymity and control over their coming-out process. Teachers and fellow students are less likely to know of a person's participation in a community-based GSA unless he or she wants them to know. A community-based group also provides the opportunity for GLBT youth to meet youth from other schools. This is particularly important in rural areas, where the numbers of persons willing to participate in school-based GSAs may be very small and the climate may be more harsh than in urban areas. Furthermore, community-based GSAs provide opportunities for youth to meet a variety of GLBT adults and adult allies who can act as mentors.

Because youth may not know any GLBT adults, they sometimes struggle to envision what options are available to them as GLBT persons. Few GLBT teachers, school administrators, and staff are "out" in school environments because of homophobic anxiety among parents about what influence GLBT persons might have on their children's development, the fact that many school districts still do not include sexual orientation in their nondiscrimination policies, and previous firings of school personnel due to their sexual orientation (Anderson, 1997; Uribe, 1994). Adult mentors provide examples of healthy, successful GLBT adults. Further, a community-based GSA provides opportunities for GLBT youth and adults to meet in a healthy atmosphere–a safe alternative to bars and other high-risk environments (Robinson, 1991).

Youth members can also play a greater role in decision making in a community alliance because participants are not limited by school governance regarding the advisors' role, how and when the group may meet, the group's activities, or what may be discussed in the group setting. To the extent that community-based alliances incorporate gay rights activism, they provide important opportunities for youth to assume leadership roles and participate as constructive community members or agents of change. According to Van Wormer, Wells, & Boes (2000), "Unfortunately, it would appear that for lesbian and gay adolescents to experience leadership through social interaction they would have to be perceived as heterosexual" (p. 71). Community alliances provide a mechanism for youth to be leaders if they choose, while expressing authenticity as GLBT persons in the company of affirming adults.

PRISM: A NEW COMMUNITY-BASED ALLIANCE

In the wake of Matthew Shepard's death, Prism was founded in November 1998 by young adult residents of Columbia, Missouri, who wanted to create a safe place for GLBTQQA youth of central Missouri. Some early leaders of the group were undergraduate, upper-class students at the University of Missouri-Columbia. The group met informally once a week for two years to discuss diversity and social justice issues related to sexuality and gender, as well as what it is like to grow up in central Missouri. Youth from surrounding rural communities heard about Prism and began to attend meetings, some driving between 30 and 45 minutes each way. As a result of these consciousness-raising meetings, some of the persons involved with Prism successfully lobbied during the summer of 1999 to have sexual orientation added to the Columbia Public Schools' nondiscrimination policy.

In autumn 2000, Prism established a formal board of adult alliance members to provide guidance and support for the physical and emotional safety of group members and assist them in accomplishing their goals. The youth members continue to meet on a weekly basis to experience friendship and recreation and to discuss their life experiences in a safe, affirming environment. Youth members range from 13 to 20 years of age, but the most consistently active members are 15 to 17 years of age. Since this organization is youth governed, the mission and constitution were written by youth members. Any changes to the constitution are made by youth members with adult input. Because Prism is meant to be a safe harbor for youth, all meetings and activities are alcohol and drug free.

The role of members of the advisory board is to assure that a safe, affirming environment exists for GLBTQQA youth, to serve as mentors, and to provide access to resources. The 12 adults on the board are GLBT or allies from the central Missouri area who are at least 20 years of age. Each autumn, the youth members interview persons who are interested in board positions, including previous board members, and select the board for the coming year. Although several persons on the first two boards were affiliated with the local university in some capacity (faculty member, doctoral student, student life coordinator), the group is fairly diverse in regard to gender, sexuality, age, ethnocultural identity, class, and employment experiences. These adults have various degrees of experience in working with youth; some have professional experience as counselors and social workers or as teachers; others are parents or have volunteer experience. During the interview process, many have stated their commitment to GLBTQQA youth because they felt this was lacking when they were growing up. One volunteer stated, "I never had anything like this when I was growing up and if I had, it would have been great."

Although the advisory board functions with a shared leadership structure, there are some distinct roles within the group. After interviews with the youth, two or three adults are chosen to both serve on the board and to act as "coordinators." Adult coordinators take turns attending the Monday night meetings. Youth members decide on activities and plan them, but the adult coordinators typically do the background work, such as picking up a video for screening, gathering board games together, arranging for a guest speaker, or bringing snacks. Given that the coordinators are not specially trained in working with youth, they are supported by two adult board members who are either licensed as clinical social workers or professional counselors. The role of the professional helper, referred to as "liaison," is to serve as a resource for group activity ideas and facilitation techniques and to listen for warning signs that youth members may need additional support from formal services, such as therapy. When the need for formal help arises, the liaison makes referrals for assessment and treatment to persons or programs that are known to be culturally competent regarding GLBTQ youth issues. The liaisons shift responsibilities on a monthly basis. Coordinators meet as needed, usually one to two times monthly, with the liaison on duty. When not on duty, the additional liaison is available as a backup or for consultation as needed.

The activities of the Prism meetings vary from week to week. Sometimes guest speakers present talks on subjects requested by youth members, such as safer sex, queer history, alcohol and drug abuse, or verbal and physical self-defense. At other meetings, the youth watch movies on GLBTQQA-related issues. Sometimes, they go out for pizza, play pool, or just sit and chat.

In addition to holding weekly meetings, the youth and the adult board plan special activities throughout the year. During the first year of the board, Prism held a concert fundraiser, staffed a Prism booth at community events, published a newsletter, and met weekly for social and educational activities. The major project of the first year was the creation and facilitation of a community workshop on GLBT youth issues.

The workshop, "Beyond Tolerance, Building a Better Community for Our Youth," was a collaborative effort by adult and youth alliance members. Forty community residents attended the four-hour session, which consisted of a film (created by Prism youth), a youth question-and-answer panel, a small group activity, and a discussion/planning session on ways to make the local community and schools more inclusive of sexuality and gender diversity. The workshop's success brought additional invitations for community education throughout the second year. Presentations included a youth-facilitated public schoolteacher in-service and a presentation at a statewide summer academy for youth leaders.

In addition, recreational activities of the second year included a drag workshop, a trip to Pride Day at an amusement park and to other Pride events (parade/festival) in an urban area, a canoeing and camping trip, and numerous barbecues and parties. The group is currently working to coordinate a weekend "lock-in" with a GLBTQQA youth group from an urban area of the state and is recruiting adults for the third advisory board.

The weekly meetings, group activities, and informal time spent together has provided Prism youth with a strong support network. Youth members are aware that they can count on the adults to offer smiles, waves, or occasional hugs when they run into each other in public settings and to "be there" at times when more attention and advice are needed. When other adults and peers are giving youth the message that it is wrong to be who they are, such support is invaluable. As one youth member has repeatedly stated, "Prism has saved my life."

CONCLUSION

While societal conditions appear to be improving for GLBT persons, the needs of GLBT youth remain high. Coordination between informal and formal helping strategies is essential to creating strong social networks that support youth and change our communities into more affirming, inclusive places for everyone to live. Adult community members, schools, social workers, and the youth themselves all can participate in creating better communities. The first step is to fill the gaping holes in our current network of support and care for GLBT youth so that they no longer endure discrimination and violence on a daily basis and can grow up in a healthy environment. School- and community-based GSAs have an important role to play in this process. In rural settings, community-based alliances can meet an important need, connecting youth with caring adults within a safe and affirming environment. The forming of community alliances is an important new strategy in organization of the "gay community." These alliances bring diverse adults and youth together to build a network of support and create a better community for all.

REFERENCES

Anderson, J. D. (1997). Supporting the invisible minority. *Educational Leadership*, *54*(7), 65-68.

Anhalt, K., & Morris, T. L. (1998). Developmental and adjustment of gay, lesbian, and bisexual adolescents: A review of the empirical literature. *Clinical Child and Family Psychology Review*, *14*(4), 215-230.

Barton, W. H., Watkins, M., & Jarjoura, R. (1997). Youth and communities: Toward comprehensive strategies for youth development. *Social Work*, *42*(5), 483-493.

Berkman, C., & Zinberg, G. (1997). Homophobia and heterosexism in social workers. *Social Work, 42*(4), 319-331.

Blumfeld, W. J. (1994). "Gay/straight" alliances: Transforming pain to pride. *The High School Journal, 77*(1-2), 113-121.

Boulden, W. T. (2001). Gay men living in a rural environment. *Journal of Gay and Lesbian Social Services, 12*(3-4), 63-75.

Cody, P. J., & Welch, P. L. (1997). Rural gay men in northern New England: Life experiences and coping styles. *Journal of Homosexuality, 33*(1), 51-67.

D'Augelli, A. R., & Dark, L. J. (1994). Lesbian, gay, and bisexual youths. In L. D. Eron, J. H. Gentry, & P. Schlegel (Eds.), *Reason to hope: A psychosocial perspective on violence and youth* (pp. 177-196). Washington, DC: American Psychological Association.

D'Augelli, A. R., & Hart, M. M. (1987). Gay women, men and families in rural settings: Toward the development of helping communities. *American Journal of Community Psychology, 15*(1), 79-93.

D'Augelli, A. R., & Hershberger, S. L. (1993). Lesbian, gay, and bisexual youth in community settings: Personal challenges and mental health problems. *American Journal of Community Psychology, 21*(4), 421-443.

Finn, J. L., & Checkoway, B. (1998). Young people as competent community builders: A challenge to social work. *Social Work, 43*(4), 335-344.

Foster, S. J. (1997). Rural lesbians & gays: Public perceptions, worker perceptions and service delivery. *Journal of Gay & Lesbian Social Services, 7*(3), 23-35.

Ginsberg, L. H. (1998). Introduction: An overview of rural social work. In L. H. Ginsberg (Ed.), *Social work in rural communities* (3rd ed., pp. 3-22). Alexandria, VA: Council on Social Work Education.

Gay, Lesbian and Straight Education Network (2001a). GLSEN 2001 school climate survey. Retrieved November 25, 2001, from <http://glsen.org/templates/news/record.html?section=20&record=1029>.

Gay, Lesbian and Straight Education Network (2001b). GLSEN tallies 1,000 gay-straight alliances. Retrieved November 25, 2001, from <www.glsen.org/templates/news/record.html?section=13&record=1067>.

Gustavsson, N. S., & MacEachron, A. E. (1998). *Violence and lesbian and gay youth. Journal of Gay & Lesbian Social Services, 8*(3), 41-50.

Henry J. Kaiser Family Foundation (2001). *Inside-OUT: A report on the experiences of lesbians, gays, and bisexuals in America and the public's views on issues and policies related to sexual orientation* (Publication No. 3193). Menlo Park, CA: Author.

Herek, G. M. (1984). Beyond "homophobia": A social psychological perspective on attitudes toward lesbians and gay men. *Journal of Homosexuality, 10*(1-2), 1-21.

Human Rights Watch (2001). Hatred in the hallways: Violence and discrimination against lesbian, gay, bisexual, and transgender students in U.S. schools. New York: Author.

Hunter, S., Shannon, C., Knox, J., & Martin, J. I. (1998). *Lesbian, gay, and bisexual youths and adults: Knowledge for human service practice*. Thousand Oaks, CA: Sage.

Levitt, M. J., Guacci-Franco, N., & Levitt, J. L. (1993). Convoys of social support in childhood and early adolescent structure and function. *Developmental Psychology, 29*(5), 811-818.

Lindhorst, T. (1997). Lesbian and gay men in the country: Practice implications for rural social workers. *Journal of Gay & Lesbian Social Services, 7*(3), 1-11.

McCarthy, L. (2000). Poppies in a wheat field: Exploring the lives of rural lesbians. *Journal of Homosexuality, 39*(1), 75-94.

McWhirter, J. J., McWhirter, B. T., McWhirter, A. M., & McWhirter, E. H. (1998). *At-risk youth: A comprehensive response* (2nd ed.). Pacific Grove, CA: Brooks/Cole.

Morrow, D. F. (1993). Social work with gay and lesbian adolescents. *Social Work, 38,* 655-660.

Moses, A. E., & Buckner, J. A. (1982). The special problems of rural gay clients. In A. E. Moses & R. O. Hawkins, Jr. (Eds.), *Counseling lesbian women and gay men: A life-issues approach* (pp. 173-180). St. Louis: C. V. Mosby Company.

Platt, L. (2001). Not your father's high school club. *The American Prospect,* 37-39.

Pretty, G. M. H., Andrewes, L., & Collett, C. (1990). Exploring adolescents' sense of community and its relationship to loneliness. *Journal of Community Psychology, 22,* 346-358.

Rein, A. S. (1999). Sexual orientation and suicidal behavior among adolescents (Doctoral Dissertation, Simon Fraser University). *Dissertation Abstracts International, 60,* 2931.

Robinson, K. E. (1991). Notes for the field, gay youth support groups: An opportunity for social work intervention. *Social Work, 36*(5), 458-459.

Russell, S. T., & Joyner, K. (2001). Adolescent sexual orientation and suicide risk: Evidence from a national study. *American Journal of Public Health, 91*(8), 1276-1281.

Safren, S. A., & Heimberg, R. G. (1999). Depression, hopeless, suicidality, and related factors in sexual minority and heterosexual adolescents. *Journal of Consulting and Clinical Psychology, 67*(6), 859-866.

Saulnier, C. F. (1998). Prevalence of suicide attempts and suicidal ideation among lesbian and gay youth. *Journal of Gay & Lesbian Social Services, 8*(3), 51-68.

Savin-Williams, R. C. (1994). Verbal and physical abuse as stressors in the lives of lesbian, gay male, and bisexual youths: Association with school problems, running away, substance abuse, prostitution, and suicide. *Journal of Consulting and Clinical Psychology, 62*(2), 261-269.

Sears, J. T. (1991). *Growing up gay in the south: Race, gender, and journeys of the spirit.* New York: Harrington Park Press.

Smith, J. D. (1997). Working with larger systems: Rural lesbians and gays. *Journal of Gay & Lesbian Social Services, 7*(3), 13-22.

Smith, J. D., & Mancoske, R. J. (1997). Preface. *Journal of Gay & Lesbian Social Services, 7*(3), xvii-xx.

Uribe, V. (1994). The silent minority: Rethinking our commitment to gay and lesbian youth. *Theory into Practice, 33*(3), 167-172.

Van Wormer, K., Wells, J., & Boes, M. (2000). *Social work with lesbians, gays, and bisexuals: A strengths perspective.* Boston: Allyn and Bacon.

Grassroots Meet Homophobia: A Rocky Mountain Success Story

Audrey Olsen Faulkner
Ann Lindsey

SUMMARY. This case study highlights the challenges and successes of a small grassroots effort to change the learning environment for GLBT youth in a local public school district located within the conservative social climate of a small city in Colorado. Strategies included tailoring the social action agenda to the unique characteristics of the conservative community; finding allies in the school district; recruiting volunteer professional talent; and reframing social justice issues to focus on the educational value that every child is entitled to a physically and psychologically safe and supportive learning environment in order to achieve full academic potential. *[Article copies available for a fee from The Haworth Document Delivery Service: 1-800-HAWORTH. E-mail address: <docdelivery@haworthpress.com> Website: <http://www.HaworthPress.com> © 2004 by The Haworth Press, Inc. All rights reserved.]*

Audrey Olsen Faulkner, PhD, is Core Professor, College of Interdisciplinary Arts and Sciences, The Union Institute and University, 731 West Olive Street, Fort Collins, CO 80521 (E-mail: audreyof@verinet.com).

Ann Lindsey, MSW, can be contacted at #10, 51511 RR 264, Spruce Grove, Alberta T7Y 1C7, Canada (E-mail: ann484@yahoo.com).

[Haworth co-indexing entry note]: "Grassroots Meet Homophobia: A Rocky Mountain Success Story." Faulkner, Audrey Olsen, and Ann Lindsey. Co-published simultaneously in *Journal of Gay & Lesbian Social Services* (Harrington Park Press, an imprint of The Haworth Press, Inc.) Vol. 16, No. 3/4, 2004, pp. 113-128; and: *Gay and Lesbian Rights Organizing: Community-Based Strategies* (ed: Yolanda C. Padilla) Harrington Park Press, an imprint of The Haworth Press, Inc., 2004, pp. 113-128. Single or multiple copies of this article are available for a fee from The Haworth Document Delivery Service [1-800-HAWORTH, 9:00 a.m. - 5:00 p.m. (EST). E-mail address: docdelivery@haworthpress.com].

KEYWORDS. Lesbian and gay youth, social change, grassroots organizing, queer, schools

This case study presents the story of the challenges and successes of a grassroots effort to improve a school district's educational environment for gay, lesbian, bisexual, and transgender (GLBT) students. These social change activities were carried out in the conservative social climate of a small city in Colorado, where both the state and city are home to social and political attitudes and organizations that are militantly anti-gay. Grassroots activists must factor the social and political climate into their efforts, often having to be satisfied with outcomes that other communities might consider merely preludes to action.

GLBT YOUTH AND SCHOOL

Only in recent years has the issue of GLBT youth and their experiences been studied. There is very limited research on the activism of external grassroots agents to change school systems' attitudes and actions. The majority of research centers on the results of homophobia and heterosexism on GLBT youth and/or the implementation of supportive services and programs instituted from within a school system. Uribe and Harbeck (1992) report on Project 10, a successful program created and instituted from within a school system in response to the harassment of an openly gay student who subsequently dropped out of a California public school. Uribe and Harbeck acknowledge that litigation is often needed to bring about change, because school districts are not always responsive to the needs of GLBT students and not all schools have the option of creating or implementing a program without great struggle.

Students and others who are merely perceived as GLBT often suffer, and such intolerant attitudes go unaddressed and even unnoticed. Harbeck (1995) takes a more optimistic view. He believes that these concerns of GLBT youth now have people's attention, and that it is the job of activists and service providers to educate the schools and facilitate attitudinal change.

GLBT youth have the burden of recognizing and accepting a sexual identity different from what mainstream culture considers normal. They are challenged to create a healthy alternative sexual identity. Schools have never been havens of safety for GLBT youth, but they have provided a hiding place. Rofes (1997) proposes that mainstream education and exposure to GLBT life, community, and issues may in fact have worsened life for LGBT youth, and that "As knowledge of the existence of lesbian athletes and gay pop singers spreads throughout popular culture, it becomes increasingly difficult for youth constructing counter-hegemonic identities to find cover" (p. xvi).

Many GLBT youth are not able to avoid problems such as poor grades, dropping out of school, drug/alcohol use, homelessness, social isolation, alienation, and suicide (Remafedi, 1991, as cited in Lipkin, 1995; Remafedi, 1994, as cited in Snowder, 1996; Savin-Williams, 1994; Sears, 1991; Walling, 1993). There is consensus that schools are not welcoming and friendly places for GLBT youth, whether they are visible or closeted. Teachers, counselors, and administrators share in creating that situation. While school-initiated programs exist, they are typically in large, metropolitan areas and are not always an option for smaller or conservative communities.

CONTEXT FOR THE GRASSROOTS EFFORT

Colorado is a Rocky Mountain state, connected to images of majestic mountains, horses, cattle, gold mines, cowboys still riding the range. Like its neighbor Wyoming, Colorado takes pride in its citizens' self-sufficiency and rugged individualism. Colorado is also the state where the governor opened the 2000 General Assembly with a speech declaring that marriage was meant to occur between one man and one woman. Subsequently that session of the Legislature passed a bill declaring " . . . a marriage is valid in this state only if . . . it is between one man and one woman . . . " (Colorado Revised Statute, 2000).

In the early 1990s Colorado made national headlines with Amendment 2, which disallowed any laws by the state or cities that would have created legal protections for GLBT citizens. The amendment, initiated and advanced by conservative forces and passed by citizen vote, was subsequently overturned by the U.S. Supreme Court in May of 1996.

Colorado is home to Focus on the Family, the fundamentalist religious organization founded by James Dobson. This organization has a multimillion-dollar budget, and its local and national networks of fundamentalist churches and organizations make it a formidable enemy of civil rights and progressive causes. Focus on the Family often sets the tone for thought and expression at a local level in Colorado, especially in regard to local politics and schools. This powerful organization actively and effectively discourages individuals, churches, and groups from any effort to hold open and frank discussions about sexual orientation, acceptance of GLBT individuals, or civil rights for the GLBT community.

Of special interest for this case study, Focus on the Family also targets public schools as "promoting homosexuality." The organization's CitizenLink Website makes the following claim:

Teachers across America are sparking students' curiosities in subjects like history, mathematics, English . . . and homosexuality. But are they presenting all of the facts, or simply pushing a seductive agenda upon young minds? As more and more public schools promote homosexuality as an alternative lifestyle without consulting parents, families need to proactively monitor school activities and policies. Many of these "academic opportunities" sound nice–but actually protect and promote sexual promiscuity. (CitizenLink, n.d.)

Focus on the Family considers the following as "warning" signs within a public school: a "safe-schools" nonharassment program; a homosexual student club; a nondiscrimination policy based on "sexual orientation"; programs to stop "homophobia," "hate," or "bias"; pro-homosexual literature added to curricula and libraries with pro-family material bypassed or discarded; and AIDS and "safe sex" education programs. In regard to the "homosexual student club" the CitizenLink Website tells readers, "A club provides a venue where students curious about this behavior but who have not yet engaged in it can readily meet students and even adult advisors to begin homosexual relationships–with school support!" (Harvey, 2000).

The Local Area

Rightville, the subject of this case study, is a mid-size city near the foothills of the Rocky Mountains. (Geographical, organizational, and individual names and some minor details have been changed to protect the identities of the community and participants.) Rightville prides itself on "diversity" but fewer than 10 percent of its citizens are minorities of color, and the majority of diversity exists within the local university community, not the larger city. The majority of the GLBT population is closeted, especially in their work settings. Metropolitan Denver, where the GLBT population is larger and more visible, is nearby, and many GLBT individuals travel there for social and community activities.

Since 1993, the city has had a nonprofit GLBT Community Resource Center, which was established in response to Colorado's Amendment 2. The Center provides referral services, social opportunities, education, information, and advocacy. It struggles for members and financial support in the relatively hostile community environment, where GLBT citizens are reluctant to reveal their sexual orientation for fear of losing jobs or housing.

The School District

The public school district serves the city and neighboring towns, covering four high schools, six junior highs, and more than two dozen elementary schools, and serving over 20,000 students. The district reflects the larger community. A small vocal minority of religious conservatives regularly attend school board meetings and attempt to promote their agenda around issues of policy and curriculum. The school board often feels compelled to defer to them, under threat of losing resources by having children removed to home schooling or private religious schools.

There are no "out" teachers or administrators because the climate in the schools and the community is such that they do not feel safe revealing their sexual orientation. This atmosphere allows many school personnel to believe that there are no gay students in the Rightville School District.

History of Human Rights Activity in Rightville

In 1992, when Amendment 2 was on the ballot, Rightville citizens approved it by a narrow margin. Because opinion on the amendment was almost evenly divided, pro-human rights activists were encouraged that the city's climate was changing. The amendment was struck down by the Supreme Court in 1996. At that point, in spite of well-founded fears about the continued power of the conservative religious movement, activists believed its control could be successfully challenged (Perrotti & Westheimer, 2001).

The city's Human Rights Commission worked for two years to bring the city's Human Rights Ordinance up to federal standards, by adding categories such as the aged and the physically challenged. In addition, they added sexual orientation as a protected category in housing and employment. After public forums and intensive educational efforts by the Human Rights Commission, the GLBT community, and their allies, the city council unanimously approved the additions to the ordinance. The fundamentalist church network and some factions of the business community countered this unanimous vote by gathering sufficient signatures to successfully petition for a public referendum on the issue.

A fierce political battle ensued. Several progressive foundations gave substantial financial support to the Rightville Coalition for Human Rights, and a broad-based citizen group organized to help support the ordinance's passage. A large progressive church and a significant number of individual clergy supported the ordinance, as did GLBT citizens and their allies. Similarly, educators, students, progressive business owners, and many community organizations backed the ordinances. To lead the campaign in support of the ordinance, the GLBT Community Resource Center and the Rightville Coalition for Human Rights hired a campaign director with successful experience in winning similar struggles elsewhere. Dozens of community volunteers signed on for campaign duties.

The conservative religious churches entered the fray with money, advertisements, and printed flyers depicting Armageddon if the ordinance were passed. The pro-ordinance groups, however, had more funding than the conservative organizations, and were able to create leaflets, buy newspaper, radio, and television advertising, and hold numerous public meetings. Although many business leaders supported the ordinance, the business community generally questioned the ordinance on the basis that compliance would cost them money and reduce profits if the ordinance's opponents decided to boycott. All sides tried to exercise influence through letters to the editor of the local newspaper.

In spite of outspending their opponents, the Community Coalition lost the battle; the ordinance was defeated by a substantial majority. The reservations of the business community and the power of the fundamentalist pulpit had prevailed.

This is the geographic, political, and social setting for this case study about the grassroots effort of the Community Resource Center to change school district policies and practice in Rightsville.

THE RIGHTVILLE COMMUNITY RESOURCE CENTER TAKES ON COMMUNITY EDUCATION

When the Human Rights Ordinance was defeated, many citizens, especially those in the business community, stated publicly that they wanted the goal of nondiscrimination reached through education rather than legislation. The Community Resource Center (CRC) accepted the challenge and appointed a Social Change Committee for the huge task of creating a change in community knowledge and attitude.

Constituting a Social Change Committee

Iris Hammond, a CRC board member who was a seasoned social work community organizer, chaired the Social Change Committee. GLBT professionals and community members, allies, parents of gay students, GLBT college and high school students, representatives of faith organizations, a teacher from an adjacent school district, a program director from the local University, and a therapist joined the group. Two graduate social work interns from the university gave staff support to the committee for its first two years. Mildred Jefferson, who had been a leader in the Rightville Coalition for Human Rights, also joined the committee. The broadly based committee membership guaranteed a range of stakeholder views and knowledge.

Construing Committee Tasks

Ms. Hammond's first task was to help the committee create its vision for the future, see the potential for change with their involvement, and gain a sense of confidence that their actions would make a difference, so that in this way, they could develop the political will to act (Medoff & Sklar, 1994).

The resources were few, but the enthusiasm was high. Ms. Hammond and Ms. Jefferson guided the committee through its first discussion of how to select an issue for action (Homan, 1994). Members talked about the need for an issue that would capture the imagination of the GLBT community and their allies–one that would enlist support and unite the community rather than divide it, and one where the scope was appropriate for available resources and talents. To give heart to the GLBT community suffering from the defeat of the ordinance, and to keep the committee members engaged in a long-term effort, the project had to have a good chance for success.

In a parallel development, the Foothills Youth Group, sponsored by the CRC, came to the CRC's board with its concerns about the daily harassment the members were experiencing in Rightville high schools. CRC's board asked the youth to tell their stories to the Social Change Committee. The committee listened, and at their next meeting, they decided to focus their work on changing the climate of the high schools. Changing the high school climate, while very challenging, seemed to be a concrete issue where the committee's work might make a difference. More importantly, the committee reasoned that if they could change the attitudes of the young people in the community and the people who mentored them through high school, the changed attitudes would be passed on to following generations. This approach seemed a better way of influencing community attitudes than if the target group was older adults.

The committee had their issue. They had a vision of a school environment without harassment, and they knew the schools' negative environment would not change without their intervention. Although they had no local models for action, they believed they could find a way to create the change.

Creating Educational Packets

Eager to get started, the Social Change Committee identified a list of persons in the community whom they knew to be allies knowledgeable about GLBT issues. This included a few school counselors. The committee decided to create educational packets, which would first educate the committee members and then could be distributed to the counselors. Using resources on the Internet, newspaper articles, and materials from Parents, Families and Friends of Lesbians and Gays (PFLAG) and the Gay, Lesbian and Straight Education

Network (GLSEN), the committee collected a vast amount of material. The packet the committee made from this material included basic articles about what it means to be a GLBT youth, suggestions for making schools safe places, the myths of sexual orientation, and risks GLBT students face, as well as a bibliography of resources. The packet was focused on the educational and psychological consequences of harassment for gay students. The first version was simple and sparse because funds to produce it were limited.

The social work student intern delivered a handful of packets to a few school counselors. The committee was apprehensive about the response, but soon learned informally that the materials were welcomed. As time passed and funds became available, the packets were increased in size and scope and were more widely distributed within the high schools. Subsequently, the Counseling Department for the first time officially requested a new supply of packets, because the counselors had been giving the contents away to teachers, staff, and students.

Later, the committee acquired an article from a school board journal about a gay student and his family who had won a large settlement from their local Board of Education because of its failure to protect him from harassment. This article was included in all future packets to assist in delivering the message that schools were responsible for the protection of their GLBT students. The informational packets were developed before the committee had created a definite action strategy, but they were an effective and convenient way to disseminate information in a nonthreatening and educational manner (Perrotti & Westheimer, 2001).

Collecting Personal Stories from Youth

The next move was to collect written stories of daily harassment from Foothills Youth Group members. Committed to the need to involve students (Perrotti & Westheimer, 2001), the committee saw the stories as a way to empower the students by hearing and acknowledging their capacity for agency (Simon, 1994). Another value of the stories was that they could be expected to have a dramatic impact on school personnel.

The initial plan was to present the stories to the school board at a public meeting, as a way of beginning a dialogue at the policymaking level of the school district. Ms. Jefferson, however, suggested a preliminary conference with a well-known and respected retired school teacher. As Ms. Jefferson emphasized,

> There probably isn't a family in this community who does not have at least one member who had Sam Calhoun as a teacher. He would be a tremendous ally, if we could engage him. Everyone in the school system knows him. Let's see what he thinks we should do.

Meeting with Sam Calhoun–The Beginning of a Calculated Strategy

The meeting with Sam Calhoun was a turning point for the Social Change Committee. When the committee asked Mr. Calhoun for advice, he explained that what had seemed to be a forthright and clear path of action had many inherent dangers. School board meetings were public; by taking the students' stories there, the committee would expose its agenda to the view of religious conservatives, who always had observers at the meetings. The cause might be defeated before the work began. Mr. Calhoun reported that the school board had been under constant pressure from conservative parents around issues of sex education, birth control, and diversity education. Parents had threatened to withdraw their children from school, create a public uproar, and subject school board members to vicious verbal attacks if these issues were not handled to their satisfaction. Mr. Calhoun suggested the committee should begin with locating allies in the school system, and working quietly through them. He promised to connect the committee members with critical staff.

This was very much the approach the committee had stumbled upon with the packets, and they decided to adopt it as their long-term strategy. They made a deliberate choice not to label the school district personnel as the "enemy." They would attempt to appeal to a universal value that eventually became the core of the committee's mission statement–that every child is entitled to a physically and psychologically safe and supportive learning environment in order to achieve his or her full academic potential. The committee believed that no school board member, administrator, teacher, or counselor could fail to support such an objective. The committee could also argue that the district's broad antidiscrimination policy, while it did not specifically list sexual orientation, could easily be interpreted to extend to GLBT students. Tactically, this decision meant that the committee would work through allies they could locate in lower levels of the district hierarchy. They would forgo conflict and concentrate on networking and education. School personnel would be asked about their issues and their needs for information about GLBT students. The committee would first respond to those issues, and then provide additional information and resources. Finally, they would appeal to educators' value systems by focusing on equal learning opportunities for every student, rather than emphasizing inclusion based on sexual identity.

The committee had reached organizational maturity. It now had a cohesive strategy and guidelines for the tactics to be used (Burghardt, 1982; Kahn, 1982; Perrotti & Westheimer, 2001; Toseland & Rivas, 1987).

Meetings with School Principals Brings Promise of Cooperation

The first school principal Mr. Calhoun invited to meet with the Social Change Committee was receptive to the message and the issues. She identified the pivotal school personnel who should be contacted, and offered to set up a meeting with the committee and all of the high schools principals. The committee chose the meeting with principals as its first priority. When the group gathered, the assistant superintendent and all of the high school principals came. The committee invited older members of the Foothills Youth Group, now graduated from high school, who felt less at risk, to tell their stories about daily harassment and the effect it had on their high school career. Several of the principals expressed shock and surprise; others seemed uncomfortable. The principals shared their feelings of being under constant pressure from conservative parents. After lengthy discussion about youth who might be suicidal, the principals asked to refer such cases to the Community Resource Center with the youth's permission, and they committed themselves to taking immediate action when harassment of a GLBT student came to their attention. The committee believed that the principals' commitment to action in the presence of their peers, the youth, and the committee, provided leverage for future committee action. The administrators knew now that they were subject to scrutiny from another concerned community group. There were subsequent reports from the Foothills Youth Group that one school quickly adopted a zero-tolerance stance on harassment and rapidly and fairly handled two incidents.

In a related development, the director of the Community Resource Center secured a letter of support from a local inter-religious organization, the Interfaith Council, for the Social Change Committee's school effort. This took considerable negotiation, since the Interfaith Council's membership included representatives from several fundamentalist groups. The decision to focus on a safe and supportive school environment that allowed every student to attain his or her learning potential, rather than more generally on homophobia and heterosexism, was instrumental in obtaining the council's support. Interfaith Council members personally delivered the copies of the letter of support to all of the high school principals. The committee believed this reinforced for the principals the fact that the community, including the religious community, was watching the situation with GLBT students in the schools and believed in educational equity for all students.

Concentrating on Opportunities to Provide Training

Committee members contacted the Counseling Department, where high-level staff were receptive. They discussed training for counselors and distribution of the information packets to individual counselors, and scheduled a training session. This was unexpected, and it began to encourage the committee that possibly the staff were not purposely denying the needs of GLBT youth but rather, did not know how to begin to deal with them. Following this meeting, the school district's director of security also called to request training for his personnel.

Committee members and allies provided the in-service training session, first to security personnel and then to counseling staff for the high schools, junior high schools, and elementary schools. At each session, information packets were distributed, and a panel of GLBT individuals, a parent, and allies told their stories and experiences. A question-and-answer session followed. Security personnel expressed appreciation for the training and requested more; they said students often approached them when counselors were too busy, and they needed information and strategies for responding. The director of security was enthusiastic about the training and asked the committee to do additional sessions. One of the trainers for the counselors' session reported that the counselors were "blown away" by the information he shared. The counselors professed not to know such things were happening in the schools, and many expressed interest in more training.

Developing a Curriculum and a Training Corps

The committee had relied on ad hoc training teams recruited from its ranks and its allies, and realized it needed to move beyond that. The committee recruited a volunteer group of local professionals experienced in GLBT and other diversity training issues and asked them to develop a standard training curriculum which volunteers could use. The committee wanted to feel comfortable that all of the trainers working under the Social Change Committee sponsorship would deliver the same message using the same materials. When completed, the curriculum included three courses–introductory, intermediate, and advanced–with handouts and exercises. Heavy emphasis was placed on strategies for school personnel to use in problem solving.

When this task was completed, the committee turned to developing a roster of experienced trainers willing to use the curriculum. At the time of this article's publication, the training corps has been recruited, and their first orientation session has been held. They are enthusiastic, knowledgeable, and see themselves as a community resource, available for anticipated training assignments at schools and in the community. They will participate in the training sessions already scheduled with the school district.

DISCUSSION:
FACTORS IN THE SOCIAL CHANGE COMMITTEE'S SUCCESS

Rightville schools are not yet free of harassment for GLBT students, but progress has been made. Networks are in place, there is a more hospitable school climate in which information and education are being sought and provided, high school principals are on record as supporting a nonharassment policy, and unexpected allies have been found. The schoolroom door has begun to open.

Why has the Social Change Committee been successful in a community that defeated an ordinance protecting civil rights for GLBT citizens, and has a high-energy, vigilant fundamentalist community faction, a change-resistant school district, and a denial of GLBT students' presence in the high schools. As in most situations, the outcome is attributable to careful strategy and some good fortune.

Selecting a "Good" Issue

Homan (1994) stresses the importance of distinguishing good issues from bad issues when attempting to move people to action. Factors to consider when selecting a good issue include the importance of clarity, capturing the imagination, immediacy, self-interest, emotional as well as intellectual attachment, limited challenge, and the possibility of success. By these criteria, the Social Change Committee chose a good issue. It captured their imagination, was limited in scope, and members were emotionally and intellectually committed. The committee believed they could succeed.

Tailoring Strategy and Tactics to the Specific Community Situation

Probably the Committee's most important step was to stop ad hoc decision making and create a deliberate long-term strategy, with accompanying tactics, to accomplish the goal. They tailored the strategy to the unique social and political characteristics of Rightville, and the resources and talents available. Staples (1984) discusses the need to make decisions on a strategic basis in order to achieve a goal and the greater importance of this when the resources and power of the action group are limited. The committee had no real power to press the school district for change. They did not initially consider that if they confronted the school board, they did not have the resources or the power to escalate the challenge to a higher level of conflict (Kahn, 1982). Mr. Calhoun pointed out that public denunciation of the school policy and practices would reveal the agenda to the community's fundamentalist faction, and the school board would feel compelled to dismiss the committee's issue. This led the committee to develop a "presumption of interest and concern" strategy for reaching teachers, counselors, and administrators–the people in the district who were in the closest contact with the youth, and who were invested in their success on a personal, rather than a simply a policy basis.

In developing strategy and tactics, the committee looked at their goal, their information, their alternatives, and their resources, in steps that closely paralleled the Perrotti and Westheimer (2001) model. They recognized the central role of GLBT students and acknowledged their agency by using their stories as a way to create a receptive climate for change; they collected and used data effectively, built on the core values of the educators they were targeting by reframing their issue in terms more acceptable to the educators, studied the local school policies that would support their position, and utilized existing networks and developed new ones to create visible support for their work.

Cultivating and Utilizing Allies

The committee understood that it would take the support of many allies to claim the moral high ground and create change (Brooks, 2001). The committee recognized and honored allies, utilized them extensively in their work, and tried to create new allies in the school district. Bicklin (1983) describes tasks for allies, among them becoming informed about the issue, aligning themselves with the cause, and speaking out in support. The organizers included both GLBT and allies on the committee, all of whom participated in the same activities. This helped gain the committee members acceptance in both communities, and also demonstrated that the educational risk for GLBT students was of total community concern, not just a gay community issue. Members were recruited from a number of community sectors, including religious groups. The allies on the Interfaith Council helped get the council's support for the letter to the principals. The ally networks helped to multiply the committee's resources. While some committee members came and went for various reasons, when one talent was lost, another was usually gained.

Enlisting Established Community Leadership

Mr. Calhoun's advice saved the committee from an initial blunder that would have undermined and perhaps defeated their efforts. Ms. Jefferson was absolutely critical to the committee's success: She had stature in the community and among local educators, she was known for years of social justice work, and her motives could not be questioned. She made many phone calls and visits to school and community contacts, and was an endless source of help with strategic planning.

Creating Resources Through Utilizing Volunteers

The committee identified the skills and abilities of individuals as they looked for resources, utilizing an informal "capacity index" (McKnight & Kretzman,

1998) to identify and recruit volunteers. Many professionals with busy lives volunteered their time for the training, the curriculum development, and the training corps. Two graduate social work interns (one in each of two years) did far more than their school assignment called for, researching material for the packets, planning meetings, preparing committee minutes, making phone calls, and developing mailing lists. They also added many insights and suggestions and made critical community contacts. They established warm relationships with the rest of the committee, adding to the camaraderie that kept the process moving.

The importance of the committee members' commitment to social justice cannot be overlooked. They never took their eyes off the goal of a safer, more nurturing and productive educational environment for all of the city's children. Fortune favored the committee's early work.

The committee stumbled onto what became its deliberate, long-term strategy when they first chose to identify allies and give them educational materials. It was originally a way for the members to "do something" while they were developing cohesion and purpose. Having organized packets filled with easy-to-read materials focusing on the educational issues was a low-budget way to deliver an educational message. These activities–identifying counselor allies and creating and distributing packets–helped get the committee energized, informed them about the issues, and educated a cadre of counselors who remained sympathetic and helpful.

Accepting Slow Change

The committee was persistent. Without staff, they had to limit efforts to what busy volunteers could do, so the pace was sometimes excruciatingly slow. The committee's tasks were not the highest priority for their school allies, whose job demands took precedence over social change activities. But the committee had a basic strategy from which it did not deviate, and stayed with it long enough to be successful, even though the wait was tedious.

In summary, the committee's work reflected social work community's organizing theory and principles. They tailored their strategy to a community situation in which they had very limited power, gathered a diverse grassroots committee representative of many areas of the GLBT and the allied community, and utilized scarce resources to the fullest. They enlisted existing community leadership, used familiar community networks and created new ones, accepted that change is a process not an event, and recognized that community change is slow and incremental.

REFERENCES

Bicklin, D. P. (1983). *Community organizing: Theory and practice.* Englewood Cliffs, NJ: Prentice-Hall, Inc.

Brooks, F. (2001). Innovative organizing practices: ACORN'S campaign in Los Angeles organizing workfare workers. *Journal of Community Practice, 9*(4), 65-85.

Burghardt S. (1982). *Organizing for community action.* Beverly Hills: Sage.

CitizenLink: A web site of Focus on the Family (n.d.). *Homosexuality in schools.* Retrieved July 31, 2002, from <www.family.org/cforum/topics/a0018824.cfm>.

Colorado Revised Statute, Concerning the restriction of valid marriages to those only between one man and one woman, 14-2-104 (2000).

Harbeck, K. M. (1995). Invisible no more: Addressing the needs of lesbian, gay, and bisexual youth and their advocates. In G. Unks (Ed.), *The gay teen: Educational practice and theory for lesbian, gay, and bisexual adolescents* (pp. 125-133). New York: Routledge.

Harvey, L. (2000). CitizenLink: A web site of Focus on the Family. *A checklist to assess your school's risk for encouraging homosexuality.* Retrieved July 31, 2002, from <www.family.org/cforum/tempforum/A0015282.html>.

Homan, M. S. (1994). *Promoting community change.* Pacific Grove, CA: Brooks/Cole.

Kahn, S. (1982). *Organizing: A guide for grassroots leaders.* New York: McGraw-Hill.

Lipkin, A. (1995). The case for a gay and lesbian curriculum. In G. Unks (Ed.), *The gay teen: Educational practice and theory for lesbian, gay, and bisexual adolescents* (pp. 31-52). New York: Routledge.

McKnight, J., & Kretzmann, J. P. (1998). Mapping community capacity. In M. Minkler (Ed.), *Organizing and community building for health* (pp. 157-172). New Brunswick, NJ: Rutgers University Press.

McLaren, P. (1995). Moral panic, schooling, and gay identity: Critical pedagogy and the politics of resistance. In G. Unks (Ed.), *The gay teen: Educational practice and theory for lesbian, gay, and bisexual adolescents* (pp. 105-123). New York: Routledge.

Medoff, P., & Sklar, H. (1994). *Streets of hope: The fall and rise of an urban neighborhood.* Boston: South End Press.

O'Conor, A. (1995). Who gets called queer in school: Lesbian, gay, and bisexual teenagers, homophobia, and high school. In G. Unks (Ed.), *The gay teen: Educational practice and theory for lesbian, gay, and bisexual adolescents* (pp. 95-101). New York: Routledge.

Perrotti, J., & Westheimer, K. (2001). *When the drama club is not enough.* Boston: Beacon Press.

Rofes, E. (1997). Schools: The neglected site of queer activists. In M. B. Harris (Ed.), *School experiences of gay and lesbian youth: The invisible minority* (pp. xiii-xviii). New York: The Harrington Park Press.

Savin-Williams, R. C. (1994). Verbal and physical abuse as stressors in the lives of lesbian, gay male, and bisexual youths: Associations with school problems, running away, substance abuse, prostitution and suicide. *Journal of Consulting and Clinical Psychology, 62,* 261-269.

Sears, J. T. (1991). Helping students understand and accept sexual diversity. *Educational Leadership*, 54-56.

Simon, B. L. (1994). *The empowerment tradition in American social work*. New York: Columbia University Press.

Snowder, F. (1996). Preventing gay teen suicide. In D. R. Walling (Ed.), *Open lives–safe schools: Addressing gay and lesbian issues in education* (pp. 261-268). Bloomington, IN: Phi Delta Kappa Educational Foundation.

Staples, L. (1984). *Roots to power: A manual for grassroots organizing*. New York: Praeger.

Toseland, R. W., & Rivas, R. F. (1987). Working with task groups: The middle phase. In F. M. Cox, J. L. Erlich, J. Rothman, & J. E. Tropman (Eds.), *Strategies of community organization* (4th ed., pp. 114-142). Itasca, IL: F. E. Peacock Publishers, Inc.

Uribe, V., & Harbeck, K. M. (1992). Addressing the needs of lesbian, gay, and bisexual youth: The origins of PROJECT 10 and school-based intervention. *Journal of Homosexuality, 22*, 9-27.

Walling, D. R. (1993). *Gay teens at risk*. Bloomington, IN: Phi Delta Kappa Educational Foundation.

INNOVATIVE STRATEGIES FOR A NEW ERA

The Importance of GLBT Think Tanks to Our Agenda of Equality and Liberation

Sean Cahill

SUMMARY. The gay, lesbian, bisexual, and transgender (GLBT) movement should support research, policy analysis, and strategy development to advance greater understanding and equality of GLBT people. Most public policy frameworks affect GLBT people in particular ways, but we have not yet developed analyses of these frameworks, let alone articulated perspectives in critical policy debates affecting us. This article illustrates how the National Gay and Lesbian Task Force works on

Sean Cahill is Director of the Policy Institute, National Gay and Lesbian Task Force, 121 West 27th Street, Suite 501, New York, NY 10001.

[Haworth co-indexing entry note]: "The Importance of GLBT Think Tanks to Our Agenda of Equality and Liberation." Cahill, Sean. Co-published simultaneously in *Journal of Gay & Lesbian Social Services* (Harrington Park Press, an imprint of The Haworth Press, Inc.) Vol. 16, No. 3/4, 2004, pp. 129-146; and: *Gay and Lesbian Rights Organizing: Community-Based Strategies* (ed: Yolanda C. Padilla) Harrington Park Press, an imprint of The Haworth Press, Inc., 2004, pp. 129-146. Single or multiple copies of this article are available for a fee from The Haworth Document Delivery Service [1-800-HAWORTH, 9:00 a.m. - 5:00 p.m. (EST). E-mail address: docdelivery@haworthpress.com].

Journal of Gay & Lesbian Social Services, Vol. 16(3/4) 2004
http://www.haworthpress.com/store/product.asp?sku=J041
© 2004 by The Haworth Press, Inc. All rights reserved.
10.1300/J041v16n03_09

identifying the concerns of GLBT people through research and policy analysis to provide the basis for more effective and proactive organizing. *[Article copies available for a fee from The Haworth Document Delivery Service: 1-800-HAWORTH. E-mail address: <docdelivery@haworthpress.com> Website: <http://www.HaworthPress.com> © 2004 by The Haworth Press, Inc. All rights reserved.]*

KEYWORDS. Gay, lesbian, public policy, research, organizing

> The mainstream movement had been pushing as hard as it could against the doors of federal power since 1972. Suddenly, we broke through. And like characters in a slapstick comedy, we came tumbling through the door, falling on top of each other and stumbling for footing as we adjusted to the sudden lack of resistance.
>
> –Urvashi Vaid on the gay rights movement following the presidential election of Bill Clinton in 1992

The transition from the Clinton-Gore to Bush-Cheney administrations was illustrative of the influential role of conservative think tanks in the structuring of public policy agendas. Social Security privatization, the estate tax repeal, the faith-based initiative, and the post-9/11 corporate welfare "stimulus" package involving the retroactive repeal of the alternative minimum tax–these and other policy ideas did not just occur to Governor George W. Bush on the campaign trail, but were incubated over decades in conservative research institutes. These ideas were strategically placed into the nation's political discourse through coverage in sympathetic mass media outlets and articulation by elected and appointed officials. When Republicans took back the Congress in 1994 and the White House in 2000, conservative think tanks were ready with a comprehensive, well-thought-out agenda framed to appeal to the majority of Americans.

We have also witnessed a number of people from conservative think tanks take key positions within the Bush-Cheney administration. For example, Labor Secretary Elaine Chao was a distinguished fellow at the Heritage Foundation from 1996 to 2001. Vice President Dick Cheney is a former senior fellow and trustee of the American Enterprise Institute. Key Department of Health and Human Services policymaker Wade Horn was an affiliate scholar with the Hudson Institute in between stints with the first Bush administration and the current Bush administration. Robert Rector, senior fellow at the Heritage Foundation, is described by the *San Francisco Chronicle* as "one of the authors of the welfare reform act" of 1996, and was expected to play a major role in the reauthorization of welfare reform in 2002 (Wildermuth, 2001).

A recent study estimated that the nation's top 20 conservative think tanks spent $1 billion during the 1990s alone (Callahan, 1999). Many of these think tanks represent a conservative movement that started organizing in the 1950s and early 1960s, and that did not see its policy vision enacted until the election of Ronald Reagan in 1980 and the election of Newt Gingrich's Congressional Republican majority in 1994. The gay, lesbian, bisexual, and transgender (GLBT) and allied progressive communities need to be as strategic and as long range in our vision.

WHERE WE ARE POLITICALLY, AND THE LIMITS OF "VIRTUAL EQUALITY"

The 1990s were a time of incredible growth in cultural visibility for gay and lesbian Americans, and to a lesser extent, transgender and bisexual Americans. Although often these cultural representations were hostile, increasingly we are portrayed as complex, sympathetic individuals on television, in film, and in the print media.

At the dawn of the 21st century, some 103 million Americans live in cities, counties, or states that outlaw sexual orientation discrimination; in 1990, fewer than 20 million did (van der Meide, 2000). In 2001 Rhode Island became the second state to expand its nondiscrimination law to include gender identity; more than two dozen municipalities have also adopted such laws. This expansion of nondiscrimination laws results from the hard work of thousands of grassroots activists, but also from the increased support of the general public for such laws. Over the past decade, strong majorities have emerged in public opinion polls in support of the right to serve in the military, employment nondiscrimination, and equal benefits for same-sex partners. In the 2000 National Election Study, a majority of Republicans (55.6 percent) supported sexual orientation nondiscrimination laws, as did two-thirds of independents and three-quarters of Democrats (Yang, 2001). In short, equal treatment of gays and lesbians now enjoys strong majority support–and city, county, and state governments all over the country are leading the way in passing laws to mandate equal treatment. In this respect, the Republican Party leadership is out of sync not only with the views of a solid majority of American voters, but also even with a majority of rank-and-file Republican voters.

Of course, our advances evoke parallel and vigorous efforts by opponents of GLBT equality to entrench unequal treatment. We have lost dozens of ballot initiative campaigns aimed at overturning or preempting pro-gay legislation, and 35 states have banned same-sex marriage. Our most basic rights are still regularly contested in the political arena. But compared to 10 years ago, there are significant improvements in local nondiscrimination laws and public opinion.

It was also during the 1990s that gays emerged as a sizable voting block. At the national level, between four and five percent of all voters identified themselves as "gay, lesbian or bisexual" (GLB) in the last three Congressional elections, according to analysis of Voter News Service exit poll data by political scientist Robert W. Bailey. In the 1998 elections, one in three GLB voters backed Republican candidates for Congress; in 2000, one in four gay voters backed Bush (Bailey, 2000). The GLB vote is as critical a constituency as the ethnic voting blocs traditionally courted by the major political parties. In a close race, the GLB vote can swing an election.

The gains of the 1990s are testament to the power of grassroots organizing at the local and state level, where most of these advances were achieved. During the 1990s the GLBT movement witnessed the emergence and strengthening of local and statewide gay political groups. There was also a growth in organizing within GLBT communities of color, among youth and elders, immigrants, and parents, and within religious communities.

The National Gay and Lesbian Task Force (NGLTF) is the oldest national GLBT rights organization. In addition to the NGLTF Policy Institute, which was founded by John D'Emilio in 1995, several other university-based think tanks also conduct research on GLBT issues, including the Institute for Gay and Lesbian Strategic Studies at the University of Massachusetts, the Institute for the Study of Sexual Minorities in the Military at University of California-Santa Barbara, and the Center for Lesbian and Gay Studies at City University of New York. At the national level, NGLTF has worked with countless other organizations to advance equality and greater understanding of GLBT people, including the Gay and Lesbian Advocates and Defenders, Lambda Legal Defense and Education Fund, the Human Rights Campaign, and the American Civil Liberties Union Gay and Lesbian Rights Projects.

Despite the fact that we had the most pro-gay presidential administration in U.S. history in power from 1993 through 2001, the GLBT community has little concrete to show for eight years of Clinton-Gore. And now we are facing the "kinder, gentler homophobia" of President George W. Bush, who opposes every major initiative of the gay rights movement. (In fairness, Bush has not repealed Clinton's executive orders banning sexual orientation discrimination in the federal workforce and banning the denial of security clearances based upon sexual orientation. But during the 2000 presidential campaign Bush spoke out against gay adoption, same-sex marriage, hate crimes legislation, nondiscrimination laws, and sex education. In one debate with Gore, he repeatedly characterized nondiscrimination laws based on sexual orientation as "special rights," the catch-phrase of the anti-gay right.) This is the context in which GLBT activists organize for equal rights and liberation in the United States.

It is important to remember, as Urvashi Vaid notes in *Virtual Equality*, that all of the GLBT movement's accomplishments are "incomplete, conditional, and ultimately revocable" (Vaid, 1995). Amazingly, some people in our movement–most of them gay white men–have such a narrow understanding of what needs to change to achieve gay equality that they call for an "end to identity politics" and announce the dawning of a "post-gay" era in which sexual orientation does not matter (Tafel, 2001).

Vaid argues that the GLBT movement's focus on achieving tolerance and visibility, instead of more fundamental changes, has won us a "virtual equality . . . [that] simulates genuine civic equality but cannot transcend the simulation." A more real and meaningful equality can be achieved, she argues, only by linking up with other progressive movements for social change, focusing especially on the racial and economic injustice which plagues U.S. society and which anti-gay politics succeeds so well in exploiting. At the Policy Institute of the National Gay and Lesbian Task Force, which Vaid directed from 1997 to 2000, we are conducting research, policy analysis, strategy development and coalition building to meet this challenge.

How should we engage this dramatically changed political context? I have three suggestions. First, we should focus on local and state activism. This is where most of our political gains have been won over the past decade, and where we have the best chance of moving our agenda forward. This certainly does not mean abandoning federal advocacy, which is often most effective when done by constituents in the home districts of members of Congress. But we need to build our capacity at the local and state level–through grassroots organizing, training, and advocacy–to continue the advances we are making in towns and cities across the country.

Second, we must be progressive. This means supporting our allies in the civil rights organizations, the women's movement, labor, and other constituencies representing populations whose basic rights are contested in the political arena. Progressive coalitions formed to oppose Ashcroft and Norton, and are now opposing Bush's tax cut and faith-based initiative. Research and policy analysis on issues of concern to low-income GLBT people, GLBT people of color, elders, and others can provide the basis for organizing strategies that strengthen coalitions among different but overlapping constituencies with a shared interest in progressive political and social change.

Third, we must be strategic. We must develop analyses of all of the policy frameworks affecting GLBT people and assert our right to articulate a pro-gay perspective in policy debates. We must be proactive. Instead of waiting for Republican-backed fatherhood and marriage promotion initiatives to undermine and stigmatize gay and lesbian families with children, gay activists should challenge such initiatives while in their formulative stages. We should seize upon Bush's proposal to "reform" Social Security and demand that any reforms address the unequal treatment of same-sex couples, who pay into Social Security all their lives but are denied hundreds of millions of dollars a year in spousal benefits and survivor benefits. We must push for new, more effective strategies to combat the spread of HIV/AIDS, which is devastating African American and Latino communities in particular. It is appalling that as we enter the third decade of the AIDS epidemic, a U.S. administration not only limits sex education within the U.S. but threatens disease prevention efforts around the world by its insistence on "abstinence-only-until-marriage" in international forums. We must reject the assault on the separation of church and state, and the wholesale privatization and desecularization of the social services infrastructure represented by Bush's faith-based initiative. We must resist the attacks on GLBT families, and defend and proliferate the few pro-GLBT education initiatives in place across the country. In short, we must expand our understanding of what constitutes a "gay" issue.

THE PROBLEM: A LACK OF BASIC INFORMATION ON OUR COMMUNITY'S DEMOGRAPHICS AND POLICY PRIORITIES

We know next to nothing about the GLBT community. Although many researchers, both gay and straight, have made valiant efforts to increase our knowledge base, we still cannot answer with certainty some basic questions: How many gay, lesbian, bisexual, and transgender people are there? How many of us have children? How many of us are partnered, and how many are single? Does being "gay" involve same-sex attraction, same-sex sexual experiences, and/or identity? How does identity vary across demographic variables? How many of us are on welfare, or serve in the military, or live in undocumented immigrant communities? The questions are endless, and the answers few.

Part of the reason we know so little about our community is that most research surveys do not include questions about sexual orientation or gender variance. This is true of most government studies like the U.S. Census or Elder Abuse and Neglect Survey, as well as academic research studies like the University of Chicago National Opinion Research Center's study of racial attitudes. The addition of a self-identifier on the Census, allowing people to note their sexual orientation, would afford us a better understanding of the basic demographics of gay people, just as the addition of a question on the Voter News Service exit poll in 1990 has allowed us to document the existence of a sizable gay voting block, and describe the voting behavior of that block. If the Department of Health and Human Services were to add a sexual orientation question to the Elder Abuse study, we might be able to say whether there are particular experiences of abuse and neglect among GLBT elders. A similar question on the National Opinion Research Center's General Social Survey, which asks questions about people's racial attitudes, would allow us to examine the particular dynamics of racism within the GLBT community.

Although some of the pioneers of early research into the gay and lesbian community have provided critical information on family structure, partnership and singlehood, income, and other demographics from relatively small samples, much of what we know about our community is skewed toward white, young or middle-aged, male, and urban populations.

The lack of information on our community's demographics is compounded by a relatively narrow understanding of what constitutes "gay" issues, and a lack of analysis of how a broad array of policy frameworks affect GLBT people, including those not usually thought of as "gay" issues, such as welfare policy and criminal justice policy. On the one hand, it is understandable that core issues like nondiscrimination, preventing and punishing hate violence, repealing sodomy laws, and obtaining domestic partner benefits have been the main focus of the GLBT rights movement in the early decades of our community's emergence. But it is important that other policy frameworks that have an impact on our community be analyzed and engaged.

Social science research and policy analysis to identify the particular concerns of GLBT people can serve as the basis of informed, strategic, and effective grassroots organizing for social change. It is critical that we document the demographics, unmet needs, and policy priorities of all GLBT people, particularly members of our community in traditionally marginalized and underserved groups, such as low-income people, people of color, youth and elders, people with disabilities, and immigrants. Such efforts can also identify spheres of common interest with heterosexuals with whom we share common political interests for progressive policy reform. A few examples will illustrate how effective such a strategy can be.

HOW RESEARCH, POLICY ANALYSIS, AND STRATEGY DEVELOPMENT CAN ADVANCE GLBT EQUALITY AND LIBERATION

The Policy Institute of the National Gay and Lesbian Task Force is a think tank which conducts research, policy analysis, strategy development, and coalition building to advance the equality and greater understanding of gay, lesbian, bisexual, and transgender (GLBT) people. In coalition with other organizations and individual researchers, the Policy Institute is helping create the knowledge base that our movement needs to conduct informed public education, organizing, and advocacy campaigns to ensure that policy frameworks treat our community and our relationships fairly.

The Policy Institute seeks change on a number of levels: (a) *governmental*, through legislation, administrative regulations, new initiatives, and broadened access to services, (b) *education and research*, through the incorporation of GLBT issues into the standard curricula of professional training programs like health care, law, and social work and via the routine gathering of demographic information on GLBT people in all types of research, and (c) *private sector*, including changes in corporate policies (e.g., benefits, nondiscrimination policies, family leave provisions), foundation funding policies, and other practices and agendas in the nonprofit sector, such as the inclusion of GLBT aging issues into the agenda of the AARP and the American Society on Aging.

The Policy Institute has prioritized research in a number of areas, including family policy; racial and economic justice issues, including issues of concern to GLBT people of color and low-income gay people of all ethnic backgrounds; aging policy; youth and education policy; voting behavior and political representation; public opinion; and workplace benefits and discrimination. Here are a few examples which illustrate how research and policy analysis can identify critical pressing policy concerns and serve organizing goals.

Outing Age: *Public Policy Issues Affecting GLBT Elders*

Outing Age, released in November 2000 by the NGLTF Policy Institute, provides an overview of social science research on GLBT seniors, analyzes a wide range of aging policy frameworks, and makes detailed recommendations for how they must be changed to meet the needs of GLBT elders. Since the report's release, our aging policy advocacy has been covered in the *New York Times*, *Newsweek*, and hundreds of other gay and mainstream media outlets. It was distributed to 1,400 local, state, and national aging and GLBT policy advocates. *Outing Age* served as the basis for the first-ever briefing on gay aging issues at the national headquarters of AARP on March 2, 2001, which was attended by several national aging organizations. A new U.S. Administration on Aging Website devoted to "Lesbian, Gay, Bisexual, and Transgender Older Persons" is based almost verbatim on *Outing Age*. The Older Women's League and other non-gay-identified aging organizations are increasingly including GLBT elder concerns in their advocacy and analysis–a key goal of NGLTF's Aging Initiative. Based on this study, the American Society on Aging is lobbying the Joint Committee on Accreditation of Health Care Organizations to include treatment of GLBT elders in the criteria it uses to accredit nursing homes, long-term care facilities, and hospitals. A Congressional briefing on GLBT elder issues was held in January 2002. Following a briefing with NGLTF, the Democratic National Committee passed a resolution calling for equal treatment of same-sex partners under Social Security. In collaboration with both gay and straight aging activists, an organizing agenda has been developed and is currently being implemented, with a long-term strategy of working in partnership with mainstream aging organizations to change aging policy in the U.S. to treat GLBT elders equally.

According to the study's key findings and recommendations (Cahill, South, & Spade, 2000), an estimated one to three million Americans over 65 are gay, lesbian, bisexual, or transgender, based on a range of 3 percent to 8 percent of the population. By 2030, one in five Americans will be 65 or older. Roughly four million of these will be gay, lesbian, bisexual, or transgender.

GLBT elders face a number of particular concerns as they age. They often do not access adequate health care, affordable housing, and other social services that they need, due to institutionalized heterosexism. Existing regulations and proposed policy changes in programs like Social Security or Medicare, which affect millions of GLBT elders, are discussed without a GLBT perspective engaging the debate. By releasing *Outing Age*, NGLTF is changing this dynamic, and intervening in these critical policy discussions.

Several studies–of nursing home administrators, of Area Agency on Aging directors, of health care providers–document widespread homophobia among those entrusted with the care of America's seniors. Most GLBT elders do not avail themselves of services on which other seniors thrive. Many retreat back into the closet, reinforcing isolation.

Several federal programs and laws blatantly treat same-sex couples differently from married heterosexual couples. For example,

- Social Security pays survivor benefits to widows and widowers, but not to the surviving same-sex life partner of someone who dies. This may cost GLBT elders $124 million a year in unaccessed benefits.
- Married spouses are eligible for Social Security spousal benefits, which can allow them to earn half their spouse's Social Security benefit if it is larger than their own Social Security benefit. Unmarried partners in life-long relationships are not eligible for spousal benefits.
- Medicaid regulations protect the assets and homes of married spouses when the other spouse enters a nursing home or long-term care facility; no such protections are offered to same-sex partners.
- Tax laws and other regulations of 401(k)s and pensions discriminate against same-sex partners, costing the surviving partner in a same-sex re-

lationship tens of thousands of dollars a year, and possibly over $1 million during the course of a lifetime. Unequal treatment of same-sex couples under Social Security and retirement plan regulations denies us access to funds we are entitled to, from systems we all pay into all our lives, but which we cannot access due to the heterosexism of current policies. These unaccessed income sources could help ensure our economic security in old age.
- And even the most basic rights such as hospital visitation or the right to die in the same nursing home as one's partner are regularly denied same-sex partners.

Many GLBT elders experience social isolation and ageism within the GLBT community itself. As GLBT people grow older, they enter a world of services that may not be familiar with GLBT people. Some activists have created GLBT-specific service organizations for the aged, such as Senior Action in a Gay Environment (SAGE), Gay & Lesbian Outreach to Elders (GLOE), Pride Senior Network, Griot Circle, and others. These types of programs are not available in all parts of the country and cannot provide all the services needed. This is particularly true in rural areas.

A number of the problems faced by GLBT elders stem from the fact that they often do not have the same family support systems as do heterosexual people. This is compounded by the failure of the state to recognize their same-sex families. Many gay men and lesbians already have experience providing care. Despite the attempts of the right wing to construct "family" and "gay" as mutually exclusive categories, one in three gay men and lesbians provide some kind of caregiving assistance–either to children or to adults with an illness or disability (Fredriksen, 1999). Since a disproportionate number of GLBT elders live alone, innovative support networks are critical.

GLBT elders are among the most invisible of all Americans. Little is known about GLBT elders because of the widespread failure of governmental and academic researchers to include questions about sexual orientation or gender identity in studies of the aged. Legal and policy frameworks which have traditionally excluded GLBT people engender social and economic consequences that deny GLBT elders access to financial resources and community support networks.

The need to make broad assumptions about the size of the GLBT elderly population underscores one of the major problems in understanding the needs of this population. GLBT elders are not only underserved, they are also understudied. Although pioneering social scientists have been studying gay elders since the 1960s, most of these studies–while offering important insights–represent small samples which do not reflect the racial, economic, or gender diversity of GLBT elder populations (Herdt, Beeker, & Rawls, 1997). In addition to a policy agenda, a research agenda is urgently needed.

A number of *Outing Age's* concrete suggestions for public policy change and intracommunity change are challenging young and middle-aged GLBT activists, as well as heterosexual aging activists, to join with GLBT elders and play a more active role in overcoming the barriers which exist. These include:

- Government agencies charged with serving the needs of older Americans must fund and actively initiate research on GLBT seniors and should amend their mandates to encompass GLBT people.
- Amend the Older Americans Act to explicitly include services, training, and research on issues of concern to GLBT seniors; to prohibit discrimination in services on the basis of sexual orientation and gender identity; and to incorporate the inclusive definition of family in Part E of the National Family Caregiver Support Program.
- Legally recognize and support GLBT families to ensure equal access to Social Security benefits by partners and children and to minimize discrimination against GLBT seniors in nursing homes and senior housing. The Democratic National Committee took a step in this direction in January 2002 when it passed a resolution calling for equal treatment of same-sex couples under Social Security.
- Expand social services to the GLBT elder population.
- Pass nondiscrimination laws to ensure GLBT people, including seniors, are not vulnerable to discrimination because of sexual orientation or gender identity.
- Mainstream aging organizations should expand programs and missions to incorporate an awareness and response to the needs of GLBT elders.

Through a combination of policy reform, education, increased research and training, and organizing, advocates can address the pressing needs of GLBT seniors in a tangible and meaningful way.

Welfare Reform's Threat to GLBT Families and Individuals

Although few currently view welfare policy as a "gay" issue, the GLBT community has much at stake in the welfare reauthorization debate. Four elements of welfare reform–first passed in 1996 and undergoing significant expansion in 2002–pose a particular threat to GLBT people of all economic classes–not only low-income GLBT people. These are (a) *marriage promotion* and the proposed privileging of heterosexual married couples over other families in social service provision and adoption proceedings, (b) *fatherhood ini-*

tiatives, which claim that children cannot be properly raised without a father and stigmatize homosexuality and lesbian and gay families, (c) the promotion of *abstinence-only-until-marriage* "sex education," which posits heterosexual sex in the context of marriage as the only acceptable and safe form of sexual activity, and (c) the "charitable choice" *faith-based initiative*, under which religious institutions will contract to provide a broad array of social services with billions in federal and state funds over the next decade, and could discriminate in service provision and employment on the basis of sexual orientation, race and religion.

As part of its Racial and Economic Justice Initiative, NGLTF issued *Leaving Our Children Behind: Welfare Reform and the GLBT Community* in December 2001 (Cahill & Jones, 2001). This study analyzes the impact of the changes brought about by the welfare reform act of 1996, officially called the Personal Responsibility and Work Opportunity Reconciliation Act. It also examines the proposals advocated in recent years by several conservative movement leaders who are now in key policymaking positions within the administration of George W. Bush, or in think tanks like the Heritage Foundation and the Institute for American Values, which have influence over administration policy. The House Republican welfare reauthorization bill–H.R. 4090–claims that children of cohabiting parents are at higher risk of child abuse, and that children raised without fathers are more likely to experience educational, health, and psychological problems. This includes, of course, millions of children raised by same-sex couples and single gay parents. Marriage and fatherhood initiatives which make such claims implicitly question the value and functionality of gay families with children.

As we go to press, Congress is considering hundreds of millions for state experimentation with "innovative programs to promote and support healthy, married, two-parent families and reduce out-of-wedlock births." Given the reactionary proposals recently advocated by Wade Horn, Andrew Bush, Don Eberly–now in the Bush administration–and given the inappropriate and often unconstitutional marriage promotion efforts already underway in Florida, West Virginia, Louisiana, Tennessee, and New Jersey, we predict a proliferation of policies which privilege heterosexual married families with children over single-parent and cohabiting parent families.

Congressional conservatives are also seeking to renew and increase funding for abstinence-only-until-marriage education, which teaches that sex outside the context of marriage is intrinsically dangerous, both physically and psychologically. Today one in three school districts teach abstinence only, while many other school districts teach sexuality education that only covers heterosexuality. This is certainly a factor in the spike in HIV transmission among young homosexually active men, especially black and Latino gay and bisexual men.

Demonizing low-income single parents as the cause of many of our social problems—as many conservative welfare reformers have done—should deeply concern the GLBT community, who have been scapegoated as well. Much of the rhetoric we have heard in the welfare reform debate is reminiscent of the "blame-the-victim" claims made about gay men at the height of the HIV/AIDS epidemic. We must also see welfare programs in the context of a multi-trillion dollar federal budget, which contains billions in tax breaks, subsidies, and "pork" to corporations.

Some welfare reform proposals raise issues of racial justice. Because single-parent families are more prevalent within African American and Latino communities than in other ethnic communities, proposals to prioritize or limit access to benefits to married couple families—made by several Bush appointees prior to entering the administration—pose a disproportionate threat to black and Latino families. Some 39 percent of black families with children and 25 percent of Latino families with children are headed by single parents. This compares with only 11 percent of white non-Hispanic families with children, according to the 2000 Census (U.S. Census Bureau, 2000). The acknowledgment of this connection between GLBT equality and broader issues of racial justice can serve as the basis for a coalitional politics of resistance among predominantly white gay rights groups and predominantly straight people of color organizations like the NAACP and the Mexican American Legal Defense Fund.

Although NGLTF worked hard to improve the welfare reauthorization legislation, as this journal went to press it appeared that many of the worst aspects of welfare reform were headed for approval. Assuming the worst-case scenario that the Republican-backed welfare reauthorization bill is passed with hundreds of millions for marriage, fatherhood, and abstinence-only-until-marriage initiatives, and that the faith-based initiative is also passed without the nondiscrimination language we are seeking, the National Gay and Lesbian Task Force will work with a network of state and local organizations to closely monitor the implementation of these policies at the state level. Implementation of welfare reauthorization will occur in several venues. Legislatures will hold the key to authorizing funding and setting high-level goals and objectives for each of the states' programs. However, the real implementation will be with nonlegislative bodies in all 50 states. Literally hundreds of state departments and agencies on health and human services, family needs, women's issues, children's issues, and others will be writing regulations and rules. NGLTF will work with state and local organizations and activists to monitor and challenge abuses under these initiatives.

Documenting Other Issues:
Redistricting, Public Opinion, Health, and the Census

Several other projects of the NGLTF Policy Institute provide much-needed research and analysis to support organizing:

Redistricting and the GLBT Community: A Strategy Memo provides tools to state and local GLBT activists for engaging the critical process of redrawing city council, state legislative, and Congressional House district lines to push for progressive, pro-gay districts (Bailey, Magpantay, & Rosenblum, 2000). In states like Illinois and New York, which lost U.S. House seats in the 2000 redistricting, NGLTF provided technical support and information to state and local activists, so that they can work to ensure that the seats we lose are not those of pro-GLBT Congresspeople, and that the new district lines make it likely that progressive, pro-gay candidates will be elected–and, wherever possible, women and/or candidates of color. (This is in part out of a principled commitment to a more diverse and representative elected government, but also because electing more women and people of color is generally in the gay community's self-interest, as elected officials who are ethnic minority and/or women have consistently supported GLBT equality at higher rates than have white men.) In Florida and other states gaining seats, we are working with activists to ensure that the new votes in Congress from those states are pro-gay votes.

The 2000 National Election Study and Gay and Lesbian Rights: Support for Equality Grows uses data from the 2000 National Election to document steadily increasing support for sexual orientation nondiscrimination laws, the right to serve in the military, and the right to adopt children (Yang, 2001). Yang's study bears mostly good news for the GLBT community: Over the past decade or so, support for equal rights for gay men and lesbians has increased substantially among people of all political ideologies. For the first time in 2000, a solid majority of Republicans (55.6 percent) support sexual orientation nondiscrimination laws, as do overwhelming majorities of the public at large. Yang's analysis establishes that elected officials like George W. Bush and the Republican Congressional leadership, who oppose sexual orientation nondiscrimination laws, are out of touch not only with a majority of the U.S. public, but also with a majority of rank-and-file Republicans. In fact, a broad consensus in support of nondiscrimination laws has emerged across the political spectrum. These most recent data will provide useful ammunition in our fight for equal rights.

Yang also reports good news regarding military service and adoption rights. More than 70 percent of Americans, including 66 percent of Republicans, support our right to serve. The public still narrowly opposes the right of same-sex couples to adopt children, but sentiment on the issue is rapidly shifting. Of those surveyed, 41.4 percent support the right of gay men and lesbians to adopt, 50.5 percent are opposed, and 8.2 percent are undecided. Activists can use the good news about improvements in public opinion toward lesbians and gay men to push policymakers and corporate managers to adopt laws and policies that treat GLBT people equally. Yang has also documented that solid majorities support equal inheritance rights and Social Security benefits for same-sex partners (in 1997 Princeton Survey Research Associates found 62 percent support for the former and 57 percent support for the latter) (Yang, 1999). This will help convince lawmakers to adopt the changes we seek in pension and 401(k) regulations and Social Security policies.

Social Discrimination and Health: The Case of Latino Gay Men and HIV Risk documents the correlation among homophobia, racism, poverty, and HIV risk, and has significant implications for prevention strategies which have not worked as well as they should in communities of color (Diaz & Ayala, 2001). This analysis of the *Nuestras Voces* study, which interviewed 900 Latino gay men in Los Angeles, Miami, and New York, was authored by the study's principle investigators, Rafael Diaz of San Francisco State University and George Ayala of UCLA. NGLTF translated this report into Spanish and for the first time released a substantive report in a language other than English.

Social Discrimination and Health documents a strong correlation between high-risk sexual behaviors and experiences of social discrimination. People engaging in high-risk sexual behaviors, such as anal sex without a condom, were more likely than those who reported low-risk sexual practices to have experienced homophobia, racism, and insufficient economic resources, both in childhood and adulthood. However, the presence of an openly gay adult role model during childhood and the acceptance of one's homosexuality by one's family correlated with lower incidence of high-risk behaviors. These resiliency factors have significant policy implications, not only for HIV transmission, but also for the Boy Scouts controversy and for safe schools initiatives to combat homophobia. Diaz and Ayala also critically examine the shortcomings of currently dominant HIV-prevention strategies, which focus on reforming individual behavior and do not take account of the social context that can structure self-esteem and limit individual agency.

Make Your Family Count!, a public education campaign encouraging same-sex households to identify as unmarried same-sex partners on the 2000 U.S. Census, was conducted by the Policy Institute in collaboration with the Institute for Gay and Lesbian Strategic Studies. This is an example of organizing supporting research. The Policy Institute has also worked with Dr. Judith Bradford, Dr. Kirsten Barrett, Dr. Julie Honnold, and survey methodologist Jim Ellis of Virginia Commonwealth University's Survey Evaluation and Research Lab (SERL) to analyze the 1990 Census data on same-sex households.

In particular, we have looked at income, race, family structure, veteran status, and other demographic factors. A report was released at the Lesbian Health Conference in San Francisco in June 2001. *Census 2000's Same-Sex Household Data: A Users' Manual*, aimed at activists and policymakers, was published by the NGLTF Policy Institute in summer 2002 (Barrett & Bradford, 2002). A comparison of the 1990 Census data with the 2000 Census data will be conducted following the release of the actual household data by the Census in late 2002 and 2003.

Initial results from the 2000 Census showed a fourfold increase in same-sex coupled households, from 150,000 in 1990 to 600,000 in 2000. The largest increases were in rural, sparsely populated communities and more conservative states. The smallest increases were in more densely populated communities and urban states. The 1990 Census reported same-sex cohabiting couples in just over half of U.S. counties. In the 2000 Census, same-sex cohabiting couples occupied 99.3 percent of U.S. counties; only 22 counties out of 3,219 did not report same-sex couples.

Although the Census has its limitations, as it does not begin to capture the full racial, economic, and age diversity of the GLBT community, it is one of very few national data sets that gather information on GLBT people. There is great potential for use of these data in public education campaigns and coalition building. For example, according to the 1990 Census, lesbians of color and older lesbians are more likely to have given birth. Twenty-three percent of white lesbians compared to 60 percent of black lesbians have given birth. One in five lesbian households had children under 18 years of age. Thirty-one percent of lesbians and bisexuals in same-gender relationships and 19 percent of gay or bisexual men in same-gender relationships were once married to a person of the opposite sex.

These findings are pertinent to family policies such as "covenant marriages," which could trap GLBT people in heterosexual marriages. Covenant marriage is essentially a stricter version of marriage that is harder, legally, to enter into and to leave. GLBT people who discover or come to terms with their sexual orientation or gender identity/expression after they marry could find it difficult to divorce their spouse without their spouse's consent, thereby hindering their ability to live open and honest lives. The proposed marriage and divorce laws would also affect millions of heterosexuals, effectively trapping them and their children in unhappy marriages. The differences in parenting patterns between black lesbians and white lesbians, coupled with the fact that black children are overrepresented in the nation's foster care system, indicate that anti-gay parenting bills may have a disproportionate impact upon lesbians of color, making these proposals a matter of racial justice as well as a GLBT issue and a basic human rights issue. The fact that anti-gay adoption bills may disproportionately threaten black children and black lesbians could serve as the basis for coalition politics between predominantly white GLBT activists and predominantly straight civil rights activists to defeat such bills.

CONCLUSION

Ideas matter. They have the power to change how we understand ourselves and the world around us. Ideas take on even more power when they are connected to action. The Policy Institute of the National Gay and Lesbian Task Force serves as a national clearinghouse for information and research on GLBT people's lives, and the impact of a broad array of policy issues affecting them. With publications like *Income Inflation: The Myth of Affluence Among Gay, Lesbian and Bisexual Americans* (Badgett, 1998), copublished with the Institute for Gay and Lesbian Strategic Studies, we respond to the cultural myths and misinformation of the right with accurate data and facts. Our research, policy analysis, and strategy development brings new perspectives to the issues affecting our diverse communities; produces information that grassroots activists, policymakers and the media can use to advance GLBT equality; and strengthens coalitions with other progressive constituencies.

A generation ago, conservatives consciously and deliberately chose to invest in their future. They made the molding of ideas, public opinion, and public policy their priority, and they generously funded a large number of research institutes whose influence has grown steadily, and many of whose scholars are now ensconced in the second Bush Administration. Through its long-term commitment to the Policy Institute, NGLTF borrows unashamedly from the successful strategy of those who most often attack our communities. We need smart and strategic thinking to guide the GLBT movement through a challenging, but also potentially promising, future.

REFERENCES

Badgett, M. V. L. (1998). *Income inflation: The myth of affluence among gay, lesbian and bisexual Americans.* New York: Policy Institute of the National Gay and Lesbian Task Force and Institute for Gay and Lesbian Strategic Studies.

Bailey, R. W. (2000). *Out and voting II: The gay, lesbian and bisexual vote in Congressional elections, 1990-1998.* New York: Policy Institute of the National Gay and Lesbian Task Force.

Bailey, R. W., Magpantay, G., & Rosenblum, D. (2000). *Redistricting and the gay, lesbian, bisexual and transgender community: A strategy memo.* New York: Policy Institute of the National Gay and Lesbian Task Force.

Barrett, K., & Bradford, J. (2002). *Census 2000 and same-sex household data: A user's manual.* New York: Policy Institute of the National Gay and Lesbian Task Force.

Cahill, S., & Jones, K. T. (2001). *Leaving our children behind: Welfare reform and the gay, lesbian, bisexual and transgender community.* New York: Policy Institute of the National Gay and Lesbian Task Force.

Cahill, S., South, K., & Spade, J. (2000). *Outing age: Public policy issues affecting gay, lesbian, bisexual and transgender elders.* New York: Policy Institute of the National Gay and Lesbian Task Force.

Callahan, D. (1999). *$1 billion for ideas: Conservative think tanks in the 1990s.* Washington, DC: National Committee for Responsive Philanthropy. Cited in Callahan, D. (1999, April 26). $1 billion for conservative ideas: Gifts to right-wing think tanks have become a form of political donation. *The Nation,* pp. 21-23.

Diaz, R., & Ayala, G. (2001). *Social discrimination and health: The case of Latino gay men and HIV risk.* New York: Policy Institute of the National Gay and Lesbian Task Force.

Fredriksen, K. I. (1999). Family caregiving responsibilities among lesbians and gay men. *Social Work, 44,* 142-155.

Herdt, G., Beeker, J., & Rawls, T. (1997). Life course diversity among older lesbians and gay men: A study in Chicago. *Journal of Gay, Lesbian, and Bisexual Identity, 2*(3/4), 231-246.

Tafel, R. (2001, November 29). United we stand: Gay politics after 9/11. Liberty Education Forum. Retrieved August 18, 2002, from </www.libertyeducationforum.org/cgi-data/opinion/files/4.shtml>.

U.S. Census Bureau. (2000). Table FG6. One-parent family groups with own children under 18, by marital status, and race and Hispanic origin/1 of the reference person: March 2000. Retrieved October 20, 2002, from <www.census.gov/population/socdemo/hh-fam/p20-537/2000/tabFG6.pdf>.

Vaid, U. (1995). *Virtual equality: The mainstreaming of gay and lesbian liberation.* New York: Anchor Books.

van der Meide, W. (2000). *Legislating equality: A review of laws affecting gay, lesbian, bisexual and transgendered people in the United States.* New York: Policy Institute of the National Gay and Lesbian Task Force.

Wildermuth, J. (2001, November 4). Welfare reform heading back to Congress next year. *San Francisco Chronicle,* pp. A11.

Wockner, R. (2001, November 28). Post-Gay. November 28, 2001. <www.planetout.com/pno/news/feature.html?sernum=334>.

Yang, A. (1999). *From wrongs to rights, 1973-1999: Public opinion on gay and lesbian Americans moves toward equality.* New York: Policy Institute of the National Gay and Lesbian Task Force.

Yang, A. (2001). *The National Election Study and gay and lesbian rights: Support for equality grows.* New York: Policy Institute of the National Gay and Lesbian Task Force.

Assessing Health and Social Service Needs in the GLB Population: The Norwegian Experience

Berge-Andreas Steinsvåg
Bjørg Sandkjær
Ingvill Størksen

SUMMARY. Norway has been a leading nation when it comes to lesbian, gay, and bisexual (LGB) rights. With the majority of LGB people enjoying a high quality of life, Norway has turned its attention to a minority of the LGB population experiencing a clustering of chronic and other life

---

Berge-Andreas Steinsvåg, MA, is Manager of Kontekst Kommunikasjon and a licensed social worker.
Bjørg Sandkjær, MA, is a project manager in Kontekst Kommunikasjon and a demographer.
Ingvill Størksen, BA, is a project manager in Kontekst Kommunikasjon.
Address correspondence to: Berge-Andreas Steinsvåg, Kontekst Kommunikasjon, Motzfeldtsgt. 1, 0187 Oslo, Norway (E-mail: berge@kontekst.no).
This research review was produced by Kontekst Kommunikasjon (Context Communication), Oslo, Norway. Kontekst Kommunikasjon has for the last 5 years worked with the health and social service sector and NGO's in Norway. The consultancy has carried out several needs assessments for minority populations, and stresses an international perspective in its work. GLBT and HIV issues are among the main topics of their research. They are currently working on an evaluation of the City of Oslo's public health center for GLB youth.

[Haworth co-indexing entry note]: "Assessing Health and Social Service Needs in the GLB Population: The Norwegian Experience." Steinsvåg, Berge-Andreas, Bjørg Sandkjær, and Ingvill Størksen. Co-published simultaneously in *Journal of Gay & Lesbian Social Services* (Harrington Park Press, an imprint of The Haworth Press, Inc.) Vol. 16, No. 3/4, 2004, pp. 147-164; and: *Gay and Lesbian Rights Organizing: Community-Based Strategies* (ed: Yolanda C. Padilla) Harrington Park Press, an imprint of The Haworth Press, Inc., 2004, pp. 147-164. Single or multiple copies of this article are available for a fee from The Haworth Document Delivery Service [1-800-HAWORTH, 9:00 a.m. - 5:00 p.m. (EST). E-mail address: docdelivery@haworthpress.com].

Journal of Gay & Lesbian Social Services, Vol. 16(3/4) 2004
http://www.haworthpress.com/store/product.asp?sku=J041
© 2004 by The Haworth Press, Inc. All rights reserved.
10.1300/J041v16n03_10

cycle-related problems. A number of needs assessments have been initiated in order to determine how to meet these challenges. The needs assessments underscore the importance of social networks for health and well-being. An important action is, therefore, to provide arenas for network building. Partnerships between public, private, and voluntary sectors would facilitate these arenas. Existing health, social, and labor market public services need to be sensitized to LGB issues and particular challenges. *[Article copies available for a fee from The Haworth Document Delivery Service: 1-800-HAWORTH. E-mail address: <docdelivery@haworthpress.com> Website: <http://www.HaworthPress.com> © 2004 by The Haworth Press, Inc. All rights reserved.]*

KEYWORDS. Homosexual, gay, lesbian, bisexual, Norway, welfare state

Norway, with a population of 4.5 million and one of the world's highest per capita income levels, a welfare state, and a state church, has been a leading nation when it comes to lesbian, gay, and bisexual rights. A same-sex marriage law came into force in 1993. A comprehensive national study of living conditions and life quality among gay, lesbian, and bisexual persons revealed that the majority of this group in Norway live good, or even better lives than the population at large (Hegna, Moseng, & Kristiansen, 1999). However, a substantial minority struggles with coming out and *coming in*–creating a network of LGB friends and integrating old and new networks–substance abuse, and suicide-related problems. This article provides an overview of the status of lesbian, gay, and bisexual issues in Norway at the start of the new millennium. It discusses results from needs assessments and studies, and investigates how the community and the public sector could organize to chart and meet the needs in the lesbian, gay, and bisexual population in the country. The approach taken toward these issues is therefore needs based, and the suggested ways to meet these needs are largely community based.

This article focuses on the status of the self-identified lesbian, gay, and bisexual (LGB) population in Norway. The country also has a population of 200 to 400 self-identified transpersons. Although some of the findings of the studies referred to here may also be relevant to this group, the studies have not included transpersons.

LEGAL FRAMEWORK: FROM CRIMINAL OFFENCE TO PARTNERSHIP

Until 1972 sex between men was a criminal offence in Norway, while sexual relations between women has never been illegal. The formation of the LGB organization in Denmark in 1948 sparked the formation of a Norwegian chapter of the organization in 1950. There were LGB meeting places in Oslo, Bergen, and other cities, but these were extremely secretive. The LGB community was very much a hidden community. In 1972, the law criminalizing sex between men was finally abolished, and in 1977 sexual orientation was included in nondiscriminatory legislation. The Act on Registered Partnership for Homosexual Couples was adopted in 1993, establishing the right to marriage, but without the right to adopt children, and with restrictions on the right for foreigners to register (Ministry of Children and Family Affairs, 1993; Størksen, 2000). In 2000, conducting reparative therapy with LGB persons was deemed unethical by the Norwegian Psychiatrist Association (Selle, 2001). Since 2000, same-sex couples may be foster parents, and since 2002 lesbian and gay persons may adopt their partner's children. In 2001, the government published its long-awaited white paper on homosexuality (Ministry of Children and Family Affairs, 2001), detailing further action to be taken on various levels. The state budget for 2002 also provides increased funding and increased attention to LGB issues.

THE NORWEGIAN LGB COMMUNITIES

The Norwegian population is spread out over a vast geographical area, although the main concentration of population is in and around the capital city Oslo, located in the southeast. This has implications for the LGB community. There seems to be a movement toward Oslo and the LGB "scene" there among young LGB persons (Hegna, Moseng, & Kristiansen, 1999), and possibly a movement back to smaller towns and rural areas with a partner at a later stage. LGB communities outside Oslo are largely perceived as small and transparent. A failed attempt at building networks in one of these communities may have dire consequences, as there are, or at least don't seem to be, alternative LGB networks or arenas in the local community. In smaller places, there may be no LGB community at all.

There are several organizations for LGB persons. The largest is the Lesbian and Gay Association (Landsforeningen for lesbisk og homofil frigjøring–LLH), with a main office in Oslo, and local groups across the country. The association works politically, and organizes social, sports, music, and other activities. The bulk of the work is volunteer-based. There are also other LGB organizations, including fetish associations.

THE SET-UP OF THE WELFARE STATE

Norway features an active and extensive public sector, a sector that since the 1970s has claimed around 50 percent of the country's gross domestic product. The main driving force behind the development of extensive public activities has been the political authorities' ambition of developing a strong and universal welfare state. At the outset, this was based on a social democratic foundation, but for most of the time since the late 1940s, the welfare state has won the support of all major Norwegian political parties (Hansen, 1999). Everyone has the right to receive health care and welfare services when in need, meaning that a basic standard of living and economic security is guaranteed regardless of employment history or private insurance schemes.

Most welfare schemes are administered at the municipality and county level, particularly the direct delivery of welfare services such as health services, care of the elderly, daycare centers and primary education. Municipalities and counties account for two-thirds of all public services. The municipal sector has been accorded main responsibility for the production of welfare state services, while the central government administers the transfer of money through the public pension and social security system.

The main goal of the welfare state is to promote national equality in the delivery of welfare benefits. Service provision is mainly carried out at the local level as this facilitates availability of the services to users. Geographical distances in a sparsely populated country require one or another form of diffusion and local administration of services if the population is to be ensured equal rights and equal access to benefits (Hansen, 1999).

LIVING CONDITIONS OF LGB PERSONS IN NORWAY

"Living Conditions and Life Quality Among Lesbian Women and Gay Men," a report of a comprehensive national survey of living conditions among LGB persons in Norway, was published in 1999 (Hegna, Moseng, & Kristiansen, 1999). The survey collected data through questionnaires (N = 2987) and life history interviews (N = 23). The questionnaire was distributed through a range of channels. The main channels were the monthly LGB newspaper *Blikk*, which sent the questionnaire to its subscribers, and the Lesbian and Gay Association, whose members also received the questionnaire. In addition, the questionnaire was spread in other networks, including private networks, trying particularly to reach women, youth, older people, and people living in rural areas, as these are more difficult to recruit. To reach people who did not make use of LGB media, were not part of organized networks or were not open about their sexuality, the project was promoted through the mass media. People were encouraged to contact the research institution for questionnaires, or to download the questionnaire from the Internet. Other LGB-oriented Websites, as well as the large mainstream search engines, linked to the questionnaire electronically.

Thirty-eight percent of the survey respondents are women, and two-thirds of the sample are aged between 25 and 44. Around half of the sample live in the Oslo area, one-quarter live in other large Norwegian cities, and the last quarter live in smaller towns and rural areas. Forty-nine percent of the men and 41 percent of the women do not participate regularly in organized activities or societies for LGB persons. The vast majority of respondents are at least partially open about their sexuality.

The distribution of respondents is somewhat skewed compared to the population at large. Data about the population at large originate from a 1995 national survey on life quality and living conditions (Levekårsundersøkelsen, 1995, cited in Hegna, Moseng, & Kristiansen, 1999). Many of the questions in the LGB survey questionnaire were kept identical to questions in the 1995 survey, enabling comparison. Men, the 25-44 age group, and the Oslo area are overrepresented. Also, both the educational and income levels of the sample are higher than in the population at large, and respondents in the LGB survey are more socially and culturally active than the population at large. However, the researchers behind the report conclude that "There is a good breadth of respondents, and all important groups of lesbians/gays are represented" (Hegna, Moseng, & Kristiansen, 1999, p. 316). The survey results are therefore considered representative and valid enough to merit further analysis.

The study showed that living conditions and life quality of Norwegian LGB persons are as good, or even better, than for the population at large. This is important, as the remainder of this article focuses on the proportion of the LGB population that seems to experience problems. This proportion seems to experience a clustering of problems, such as mental health problems, elevated levels of alcohol and other drug use, and loneliness. Some of these may be classified as chronic, some as life phase related. We will now examine these problems in more detail.

Compared to the population at large, LGB persons judge their overall health to be less good. As data for heterosexual persons only does not exist, comparisons are made with data from surveys of the population at large, which probably also include LGB persons. This bias has not been corrected for, as the data are considered adequate for the aim of this article: to investigate more general trends and needs among LGB persons. Seventy-one percent of lesbian women and 75 percent of gay men surveyed judge their health to be good or very good, while the corresponding figures for the population at large are 87 percent and 88 percent, respectively. While gay men are no more at risk for violence than men in the population at large (5 percent among both groups experienced violence in the year before completing the questionnaire), lesbian women, especially young women, have up to twice the risk (4 percent vs. 2 percent) of experiencing violence in a given year. Both men and women surveyed experience more threats of violence than the population at large, and the majority of respondents indicate that at least one incidence of either violence or threat in the previous year was related to their sexuality.

The survey measured mental health through a battery of questions taken from the Hopkins' symptom checklist (Derogatis et al., 1974, cited in Hegna, Moseng, & Kristiansen, 1999). The answers reveal a higher risk of psychological afflictions among LGB persons, particularly nervousness, tension, melancholia, and depression. Young LGB persons and LGB persons who hide their sexual orientation have an even higher risk of experiencing these psychological afflictions. Factors associated with fewer psychological afflictions are integrating heterosexual and LGB friendship networks, and being in a stable relationship with a same-sex partner. Bisexual persons have higher risks of experiencing these afflictions than those who identify as homosexual.

Suicide-related problems are much more prevalent in the LGB population than in the population at large. Six to seven times more respondents in the LGB survey (3.4 percent) report that they have been quite or very bothered by thoughts of suicide during the previous 14 days; the number for the population at large is 0.4 percent. Twenty-five percent of the respondents under age 25 report that they have attempted suicide at least once. The four main reasons given for attempting suicide are a feeling of isolation and loneliness, a wish to escape from an intolerable situation, a feeling of powerlessness regarding the future, and difficulties accepting oneself as LGB.

Levels of alcohol and other drug use are much higher in the LGB sample surveyed than in the population at large. An indicator of problematic alcohol use is frequency of intoxication. Twenty-three percent of the men surveyed get intoxicated from alcohol at least four times a month, while the figure for men in the population at large is 10 percent. Corresponding figures for women are 12 percent for the lesbian or bisexual women compared to 3 percent of women in the population at large. Further analysis of the LGB survey data reveals that those who report frequent intoxication have higher levels of psychological afflictions such as nervousness, being worried, depression, and being tense. LGB persons also use more of every drug than the population at large. Particularly, young lesbian and bisexual women use cannabis substantially more often than both the population at large and gay men, and gay and bisexual men use more "party drugs" such as amphetamines and ecstasy.

A social network is important for coping and for mental health. A supportive network will both help prevent a crisis, and, if crisis occurs, provide support (Fyrand 1995). Ninety-six percent of the female and 93 percent of the male respondents in the LGB survey state that they have close friends, and 89 percent of the female and 93 percent of the male respondents also state that they have a quite or very good relationship with their biological family. In general, it is the people who have a good relationship with their biological family who also have a large and supportive network of friends. This indicates that the LGB "family of friends" may not be as important as a substitute for the biological family as has previously been indicated (Andersen, 1987). Lack of network and good relationships with family and friends is more common among the very young and those above age 50.

Chronic and Life Phase-Related Problems

Life history-oriented questions, both in questionnaires and interviews, provide indications of lasting problems and the factors and characteristics these may be related to. First, it seems that the people experiencing persistent problems lack a supportive network, and this is related to problematic alcohol or other drug use and psychological afflictions. Second, ability to cope with the persisting stressors resulting from being an at least partially stigmatized minority seems also to be related to a heaping of other problems. Such stressors include constantly having to decide when or if to reveal sexuality to new people, and fear of negative reactions if the sexuality becomes known (Benum, Friis, & Offerdal, 1997).

Other problems seem to be more life phase-related. These are largely centered on coming out to oneself, family, friends, and coworkers, and coming in by creating a network of LGB friends and integrating old and new networks. This article takes as a starting point the stage model for coming out, as laid out in Coleman (1981/1982). The model sets coming out as a process where the individual passes through progressive stages toward self-awareness and openness about a gay, lesbian, or bisexual identity. The stage models have been criticized for being too linear and rigid. We are aware of this criticism, but for the purposes of this analysis, we have found the stage model a useful conceptual tool, and use it with the awareness that it may not accurately describe the experiences of all LGB persons. Coming out/coming in is a life stage where LGB persons are particularly vulnerable to alcohol and other drug abuse, and mental health as well as suicide-related problems.

MEETING THE NEEDS OF THE LGB COMMUNITY

In order to deal with these problems and meet the identified challenges, an evidence-based approach is crucial. Evidence of what the problem is forms a basis for action, but in order to have an effect it is also necessary to work out what the needs of the target population are and how to best meet these needs. All too often, actors in both the voluntary and the public sector determine a problem and move directly to some sort of action without a proper analysis of what kind of action would have an effect through meeting identified needs.

To identify needs in the LGB population, and also to investigate the meaning behind the patterns identified in the large national study, comprehensive needs assessments have been, and will be, carried out. The needs assessment methodology has proved useful both in charting needs and in developing practical ways to meet those needs (Soriano, 1995; Witkin & Altschuld, 1995). In carrying out the needs assessments, emphasis has been placed on building on existing knowledge, national and international, and partnership and contact with other researchers and practitioners in relevant fields. In order to translate international findings or projects to the Norwegian context, or investigate the meanings and underlying patterns of existing quantitative data, qualitative data are collected through a variety of ways, such as community forums, focus groups interviews, online surveys, and in-depth interviews. Analyses of these data show needs in the community and among individuals. Practical ways to meet these needs are suggested, and have been presented to the community.

Strategies for Alcohol and Other Drug Use Prevention in the LGB Community

In 2000, the Lesbian and Gay Association commissioned a government-funded needs assessment in order to develop strategies for primary prevention of problematic use of alcohol and other drugs in the LGB communities (Kontekst Kommunikasjon, 2001a).

The formulation of the needs assessment was based on an extensive literature review of Norwegian, Swedish, Danish, U.S., Canadian, Australian, Dutch, and British research on alcohol and other drug use and prevention in LGB communities, as well as in the general population.

In order to better understand the underlying patterns of the high levels of use found in the large survey, four focus group interviews with a total of 40 participants, and five in-depth interviews were carried out in Norway. Interviewees were recruited to reflect the diversity in the LGB communities in Norway, ensuring variation in:

- geography (interviews were conducted all over the country);
- age (the youngest participant was 17, the oldest around 60);
- gender;
- time since coming out;
- members (but not board members) of organized LGB communities such as the Lesbian and Gay Association, LGB church groups, sports clubs,

and so on, and those who do not take part in such organized LGB activities; and
- lifestyle, including people in and out of stable relationships, with and without children, use of alcohol and other drugs.

Questions focused on the "good life." What is it? What is important in people's lives? How do people socialize? What role, if any, does alcohol and other drug use play? How important are LGB communities for a good social life? Why, or why not? When does alcohol and other drug use become a problem? What do you do if a friend's alcohol and other drug use is problematic?

Interviews were written up and analyzed, and then compared with the results of the literature review. Based on this information, it was possible to determine a range of prevention needs, and a list of suggested actions to meet the identified needs was developed. It is beyond the scope of this article to detail the needs and the suggested actions; however, the main trends are described below.

Explanation for Elevated Levels of Alcohol and Other Drug Use

While the survey determined that the alcohol and other drug consumption, at least among those surveyed, is high, the qualitative study investigated why. The explanation found may be divided into three partially overlapping parts:

1. LGB individuals experience greater stress, both chronic minority stress and life phase-related stress around coming out. Loneliness is also an issue, contributing to stress and also meaning a lack of a network to help manage stress, particularly among older men and women. For these, alcohol and other drugs may be used as self-medication.
2. While the consumption of alcohol and other drugs in the population at large drops with relationship formation and drops even further with children, the consumption in the LGB community stays high for longer. Patterns in the LGB community seem to be that alcohol and other drug consumption moves from the public (bar) to the private (dinner) sphere with formation of stable relationships, but does not decline, and fewer LGB persons have responsibility for children.
3. In pockets of the LGB community there seems to be an alcohol and other drug-using culture, where alcohol and other drug use, including "party drugs," is part of identity formation and a way of socializing.

In other countries and contexts, the role of the gay or lesbian bar as an important arena for socializing has been stressed (Heffernan, 1998; Parks, 1999; Weinberg, 1994). The bar is also important in Norway. However, only three cities in Norway have gay or lesbian bars and clubs, and in total, there are only 8 to 10 LGB bars or clubs in the country as a whole. The project found that while these bars are important as reference points, particularly during the early stages of joining an LGB community, bars are not the main places where socializing takes place. Throughout the country, LGB individuals use "straight" bars, gay or straight private networks and parties, and parties and events organized by the LGB associations as arenas for socializing. People meet through friends, or Internet chat, or at organized events.

In the early stages of LGB identity formation, particularly in what we have called the coming in phase, the project found that many suffer from misconceptions and stereotypical images of what it means to have an LGB lifestyle. For both women and men, this includes elevated levels of alcohol use. For women, it also includes smoking, while for men, it may include illegal drugs such as ecstasy or "poppers." For men, the stereotype also includes casual sex. These stereotypes seem to lead people who are new to the LGB community to higher levels of alcohol or other drug use as a way to fit in and build an LGB identity. Many of the people interviewed mentioned how becoming part of the LGB community felt like a second puberty, both in terms of a sexual awakening and in terms of insecurity and the search for identity and belonging. Several also told stories of how they consumed more alcohol or other drugs because they thought they had to as part of an LGB lifestyle. In forming these misconceptions, the bar culture plays an important part. Bars and the stereotypical image of LGB culture as a party and drug culture therefore have a larger affect on identity formation than their actual number in Norway suggests.

Strategies for Action

Of the three explanations for elevated alcohol or other drug use outlined above, the first–alcohol or other drug use as stress relief and self-medication–has been singled out for targeted action. The second, social alcohol or other drug use, is not seen as leading to as much problematic alcohol or other drug use and is therefore not a main focus for action. The third, the use and glamorizing of use of alcohol or other drugs in certain high-profile groups within LGB communities, is important for two reasons. Firstly, this use represents a risk to the people belonging to these groups. Secondly, as these groups often function as role models to other members of LGB communities, other people may try to live up to what is perceived as a norm: that use of drugs and alcohol is part of a desirable and glamorous gay life style. However, the data gathered in this more general project are not specific enough to enable working out detailed strategies for alcohol or other drug use prevention in these groups.

The main actions suggested are aimed at relieving the need for self-medication by working on the stressors that cause this need. These consist of factors in society that create homonegativity. Other stressors relate to LGB identity formation and misconceptions about having to fit in to certain stereotypes to be "properly" LGB. A supportive network protects against the harmful effect of these stressors, and therefore facilitating supportive networks is a major focus in the suggested actions.

Actions suggested include organizing a series of sustained arenas for network building. These need to be organized in rural areas as well as urban areas. The arenas may be parties, various kinds of sports groups or other interest-based groups, or other arenas. The focus of these arenas should be meeting others and forming networks, rather than alcohol or other drug use. Some of these arenas already exist. However, findings are that for such arenas to really function as network building arenas, volunteers need to be designated and trained to make contact with and include new people, so that arenas become inclusive rather than exclusive. It is particularly important to target people in the coming in phase, where an LGB identity is formed. The individual seems, in this phase, to be particularly vulnerable to elevated levels of alcohol or other drug use. This is a result of alcohol or other drug use seemingly forming an intrinsic part of gay culture and identity formation. Showing that this part of the LGB culture is only one lifestyle option among many will help prevent problematic alcohol or other drug use.

Treatment of Alcohol or Other Drug Abuse

Treatment of problematic use of alcohol or other drug use among LGB persons is an almost unaddressed issue in Norway. There are Alcoholics Anonymous groups which welcome LGB persons, and there are some therapists and other health care personnel who are knowledgeable about LGB issues. However, there is no systematic knowledge of what the specific needs of LGB persons in treatment are, and hence also no knowledge of how to meet these needs. A planned needs assessment will build on international knowledge, and also work with the target group in Norway in order to contextualize and fit programs and knowledge to Norwegian needs. There does not seem to be a need for separate services for LGB persons. There is, however, a need to work with existing services to make sure that these have a basic knowledge of LGB issues such as coming out and challenges relating to this process, as well as coming in and network building.

Facilitating the Coming Out and Coming In Process

Investigating further the needs of people coming out and coming in, the needs assessment "Out of the closet, into the network" was carried out (Kontekst Kommunikasjon, 2001b). The Oslo branch of the Lesbian and Gay Association commissioned the study, funded by the Norwegian Foundation for Health and Rehabilitation.

A review of literature from Norway and Sweden, Great Britain, the U.S., Canada, Australia, and the Netherlands formed a starting point for the data collection for this needs assessment. As this project focused on the Norwegian capital, Oslo, interviews were carried out in the Oslo area only. The target group for the project is persons aged between 18 and 30 who are coming out and/or coming in at the time of the interview, and who do not have any other significant challenges in their lives.

Seven people who had used organized services for coming out or coming in within the six months before the interview were recruited from these services and interviewed in a focus group. Four people who were in their coming out process, but who did not make contact with organized services, were interviewed individually. Recruiting these was a challenge, as several relevant people were identified and contacted, but declined to be interviewed because they felt that the phase was so confusing or difficult to deal with that an interview felt impossible. Of the four that were recruited, three were recruited through private networks, both gay and straight, and one was recruited through an Internet chatroom. These interviews were semi-structured interviews, including life history elements. In addition, twenty volunteers in three different organized coming-out services were interviewed using the community forum format, which is a structured group interview. Information gathered from 218 Internet-based questionnaires helped form a backdrop to the interview data.

Coming Out Is Not Enough

Just coming out to oneself and others does not capture the whole important process to integration in a social network. We, therefore, separate coming out and coming in, seeing coming in as the process where the individual builds networks in the LGB community or with LGB individuals, and possibly integrates old and new networks. This is a particularly important phase for well-being, as the expectations of care and support from the LGB community after coming out are often very high, while network building may be as difficult in this community as in any other. Work, therefore, needs to focus not just on coming out, but also on facilitating coming in. These two processes are linked, and often overlap. An attractive and welcoming community to come in to may, for example, facilitate and make it easier to come out.

The results of the project again underscore the importance of social arenas for meeting others. A surprising finding was that while many people still use organized activities and hotlines for the first talk with another LGB person, a seemingly increasing number already have an open LGB person in their network. This may be a friend, a colleague, a fellow pupil, a friend's older brother, a friend of a friend, or someone who in some way is part of an extended network. This is particularly true for young people in cities. Most people do not contact public services in this phase, but use private networks or arenas and activities organized by voluntary organizations such as the Lesbian and Gay Association.

Another fairly new development is the importance of the Internet and of Internet chat for contact with other LGB persons. Particularly to LGB persons in rural areas, where there is no established LGB community, the Internet and chatrooms represent a community in itself. This is particularly true for the men surveyed. Internet and chat is also important as a rehearsal space for coming out and coming in, a space for anonymous testing of borders, gathering of information, and testing out of one's own role and place in this community (see Hillier et al., 1998, for more about this issue in Australia).

The Role of the Local Community

Focus has so far been on coming in and building networks in the LGB community. However, LGB persons also belong to geographically defined local communities. Our interviewees describe how the anonymity in Oslo has facilitated coming out. One even went abroad for her first contact with an LGB community. However, interviewees also wish to integrate their LGB identity and lifestyle with their previous network and community. The local community, whether in the city or the country, therefore becomes an important arena for facilitation of coming out and coming in, this time coming in as an LGB person in an accepting local community. Local communities such as villages or municipalities are, therefore, also important partners in facilitating coming in to the population at large. Further study is needed to investigate how this can be done, but local services such as youth clubs, and arenas such as sports groups and churches may be important partners in this effort.

Coming Out and Coming In When You Are Different

Most people manage their own coming out and coming in process without assistance from organized LGB groups or public social services. Of those who do use organized groups, most need to talk once or twice to a more experienced

LGB person, and need a little direction in their search for a suitable arena for network building. However, an increasing number of people coming to organized activities in Oslo, as well as other parts of the country, are people who also belong to other minorities. These may be disabled, people who have mental health problems which require professional attention, or people with an ethnic minority background. People coming out very young, or as adults or even elderly people, also fall under this category. These groups only have one thing in common: they are different, and a planned needs assessment will work out how to best facilitate coming out and coming in for these groups. It is already clear that in meeting the needs of this group, professionals in the health and social services need to be involved to a greater degree.

Preparing for Challenges in the Years to Come

HIV/AIDS Prevention, Care, and Support

The LGB community in Norway reacted very quickly at the start of the AIDS epidemic, partnering with the public sector and initiating prevention, support, and care activities. The HIV incidence among men who have sex with men in Norway is fairly low, but is now rising, in line with trends in Western Europe and North America (Joint United Nations Programme on HIV/AIDS, 2002). In the new landscape of HIV medication and HIV prevention, there is a need for reorganization and rethinking methods. There are challenges related to organization and structure, and a need to work out who would be the constructive partners. There is also a need to work out what would be the relevant content in HIV/AIDS prevention, care, and support among men who have sex with men.

Muslim and Ethnic Minority LGB Persons

Norway has a small Muslim community, located mainly in Oslo. The majority of the Muslim community in Norway are of Pakistani or Somali origin. Being Muslim also, in most cases, therefore means belonging to an ethnic minority. Being LGB in the Muslim community poses specific challenges. The LGB community has received requests for help from LGB Muslims who experience forced opposite-sex marriages. The Norwegian government launched an action plan against forced marriages in 1998, including partnerships with the Pakistani community and other actions aimed at preventing forced marriages. The public sector would therefore be an important partner when working with Muslim LGB persons on this issue.

There are also organizational challenges in working with Muslim ethnic minority LGB. There is no organized LGB Muslim network in Norway, and LGB

Muslims are extremely secretive about their sexual orientation. According to the Norwegian Islamic Council, they do not even exist. Establishing trust therefore becomes a prerequisite to working with LGB Muslims. Some questions need to be addressed through a needs assessment before initiating activities with LGB Muslims: What are the needs of LGB Muslims in Norway? Would it be better to work through or outside established LGB channels and organizations? Should organizations work together in partnerships, and if so, which organizations should be involved? Which of the community/nongovernmental organizations should be involved, and what should be the role of the public sector and health/social services?

COMMUNICATION AND PARTNERSHIP: ORGANIZING FOR CHANGE

Selective Cooperation Between Different Types of Organizations

The needs assessments mentioned above are carried out, or will be carried out, by nongovernmental and private sector actors. Experience shows that, according to issue area, strategic alliances help further the project, as well as help further the actual implementation of the suggested actions and strategies developed.

An example of this is a needs assessment for suicide prevention, which is currently underway through a partnership between the Lesbian and Gay Association (LLH) and Kirkens SOS, a church-affiliated telephone emergency service. The partners raised the funding for the project partly from private foundations, and partly from the government. LLH, as the largest and most well-known LGB association in Norway, provides knowledge of the LGB community and an infrastructure for spreading information and recruiting people for interviews. For Kirkens SOS, the knowledge gathered through the project feeds internal capacity building in the organization, where thousands of helpline volunteers will be coached in meeting LGB callers. This is a particular challenge for a church-affiliated institution, as the State Church still views homosexual "practice" as sinful and wrong. However, there is a movement within the church toward accepting LGB relationships as well as LGB issues. Kirkens SOS wishes to meet LGB callers in the same way as other callers: listening, but not offering advice or guidance.

The findings from the needs assessments will help determine what is needed from the helpline and its volunteers, and will also support the development of course materials for Kirkens SOS volunteers. Kirkens SOS has more general knowledge of suicide prevention to bring to the needs assessment, and also provides an infrastructure to ensure implementation of the strategy developed. In addition, Kirkens SOS has credibility as a solid and dependable service for people in need, again furthering possible implementation of the project in organizations other than the two behind the project. The two organizations have never collaborated before, and this kind of surprising partnership also provides a learning opportunity for the organizations involved.

Reference networks and steering groups ensure ownership by implementers. Wide data collection through interviews and surveys or questionnaires ensure ownership also in target groups. Media coverage, especially in gay and lesbian Websites and chatrooms also ensure ownership and feedback from large part of LGB community, facilitating implementation of the eventual developed strategy.

Norway has long traditions of cooperation between the public and voluntary sectors. Community organizations have, for example, carried out some tasks associated with welfare provision, such as old age homes or youth clubs. As detailed earlier in this article, the local authorities deliver the bulk of the social services offered, and, therefore, become important partners in organizing for a change in the provision of services tailored also to the LGB community.

Capacity Building in the Health and Social Services Sector

As a result of the needs assessments that have already been carried out, the existing knowledge of needs in relation to the public health and social services sector is fairly comprehensive. The main need is for service providers to not take for granted that everyone is heterosexual, that LGB persons be met as individuals, not as a representative of LGB communities, to not have to coach service providers in what homosexuality is and what it is not, and to not be met with negative attitudes toward homosexuality.

However, more specific needs assessments are needed for some areas. As mentioned earlier, indications are that there is no need for a separate health and social services infrastructure for LGB persons. However, it is not clear how existing services should be organized to meet the needs of LGB persons. Should every part of the health and social services system be oriented also toward LGB persons, or should there be special programs set up within existing services? Should different types of services be organized differently? Is there, for example, different need for competency and knowledge of LGB issues in the mental health services, the labor market services, and youth work? If so, what are the different needs?

For meeting the identified needs among LGB persons, some patterns have emerged. Partnerships are needed between institutions with capacity and knowledge of the needs of LGB persons and labor organizations and unions.

These are very strong in Norway, and together organize the majority of the employees in the relevant public sectors. As these organizations provide courses and training, as well as communicate regularly with their members through journals and meetings, they provide an infrastructure for bringing out relevant messages. Also, it is important to bring on board educational institutions, to further inclusion of LGB issues in the respective curricula. Relevant government ministries need to become involved.

However, many questions about organizing for change still remain. At what level will partnerships work? Should partnerships be at the local, regional, or national level? Who should partner? Should the organization be more top-down, and start at the national level with ministries and the central level of unions and voluntary organizations, or should it rather be bottom-up, and consequently scale up local functioning initiatives? There may also be possibilities for new partnerships with other community-based organizations and the public sector that have not been thought of yet.

REFERENCES

Andersen, A. J. (1987). *Coming out–coming home. Vennskap som sosial strategi.* Oslo: University of Oslo.

Benum, V., Friis, E., & Offerdal, A. (Eds.). (1997). *Vite for å forstå. 10 artikler om homoseksualitet og lesbiske og homofiles livsvilkår i Norge i dag.* Oslo: The Gay and Lesbian Association.

Coleman, E. (1981/1982). Developmental stages of the coming out process. *Journal of Homosexuality*, 7(2/3), 31-43.

Fyrand, L. (1995). *Sosialt nettverk. Teori og praksis.* Oslo: Tano.

Hansen, T. (1999). *Municipal self-government in the service of the welfare state.* Oslo: Norwegian Foreign Ministry.

Heffernan, K. (1998). The nature and predictors of substance use among lesbians. *Addictive Behaviors*, 23(4), 517-528.

Hegna, K., Moseng, B. U., & Kristiansen, H. W. (1999). *Levekår og livskvalitet blant lesbiske kvinner og homofile menn i Norge.* Oslo: NOVA–Norwegian Social research. Contains the English summary "Living conditions and life quality among lesbian women and gay men in Norway."

Hillier, L., Dempsey, D., Harrison, L., Beale, L., Matthews, L., & Rosenthal, D. (1998). *Writing themselves in. A national report in the sexuality, health and well-being of same-sex attracted young people.* Australia: National Center in HIV Social Research, LaTrobe University.

Joint United Nations Programme on HIV/AIDS (UNAIDS). (2002). *Report on the global HIV/AIDS epidemic 2002.* Retrieved October 20, 2002, from <www.unaids.org/barcelona/presskit/embargo_html.htm>.

Kontekst Kommunikasjon (2001a). *Strategier for rusforebygging i homomiljø.* Oslo: The Lesbian and Gay Association.

Kontekst Kommunikasjon (2001b). *Ut av skapet, inn i nettverket*. Oslo: The Lesbian and Gay Association. English summary ("Out of the closet, into the network") available from Kontekst Kommunikasjon website, <www.kontekst.no/publikasjoner/inn-ut-eng-summ.pdf>.

Ministry of Children and Family Affairs (1993). *The Norwegian Act on Registered Partnerships for Homosexual Couples*. Oslo: Author.

Ministry of Children and Family Affairs (2001). *White paper/Stortingsmelding 25 (2000-2001), Levekår og livsvilkår for lesbiske og homofile i Noreg*. Oslo: Author.

Parks, C. A. (1999). Lesbian social drinking: The role of alcohol in growing up and living as a lesbian. *Contemporary Drug Problems, 26*, 75-129.

Selle, M. (2001). Nei til 'behandling'–ja til terapi. In M. Brantsæter, T. Eikvam, R. Kjær, & K. O. Åmås (Eds.), *Norsk homoforskning*. Oslo: Universitetsforlaget.

Soriano, F. I. (1995). *Conducting needs assessments. A multidisciplinary approach*. New York: Sage Human Services Guide 68.

Størksen, I. (2000). *Homofili og politikk. En komparativ analyse av verdiendringer og meningskoalisjoner bak vedtaket om partnerskapsloven i Danmark og Norge*. Bergen: University of Bergen.

Weinberg, T. S. (1994). *Gay men, drinking and alcoholism*. Carbondale, IL: Southern Illinois University Press.

Witkin, B. R., & Altschuld, J. W. (1995). *From needs assessment to action*. New York: Sage.

'Trans'cending Barriers: Transgender Organizing on the Internet

Eve Shapiro

SUMMARY. Drawing on in-depth interviews with 10 national transgender activists as well as analyses of movement publications and events, this article examines the use of the Internet in the development and growth of the transgender movement. The Internet, which functions both as a tool for activists and as a space within which activism can happen, reduces challenges and obstacles to mobilization and maximizes available tools and strategies for organizing. While the Internet is not a panacea, it clearly facilitates organizing, allows organizations and activists to be more productive and effective, and provides new tactics and arenas for activism. *[Article copies available for a fee from The Haworth Document Delivery Service: 1-800-HAWORTH. E-mail address: <docdelivery@haworthpress.com> Website: <http://www.HaworthPress.com> © 2004 by The Haworth Press, Inc. All rights reserved.]*

Eve Shapiro, MA, is affiliated with the University of California at Santa Barbara. Address correspondence to: Department of Sociology, Ellison Hall, Room 2834, University of California, Santa Barbara, CA 93106-9430.

Author note: I would like to thank Donna Cartwright, Sandra Cole, Sadie Crabtree, Paisley Currah, Dallas Denny, Jamison Green, Nancy Nangeroni, Pauline Park, Gwendolyn Ann Smith, and Susan Stryker, without whom this article would not have been possible. I would also like to acknowledge the outstanding guidance and support of Jodi O'Brien and Beth Schneider.

[Haworth co-indexing entry note]: "'Trans'cending Barriers: Transgender Organizing on the Internet." Shapiro, Eve. Co-published simultaneously in *Journal of Gay & Lesbian Social Services* (Harrington Park Press, an imprint of The Haworth Press, Inc.) Vol. 16, No. 3/4, 2004, pp. 165-179; and: *Gay and Lesbian Rights Organizing: Community-Based Strategies* (ed: Yolanda C. Padilla) Harrington Park Press, an imprint of The Haworth Press, Inc., 2004, pp. 165-179. Single or multiple copies of this article are available for a fee from The Haworth Document Delivery Service [1-800-HAWORTH, 9:00 a.m. - 5:00 p.m. (EST). E-mail address: docdelivery@haworthpress.com].

Journal of Gay & Lesbian Social Services, Vol. 16(3/4) 2004
http://www.haworthpress.com/store/product.asp?sku=J041
© 2004 by The Haworth Press, Inc. All rights reserved.
10.1300/J041v16n03_11

KEYWORDS. Transgender, transsexual, social movements, Internet, online organizing

> The strongest impetus of the trans movement happened with access to the Internet... You can just see the networking expansion and spreading of information dramatically influencing the social presence of transgendered individuals in our culture. (Sandra Cole, PhD, activist, Professor, founder and recently retired Director of the University of Michigan Health System Comprehensive Gender Services Program)

Leading activists in the transgender movement attribute significant movement growth to the Internet. Indeed, while one woman–Christine Jorgensen– announcing her Sex Reassignment Surgery (SRS) in 1952, introduced transgender issues into the public realm, in 2002 a simple Internet search will pull up over 800,000 trans focused Web sites, listserves, and chatrooms. Transgender issues have become a site of activism, resistance, and social change, and there has been a shift in the transgender community from a pathologized transsexual population that existed around support and informational groups to a politicized transgender community that challenges society's gender paradigms. My intent in this research is to examine how transgender activists have used the Internet to forward transgender organizing and the causes and consequences of this process. While transgender can be used in a variety of ways, I use the word, here, in its broadest sense, as an umbrella term for the community. I also use the shorthand 'trans' to refer to the same movement and groups. Transgender, and the shorthand trans, then, encompass everyone from transsexuals to cross-dressers.

While there have been many trans organizations in the past 40 years, and living 'stealth'–remaining closeted about one's transgender status–is less common than it used to be, it is still rare and difficult for transgender people to choose to risk their lives and livelihoods by being visibly out. However, the trans community as a movement has achieved a significantly large profile in public discourse. Today transgender issues are emerging within the mainstream gay and lesbian political agenda and have begun to garner attention in both state and national level forums. Movement activists explain this phenomenon, suggesting that the Internet has allowed people to educate themselves and others, to make contacts, and to organize without ever having to appear in public as a trans person–reducing the risk to which individuals must expose themselves in order to organize.

Based on a broad study of trans activism, this article shows the emergence of the theme of the transformative role of the Internet. The data revealed a striking convergence of opinion on the part of activists about the role of the

Internet in movement development and growth. The use of Web sites, listserves, and online communities have provided a critical mass of information, guidance, and space where trans people can connect. Building on the foundation laid by support groups, organizations, conferences, and publications, the Internet is a new and important site of transgender organizing that has expanded the tactics and arenas for activism. While there are significant considerations, the use of the Internet as both a tool to communicate, reduce costs, and distribute information and as a space to organize activism, network, and foster collective identity has been revolutionary within the trans movement.

METHODS

In this article my intent is to highlight activists' knowledge and understanding of the transgender movement. In-depth interviews with ten trans activists were conducted, focused on their understanding of transgender activism as a social movement and their goals for movement organizing. The activists interviewed have worked intensively with a variety of organizations, including Female to Male International (FTMI), International Foundation for Gender Education (IFGE), New York Association for Gender Rights Advocacy (NYAGRA), Gender Education & Advocacy (GEA), American Educational Gender Information Service (AEGIS), It's Time America (ITA), GenderPAC (GPAC), and Transgender Nation, among others. Collectively their work spans more than two decades, beginning in the late 1970s to the present. In addition, several types of textual data, including essays, speeches, and other materials collected from 42 issues of transgender publications as well as 10 articles from the popular press were used to broaden the scope of opinions. Materials from several transgender news services, including Gender Advocacy Internet News (GAIN), GenderPAC, In Your Face (IYF), and TransShare between October 1999 and September 2001 supplemented print media. Finally, on-site observation was conducted of the First National Conference on Gender (NCG) put on by GenderPAC in Washington, D.C., May 18-20, 2001.

The movement discussed here is not the only trans movement. Community discussions and activities highlight the multifaceted nature of the transgender community. As Pauline Park, PhD, co-founder and co-chair of NYAGRA remarked, "The transgender movement is not monolithic. It's complex, sometimes fractionalized, and often vociferous." There are a number of trans movements which are tied together by identity and issue, and separated by race, class, nationality, goal, surgery status, and other characteristics. While there are not clear and clean dividing lines between these different trans movements, the most visible movement consists of mostly white, transsexual and transgendered activists and participants with relatively stable economic situations. Presented here, then, is one view, one interpretation of the movements' development, through the eyes of activists.

LITERATURE REVIEW

Although state and national level activism and lobbying emerged as a central tactic only over the past five to ten years, there is a well-established collective movement identity within the trans community and vibrant, focused activism around issues of social and cultural change. There has not been, however, a significant amount of research on the transgender community or movement outside of examination of gender identity formation (Docter, 1988; Green, 1975, 1987; Green & Fleming, 1990; Money, 1974, 1993), gender dysphoria and its treatment and life outcomes (Bockting & Coleman, 1992; Bockting, Rosser, & Coleman, 1999; Israel & Tarver, 1998; Kirk, 1996; Miller, 1996), and more recently the use of transgenderism to explore the social construction of gender (Bem, 1993; Fausto-Sterling, 2000; Irvine, 1990; Kessler & McKenna, 1978, 2000; Lorber, 1994; Showalter, 1989; Scott, 1988; West & Zimmerman, 1987; West & Fenstermaker, 1995) and gender identity (Gagne, Tewksbury, & McGaughey, 1997; Garber, 1992; Parlee, 1996).

Few academic texts address transgender organizing or the trans social movement (see, for example, Frye, 2000; Gay and Lesbian Historical Society of Northern California, 1998; Meyerowitz, 1998; Stryker, 1998). There has been, however, significant work done within the trans community, which explores gender nonconformity, gender identity/trans identity development, and critiques of the existing medical and social environment for transgendered individuals (Jorgensen, 1968; Lesser, 1999; Martino & Martino, 1979; Rees, 1995; Stringer, 1990). In addition, there is a body of nonacademic work which theorizes transgender identity and documents legal, policy, and resource developments (Currah, Minter, & Green, 2000; Dunson, 2001; Frye, 2000; Swartz, 1997; Israel & Tarver, 1998; Kirk & Rothblatt, 1995). While these texts do not come out of academia, they offer a substantial and significant history of transgenderism and transactivism, as well as noteworthy critiques of the treatment of transgenderism over time (Bolin, 1987; Califia, 1997; Feinberg, 1996).

A SOCIAL HISTORY OF TRANSGENDER ORGANIZING

Discussions with trans activists and analyses of community publications as well as a review of the limited written history of transgender organizing

(Califia, 1997; Feinberg, 1996; Frye, 2000; Gay and Lesbian Historical Society of Northern California, 1998; MacKenzie, 1994; Shapiro, forthcoming; Wilchins, 1997) reveal three overlapping waves of organizing which moved the community from a support focus, to an educational one, and finally toward political organizing and activism. Fifty years ago, the trans movement was made up of a highly marginalized community served by trans support organizations, focused either on cross-dressers or the transition of transsexual individuals. The growth of the trans activism out of a support community is not unique to this movement but rather endemic to movements focused around highly medicalized/pathologized identities (Taylor, 1996). Other examples are the gay and lesbian rights movement, the disability rights movement, and the post-partum depression movement.

The first wave of community organizing emerged in the 1960s through support groups which developed into a significant number of support and information organizations, like Virginia Prince's Hose and Heels Club (the first support group established in 1961), Tri-Ess, and AEGIS, some of which are still in existence. Alongside this early activism, the medical community struggled to make sense of and develop treatments for transsexuals. This led to the development of and short-lived 'golden age' for gender clinics in universities such as Johns Hopkins, University of Minnesota, Stanford, and UCLA. After the Johns Hopkins program ended their sex-reassignment surgery program in 1979, the whole system of transsexual medical service providers crumbled. Not only was access to medical services devastated, but the limited social support networks built up around them were destroyed as well. Thus, the Internet helped fill the vacuum left by the medical community in more recent history through the creation of Internet support groups.

In the early to mid-1990s evolved a second wave of organizing, characterized by educational aims and local activism and modeled on civil rights-style activism of the early gay rights movement. The development of these early political organizations, such as It's Time America and GenderPAC, can be attributed to several factors: the purging of transgendered individuals from lesbian and feminist groups, a growth in the number of individuals unhappy with existing gender dysphoria practices, and a growing FTM (female-to-male) community (Califia, 1997). Finally, increased use of the Internet by the trans community and the influence of gay and lesbian direct action groups (such as ACT-UP and the Lesbian Avengers) fostered a third wave of transgender activism which blossomed in the mid to late 1990s. While direct action and Internet use conjure up different types of activism, these two tactics served distinct and complimentary needs in the trans movement. First, direct action organizing allowed for a visible transgender presence; groups such as Transgender Nation (originally a committee within QueerNation) catapulted trans *activism* into the mainstream and gay and lesbian media. Second, the Internet fostered broad community development and allowed for organizing across geographic location, thus supporting the development of new and innovative organizations.

THE ROLE OF THE INTERNET IN TRANSGENDER ORGANIZING

Critical studies of the transgender community recognize that dominant engagements with trans issues over the past forty years have been focused around attempts to medicalize gender nonconformity (Meyerowitz, 1998; Namaste, 2000; Scholinski & Adams, 1997). Two consequences of this dominance were that prior to the Internet, it was possible for transpeople to have no knowledge of anyone else like themselves, and the dominant mode of existence, which was encouraged by the medical community, was stealth. Individuals were cautioned to remain closeted about their transgender status and to disassociate from the transgender community after transition. Most gender clinics strongly advised trans people to go stealth post-transition, which consequently did not foster community. The key distinction is that before the Internet, trans people were reliant on the medical profession and the few trans support organizations for information. This meant that forces of pathologization and medicalization dominated the framing of transgender identities. The Internet, on the other hand, has become a key element in providing people access to others, allowing activists to provide their own framing and to challenge medical and social understanding of gender nonconformity. In other words, the Internet can be seen as central in the empowerment of trans subjects, who were, up until recently, the objects of medicalization. The new conceptualization of transgender identities that has emerged has come out of the community itself and is characterized by moves away from pathologization and toward social acceptance and political rights. While this move is not uniform across the community it is certainly a dominant trend.

Simply put, the use of the Internet by the trans movement has changed how organizing happens. Work that consumed trans organizations in earlier waves has migrated online, and this has changed the services organizations are called upon to provide. The networking and collective identity development that the early support groups fostered is now facilitated online, which has meant that few trans people come to support groups ignorant about transgender identities and issues–most have already accessed basic information online. Support groups, therefore, can now focus on a different type of personal and group development. Similarly, the ability of activists to use the Internet to distribute information and educational materials quickly and inexpensively has changed the need for, and tasks of, the information and education organizations which emerged in the early and mid 1990s. Finally, the direct action and political work that has dominated the past five years of organizing has benefited significantly from the Internet, because it fosters decentralized organizing and new tactics of protest.

There are two central ways in which the Internet has transformed transgender organizing. First, the Internet has become a *tool* for activists and organizations to use to reduce organizations' upstart and maintenance costs and to provide quick and efficient information distribution. Second, the Internet has become a *space* within which to facilitate networking and collective identity development and employ new tactics, leading to the further development, growth, and success of the transgender movement. Some of the major successes that can be attributed to the use of the Internet in trans organizing include the growth of broader community discussions and activism especially involving youth, FTM's, and genderqueers, and greater participation in state and national-level lobbying and activism.

The Internet as a Tool for Organizing

Within the transgender movement, the two most challenging obstacles the Internet has helped activists address are its limited financial resources and its need for extensive and geographically diverse information distribution. Transgender movement organizations cannot rely on the same internal structures or traditional activity as other, better funded, social movements. For example, in 1996 Dallas Denny found that, "only three of the seven [largest national] organizations (IFGE, Outreach Institute for Gender Studies, and Renaissance) have an actual office, and only one (IFGE) has a paid staff. The work of the other six organizations is done by volunteers (Denny, 1996, p. 8)." The low cost of communicating, organizing, and protesting online supports activism. The rise of Internet use by both organizations and individuals has allowed activists and organizations to distribute information, advertise, answer questions, and handle administrative and planning issues online. Consequently, money has become less of a constraint. While there are certainly still financial problems within the community, with the Internet limited resources can now be better utilized. Whereas ten years ago the largest transgender support organization, the International Foundation for Gender Education (IFGE), almost closed its doors due to financial trouble, transgender organizations now can and do function with much smaller budgets.

Money spent on a physical space, printing and mailing information, keeping track of membership, and other related tasks has been reduced significantly as all of these things can be done online for a fraction of the cost. In addition, the consequences for trans organizations of being homeless or operated out of an activist's homes (which was true of the majority of trans organizations for many years) are reduced if the organization lives online. For example, several trans organizations such as GEA and the National Transgender Advocacy Coalition (NTAC) exist almost exclusively online. In other words, the Internet is becoming the virtual home of many trans organizations and has helped these organizations function in a more efficient and productive manner.

Along with reducing organizing costs, the Internet facilitates the dissemination of information, a vital process in the transgender movement. The Internet has given people in rural and isolated situations access to resources, information, and community. In addition to simply facilitating communication, this change has affected the work organizations do. Information distribution was a primary job of trans activists and organizations. The Internet has changed this, freeing organizations and activists up to do other types of work. According to Dallas Denny, founder of AEGIS and long time trans activist, who was interviewed for this study,

> Ten years ago, I would work hard to get my organization's contact info into books and periodicals. Someone would see it and write a letter–if they were comfortable enough to get return mail. I would get their letter, stuff an envelope, and mail it back. Two weeks after someone sent away for information, they would get the limited amount I could afford to send. With the newly available Internet, anyone can type "transsexual" or "transgender" into a search engine and get a great deal of information instantaneously and for free.

The ease of information dissemination is especially important for activist events. The move online has allowed activists to post their events and actions more quickly and with less lead time and distribute them to a wider audience. It has also led to an explosion of online news and activism which has impacted the type and size of protest actions as well as the amount of mainstream and gay and lesbian attention these trans activities draw.

The Internet as a Space for Activism

The Internet has done more than simply change the distribution of information and reduce the cost of movement activity and development. Perhaps the most significant contribution the Internet offers social movements is the expansion of where activism happens. The Internet has developed into more than a tactic or tool social movements employ; it has become a space–albeit a virtual one–within which organizing and activism can happen. Through listservs, e-mail, message boards, and Web sites, the trans community has created an environment where the Internet's relative anonymity and safety mitigates the high social stigma and related risks which have long inhibited trans mobilization. Two outcomes of this development have been the growth and strengthening of contact between, and collective identity amongst, trans activists and community members and the development of new, Internet-specific forms of activism. These forms of activism have included the development of online letter writing campaigns, distribution of activism materials to local level activists, and online protests and boycotts of organizations, companies, and service providers.

The dissemination of information online does more than inform and organize active participants; it can also serve to recruit new members. The Internet bridges geographical boundaries, is accessible all hours of the day, and does not necessarily require simultaneous presence for communication. It is thus, an invaluable resource for activist recruitment. An activist can create a Web site, listserve, or e-mail list which can connect a diverse array of individuals. In addition, the Internet neither entails the threat of physical harm that protest often does, nor requires ones presence in the immediate physical area of mobilization.

In addition to these general incentives for mobilization, the Internet aids in community development and networking for highly marginalized groups in particularly salient ways. Because outing oneself online does not carry the same risks, many more people are willing to inquire about and become active in the community and its informational and social networks. In other words, the Internet carries fewer consequences for members of highly marginalized communities; trans people do not have to be out to access the community. According to Nancy Nangeroni, another activist interviewed:

> The Internet allows anonymous communication and so it allows people otherwise closeted to talk about things that they might not, and to talk about them with a stranger. Many cross-dressers fear discovery, they fear they'd lose their families, their jobs, or, at the very least, be socially humiliated. They can set up an e-mail account through Hotmail or some place like that and have anonymous communication or enter chat rooms, which happened in later years when the Web became big.

The Internet, then, can serve to connect people who are still closeted and/or in situations that are difficult–indeed those that often need the most information, education, and support. Professor and activist, Sandra Cole, highlighted that this is especially true for youth because they have even fewer resources available to them:

> Youth now have grown up with the Internet, they're children of the Internet. So if they had any ideas, concerns, or questions about gender for themselves, or were just snooping around on the Internet, they will

readily run into transgender sites and information. Through all types of trans-related sources they are easily able to find some relevance of social definition and meaning that can help them reaffirm and validate their own feelings and identity as well as locate new contacts and sources that will be helpful to them.

As can be seen in the significant increase in out and politicized trans people over the past five years, the ability to access resources without being out does not act as motivation to remain closeted, however. Rather, it acts to help those without access to resources or community expand their knowledge about trans issues and helps develop feelings of collective identity. This in turn helps build a support network and sense of community which may help lead trans people out of the closet and into activism.

Access to information alone is not enough to build collective identity. However, chat rooms, Billboards, and other interactive Internet mediums facilitate this type of group identification and sense of collective momentum. Like support groups in which individuals develop relationships with one another, these types of online forums work to develop a sense of collectivity and community. According to national trans activists, one of the outcomes of the Internet, then, is that there has been a significant growth in the number of individuals active in the trans community in the past few years.

Finally, the Internet has changed and aided existing means of organizing within the trans movement. Before the Internet, protest activity served as the measure by which social movement activity was evaluated by scholars and activists. The number of protests, their size, and the attention received was the primary evidence of collective action. With the Internet, however, physical mobilization for protest is no longer the only method of disobedience. While some of what goes on online is individual or identity focused, the Internet has been increasingly used as a tool for protest. Indeed, within the transgender movement, the Internet has become a place where activism can happen. Activists write, sign, and collect petitions, circulate templates for letters to legislators, and send out calls for action. Recalling her first "electronic civil disobedience," Gwendolyn Ann Smith, a San Francisco trans activist who is involved in local organizing as well as national activism through GEA, remarked in her interview for this study,

> That was really where I started to get involved with activism–in the online medium. At the time [1993], I was back on America Online and it was their terms of service at the time that you could not discuss transgender issues on AOL. I didn't feel that was quite right, so I started educating and pushed them on changing the terms which eventually did change, which eventually led to a forum, which I ended up running.

The move away from physical location is especially important for identity movements in which members are linked by a shared understanding of self rather than a shared working environment or geographic location. The ability to organize across vast distances around unifying issues is essential to these types of movements. As Nangeroni (1997) observes,

> The Internet's gift of potentially enormous power to individuals affects the rules of political engagement, remolding the activist environment experienced by prior civil rights organizers. Successful leaders today can work with a lighter hand. Deft networking outperforms ability to whoop up a crowd. Economic and political force may be unavailable, but popular consensus is more accessible than ever. (pp. 39-40)

CONSIDERATIONS

Access to the Internet, like access to surgery and related medical technology, is mitigated by social class and race in the United States. It is imperative to keep an eye on these (and other) divisions within the community, divisions that may be further accentuated by the growing use of online forums for community development and activism. Thus, it is important to temper grand notions of the Internet's current and potential use. While it is undeniable that the Internet has become a central arena for organizing around transgender issues, it is essential that both the online and offline segments of the community remain integrated. The dynamics of race, class, and nation affect who has access to the Internet. The Internet is not removed from the race and class divisions within the trans community and may indeed reinforce them. The fear, then, is that with the trans movement's move online the same people that have been marginalized within the community up to this point are again being left behind. It is also important to realize that the Internet has limitations as a tool, tactic, and space for collective action. Unlike public protest, the Internet does not reach individuals who are bystanders–individuals who are outside of the community and who are not the targets of collective action.

Furthermore, while education online has been extremely beneficial, it may have also created a false sense of movement size and safety. Because the Internet creates a space in which a large number of transpeople can congregate without having to face, directly, the social stigma and attendant consequences of being trans, the Internet can foster a false sense of security and an inflated sense of social change and acceptance. Sandra Cole argues that this is especially true for youth who have come of age within a transgender movement. She maintains that,

> The social construct of the world is changing almost faster than the rate that people can handle ... So what we are seeing now on campuses and in high schools are transgender students who are self identifying in the same way as someone who is gay coming out around that age. Because of much of the validation the transyouth have experienced through the Internet and small group discussions, they are arriving on campuses with less trepidation and fear; instead, announcing, "here I am, I need services: housing, employment, health care benefits, hormones ..." At that point they generally experience an abyss between themselves and the readiness of the campus. They do not realize and have no concept that the real world in real time around them has not caught up with the prevailing need. Basically, society is still limping along trying to understand what has happened and how should/do they respond.

Given the newness of online activism and its integration into social movements, the long-term aggregate effect of social movement reliance on the Internet and online media is unknown. Movement activists have begun to think about and address these consequences, but it is too soon to know how the dynamics of Internet activism will affect transgender social movements and communities specifically, and other social movements in general.

CONCLUSION

The Internet has been a key player in the development and growth of the trans community into a social movement. Much of the work done by early support and information organizations has been transferred online. This has freed organizations and activists to focus on other issues such as legal rights, political organizing, and direct action activism. In addition to assisting movement development directly, the Internet has alleviated many of the barriers to organizing within the trans movement. By requiring fewer financial resources, providing a more physically safe space to organize and participate in activism, developing community, and combining support and political education, the Internet has played a critical role in minimizing many obstacles to movement formation and participation.

What emerged from discussions with activists about transgender organizing is that, with the rise of the Internet, a critical mass of information, social networks, and individuals has developed that greatly aided and expanded the movement for transgender rights. Not only has the Internet allowed a highly marginalized community to advocate for change, but it has changed the nature of the community itself. While individuals may be isolated physically, there is a vibrant online community that allows for a wide distribution of information and educational materials and that builds collective identity through greater contact among trans people. The Internet has become, in many ways, a new public space within which information distribution, education, and organizing can happen. While the Internet is not without problems, it certainly facilitates organizing, allows organizations and activists to be more productive and effective, and provides new tactics and arenas for activism.

REFERENCES

Bem, S. L. (1993). *The lenses of gender: Transforming the debate on sexual inequality.* New Haven: Yale University Press.

Bockting, W., & Coleman E. (Eds.). (1992). *Gender dysphoria: Interdisciplinary approaches in clinical management.* New York: Haworth Press.

Bockting, W., Rosser, S., & Coleman, E. (1999). Transgender HIV prevention: Community involvement and empowerment. *International Journal of Transgenderism, 3.* Retrieved August 12, 2001, from <www.symposion.com/ijt/hiv_risk/bockting.htm>.

Bolin, A. (1987). Transsexualism and the limits of traditional analysis. *American Behavioral Scientist,* 31, 41-65.

Califia, P. (1997). *Sex changes: The politics of transgenderism.* San Francisco: Cleis Press.

Currah, P., Minter, S., & Green, J. (2000). *Transgender equality: A handbook for activists and policymakers.* Washington, DC: National Gay and Lesbian Task Force.

Denny, D. (1996). Vision 2001: Part 1. *AEGIS News,* 1 (6), 1-11.

Docter, R. F. (1988). *Transvestites and transsexuals: Toward a theory of cross-gender behavior.* London: Plenum Press.

Dunson, M. (2001). Sex, gender, and transgender: The present and future of employment discrimination law. *Berkeley Journal of Employment and Labor Law,* 22 (1), 465-505.

Fausto-Sterling, A. (2000). *Sexing the body: Gender politics and the construction of sexuality.* New York: Basic Books.

Feinberg, L. (1996). *Transgender warriors: Making history from Joan of Arc to Ru Paul.* Boston: Beacon Press.

Frye, P. R. (2000). Facing discrimination, organizing for freedom: The transgender community. In J. D'Emilio, W. Turner, & U. Vaid (Eds.), *Creating change: Sexuality, public policy, and civil rights* (pp. 451-468). New York: St. Martins Press.

Gagne, P., Tewksbury, R., & McGaughey, D. (1997). Coming out and crossing over identity formation and proclamation in a transgender community. *Gender & Society,* 11 (4), 478-508.

Garber, M. (1992). *Vested interests: Cross-dressing and cultural anxiety.* New York: Routledge.

Gay and Lesbian Historical Society of Northern California. (1998). MTF transgender activism in the Tenderloin and beyond, 1966-1975. *GLQ: A Journal of Lesbian and Gay Studies,* 4 (2), 349-372.

Green, R. (1975). Sexual identity: Research strategies. *Archives of Sexual Behavior,* 4 (4), 337-352.

Green, R. (1987). *The "sissy boy" syndrome and the development of homosexuality.* New Haven: Yale University Press.

Green, R., & Fleming, D.T. (1990). Transsexual surgery follow-up: Status in the 1990s. *Annual Review of Sex Research,* 1, 163-174.

Irvine, J. M. (1990). From difference to sameness: Gender ideology in sexual science. *Journal of Sex Research,* 27 (1), 7-24.

Israel, G., & Tarver, D. (1998). *Transgender care: Recommended guidelines, practical information, and personal accounts.* Philadelphia: Temple University Press.

Jorgensen, C. (1968). *Christine Jorgensen: A personal autobiography.* New York: Bantam Books.

Kessler, S., & McKenna, W. (1978). *Gender: An ethnomethodological approach.* New York: Wiley.

Kessler, S., & McKenna, W. (2000). Who put the "trans" in transgender? Gender theory and everyday life. *International Journal of Transgenderism Special Issue: What is Transgenderism.* Retrieved January 3, 2001, from <www.symposion.com/ijt/gilbert/kessler.htm>.

Kirk, S., & Rothblatt, M. (1995). *Medical, legal, and workplace issues for the transsexual.* Watertown: Together Lifeworks.

Kirk, S. (1996). *Physician's guide to transgendered medicine.* Blawnox: Together Lifeworks.

Lesser, J. G. (1999). When your son becomes your daughter: A mother's adjustment to a transgender child. *Families in Society,* 80 (2), March-April), 182-89.

Lorber, J. (1994). *Paradoxes of gender.* New Haven: Yale University Press.

MacKenzie, G. O. (1994). *Transgender nation.* Bowling Green, OH: Bowling Green University Popular Press.

Martino, M., & Martino, H. (1979). *Emergence: A transsexual autobiography.* New York: Signet.

Meyerowitz, J. (1998). Sex change and the popular press: Historical notes on transsexuality in the United States, 1930-1955. *GLQ A Journal of Lesbian and Gay Studies,* 4 (2), 159-187.

Miller, N. (1996). *Counseling in genderland: A guide for you and your transgendered client.* Boston: Different Paths Press.

Money, J. (1974). Two names, two wardrobes, two personalities. *Journal of Homosexuality,* 1 (1), 65-70.

Money, J. (1993). *The Adam principle: Genes, genitals, hormones, & gender: Selected readings in sexology.* Buffalo: Prometheus Books.

Namaste, V. K. (2000). *Invisible lives: The erasure of transsexual and transgendered people.* Chicago: University of Chicago Press.

Nangeroni, N. R. (1997). The Virtual movement. *GCN: The National Queer Progressive Quarterly,* 23 (2-3), 36-42.

Parlee, M. B. (1996). Situated knowledges of personal embodiment. *Theory and Psychology,* 6 (4), 625-645.

Rees, M. (1995). *Dear sir or madam: The autobiography of a female-to-male transsexual.* London: Cassells.

Scott, J. (1988). Gender: A useful category of historical analysis. In J. Scott (Ed.), *Gender and the politics of history* (pp. 28-50). New York: Columbia.

Scholinski, D., & Adams, J. M. (1997). *The last time I wore a dress.* New York: Riverhead Books.

Shapiro, E. (forthcoming). Trans movements: From gender clinics to internet organizing. In P. Currah, R. M. Juang, & S. Minter (Eds.), *Transgender Rights: Culture, Politics, and Law.* Minneapolis, MN: University of Minnesota Press.

Showalter, E. (1989). Introduction: The rise of gender. In E. Showalter (Ed.), *Speaking of gender* (pp. 1-13). New York: Routledge.

Stringer, J. A. (1990). *The transsexual survival guide: To transition and beyond.* King of Prussia, PA: Creative Design Services.

Stryker, S. (1998). The transgender issue: An introduction. *GLQ: A Journal of Lesbian and Gay Studies,* 4 (2), 145-158.

Swartz, L. H. (1997). Law and transsexualism. In B. Bullough, V. L. Bullough, & J. Elias (Eds.), *Gender blending* (pp. 422-429). Amherst, NY: Prometheus Books.

Taylor, V. (1996). *Rock-a-by-baby: Feminism, self-help, and postpartum depression.* New York: Routledge.

West, C., & Fenstermaker, S. (1995). Doing difference. *Gender & Society,* 9, 8-37.

West, C., & Zimmerman, D. (1987). Doing gender. *Gender & Society,* 2 (1987), 125-151.

Wilchins, R. A. (1997). *Read my lips: Sexual subversion and the end of gender.* Ithaca, NY: Firebrand Books.

"AM/FM Activism":
Taking National Media Tools to a Local Level

Kristen Schilt

SUMMARY. As a cultural approach to LGBT activism, media advocacy, such as that modeled by the Gay and Lesbian Alliance Against Defamation (GLAAD), has grown in importance in the last decade. Drawing on the tactics used to educate the media about national anti-gay defamation issues, GLAAD has recently launched "AM/FM Activism," an online resource that provides local activists with the tools necessary for responding to defamation in their own communities. Based on participant observation, in-depth interviews, and archival research, this article explores the implications of "AM/FM Activism" as a new form of media advocacy that bridges the gap between national and local activists. *[Article copies available for a fee from The Haworth Document Delivery Service: 1-800-HAWORTH. E-mail address: <docdelivery@haworthpress.com> Website: <http://www.HaworthPress.com> © 2004 by The Haworth Press, Inc. All rights reserved.]*

Kristen Schilt, MA, is affiliated with the Department of Sociology, University of California at Los Angeles, 264 Haines Hall, 375 Portola Plaza, Los Angeles, CA 90095.

The author would like to thank Bob Emerson, Laura Miller, Vincent Doyle, and the entire staff of GLAAD LA for their contributions to this paper.

[Haworth co-indexing entry note]: "'AM/FM Activism': Taking National Media Tools to a Local Level." Schilt, Kristen. Co-published simultaneously in *Journal of Gay & Lesbian Social Services* (Harrington Park Press, an imprint of The Haworth Press, Inc.) Vol. 16, No. 3/4, 2004, pp. 181-192; and: *Gay and Lesbian Rights Organizing: Community-Based Strategies* (ed: Yolanda C. Padilla) Harrington Park Press, an imprint of The Haworth Press, Inc., 2004, pp. 181-192. Single or multiple copies of this article are available for a fee from The Haworth Document Delivery Service [1-800-HAWORTH, 9:00 a.m. - 5:00 p.m. (EST). E-mail address: docdelivery@haworthpress.com].

Journal of Gay & Lesbian Social Services, Vol. 16(3/4) 2004
http://www.haworthpress.com/store/product.asp?sku=J041
© 2004 by The Haworth Press, Inc. All rights reserved.
10.1300/J041v16n03_12

181

KEYWORDS. Gay and lesbian media advocacy, Dr. Laura, online activism, gay rights movement

Since the 1950s, media and cultural activism have played a key role in the gay rights movement (Vaid, 1995). Early forms of media activism centered on creating alternative media, such as newspapers, magazines, and radio shows, that represented gay and lesbian issues. In the 1980s, gay and lesbian media sources became important sites for passing on information to the gay and lesbian community about AIDS, a disease which largely was being ignored by "mainstream" media (Vaid, 1995). As the gay rights movement gained momentum during the height of the AIDS crisis, activists began to work on new forms of advocacy that could address the treatment of gays and lesbians in the media. Before this time, as Vito Russo (1987) has pointed out, gays and lesbians were either completely ignored by mainstream media or represented negatively as perverts or disease carriers. In 1988, the first branch of the Gay and Lesbian Alliance Against Defamation (GLAAD), a media advocacy group intent on addressing the negative representation of gay men and lesbians in newsprint, formed in New York. As the landscape of media has begun to shift in a way that allows more input from media advocacy groups (Streeter, 2000), GLAAD has grown from a volunteer-run group to a national nonprofit organization that monitors all forms of media for fair, accurate, and inclusive representations of the lesbian, gay, bisexual, and transgendered (LGBT) community. With this growth, GLAAD has illustrated its ability to mobilize the LGBT community in response to anti-gay defamation in the national media and has carved out a space for LGBT voices in traditional media, as well as online (see GLAAD accomplishments, n.d.).

In working to combat anti-gay defamation through advocacy, GLAAD frequently partners with other LGBT advocacy groups, such as the Human Rights Campaign, the National Gay and Lesbian Task Force, and the National Gay and Lesbian Journalist's Association. Organizations that advocate for LGBT issues, such as hate crime legislation and gay marriage, now play a key role in educating the LGBT community about important political issues and are coming to increasingly have more power in national political arenas. However, although there is frequently overlap between the issues of these organizations and GLAAD's work, GLAAD remains the only LGBT advocacy group that focuses entirely on anti-gay defamation in all forms of national media, particularly film and television.

The majority of GLAAD's work occurs behind the scenes in the form of cooperation with media entities to ensure fair representations of the LGBT community before a film or television show airs. However, in 1997, GLAAD began a highly publicized educational campaign that brought attention to the anti-gay comments of popular radio talk show host, Dr. Laura Schlessinger. Although the media initially was slow to respond to GLAAD's concerns, the advocacy group mobilized community support for the anti-defamation issue, which ultimately dealt a severe blow to Schlessinger, as her television spin-off show, *Dr. Laura*, was canceled after only five months on the air. Although cancellation of *Dr. Laura* illustrated GLAAD's growing power as a national media watchdog, the campaign owed a great deal to the efforts of local grassroots activists who took advantage of GLAAD's online organizing tool, "Local Laura Activism." Inspired by the success of working with local activists on the *Dr. Laura* campaign, GLAAD launched "AM/FM Activism" in February 2001, an online organizing tool that provides individuals and communities with the strategies for addressing anti-gay defamation in their local media (see "AM/FM Activism": step by step, n.d.).

This article demonstrates how tools such as "AM/FM Activism" are important organizing strategies for the LGBT community, as they provide local activists with the tools, strategies, and institutional support necessary to launch effective anti-defamation campaigns. Having these tools and resources not only empowers individuals to effect change locally, but also creates political alliances that can play an integral role in future GLAAD and LGBT activism, illustrating the importance of new forms of media advocacy that bring in local activism as a counterpart for national advocacy work. I first provide a brief description of the process of media advocacy. Following an overview of the background of "AM/FM Activism" as a response to the *Dr. Laura* campaign, I discuss how this strategy can be used as a method for creating local activist networks.

The analysis is based on research conducted in the GLAAD Los Angeles office through a combination of participant observation, in-depth interviews, and analysis of archival material. I approached GLAAD in January 2001 about the possibility of doing research on the work behind media advocacy. To this end, I took a six-month, 15-hour-a-week position as an office intern, as this allowed me to participate directly in the work of GLAAD. In addition to working in the office, I recorded field notes, which totaled over 300 pages at the conclusion of my research in July 2001. After analyzing and coding some of my preliminary data, I selected several topics of interest and constructed an interview schedule. I conducted tape-recorded interviews with eight of the 15-member staff on a variety of topics. On average, the transcribed interviews were between 15 and 17 pages. Additionally, I provided interviewees with a copy of their transcript for review and revisions. Finally, data from the interviews were supplemented with archival data about the *Dr. Laura* campaign and the AM/FM initiative.

THE PROCESS OF MEDIA ADVOCACY

GLAAD recognizes five different types of defamation in the media: vicious slander, negative stereotypes, casual prejudice, deference to homophobia, and invisibility (Monitor and response, n.d.). Vicious slander includes overt attacks or abusive prejudices against the LGBT community. Negative stereotypes are instances in which the entire LGBT community is cast in a negative light, such as media portrayals of gay men as pedophiles. Casual prejudice is a case in which media representatives make offhand remarks that serve to reinforce prejudices against the LGBT community, such as blaming gay men for the AIDS epidemic. Deference to homophobia is seen in cases in which media representatives allow homophobic views to be expressed with no comment or opposing viewpoint. Finally, invisibility is a case in which LGBT individuals are completely absent from representation in a media outlet, such as radio request shows that refuse to take requests from LGBT couples.

GLAAD uses different tactics to address defamation, depending on the type of defamation taking place, the willingness of the media outlet to change their representations of the LGBT community, and the prevailing social context. Although GLAAD's early work in the 1980s relied on hostile, reactive tactics to bring attention to media defamation, the organization now embraces cooperative and proactive strategies of working with the media. Cooperative tactics are "based on rewarding the good and building relationships with the media rather than delivering threats and applying coercion" (Rossman, 2000, p. 92). GLAAD has moved toward working cooperatively with the media because they view most instances of defamation as stemming from "homo-ignorance" rather than malicious intent. Thus, it is more productive to employ educational campaigns that provide information for altering future LGBT representations than to use hostile tactics, such as boycotts, that tend to only effect the immediate issue at hand.

Once GLAAD has identified an image or story as defamatory, the first step is to contact the source of the defamation to attempt internal change by meeting with producers, executives, and media entities to explain GLAAD's position on the offending material. As GLAAD has become more influential in the entertainment industry, these attempts are usually successful, meaning that an apology or retraction is issued or a negative characterization of a LGBT character is altered. In the rare cases where these proactive tactics do not bear fruit, however, GLAAD moves to issuing press releases about the defamation and *GLAAD Alerts* (*GLAAD Alert*, n. d.), which are e-mails about instances of defamation that go out to the general membership of GLAAD. *GLAAD Alerts* provide a synopsis of the issue GLAAD is responding to, as well as contact information if GLAAD members want to write opinion letters to the source of the defamation. Additionally, as GLAAD maintains good relations with major media entities, GLAAD spokespeople are often able to appear on news programs to express their position on the defamation to which the organization is reacting. Although the majority of instances of defamation do not require this level of reaction, GLAAD has shown that it has the ability to conduct major educational campaigns with great success. The *Dr. Laura* campaign demonstrates how GLAAD incorporates proactive and cooperative–and, at times, reactive–media strategies to successfully operate a media advocacy campaign for the LGBT community.

Background of "AM/FM Activism": The Dr. Laura Campaign

The AM/FM strategy developed out of what would become known as GLAAD's "*Dr. Laura* campaign." In May 1997, Dr. Laura Schlessinger, a licensed family counselor with a popular conservative AM radio talk show and newsletter, referred to homosexuals as "biological errors" in an editorial column (Garry, 2000). As this comment was an egregious example of defamation, GLAAD issued a press statement that both outlined their opposition to Schlessinger's comment and cited past examples of defamation, such as her repeated attacks on nontraditional family forms. Exemplifying GLAAD's dedication to cooperative tactics, the organization also met with Schlessinger and her producers to discuss the incident, though the meeting brought no resolution of the issue. Realizing that this issue required community support, GLAAD began to send out *GLAAD Alerts* informing members about the Schlessinger issue and asking for help in monitoring Schlessinger's radio programs. Through this community mobilization, teams of volunteers began recording broadcasts of the show in their local areas and sending transcripts to GLAAD, which allowed the organization to keep abreast of Schlessinger's defamatory comments.

When Paramount Domestic Television announced that they planned to start production on a television talk show, *Dr. Laura*, GLAAD began to step up its efforts to mobilize the LGBT community to show Paramount that there was a great deal of opposition to Schlessinger. From March to July 2000, members of GLAAD and Stopdrlaura.com, an LGBT activist-run Website dedicated to stopping *Dr. Laura* from airing, met with community activists from across the country, as well as TV station managers who had purchased Schlessinger's show in an attempt to raise concern about her homophobic comments. In May 2000, GLAAD also launched "Local Laura Activism," an online organizing tool that provided grassroots activists with the information and resources to successfully launch an educational campaign about Schlessinger at their local level by contacting local stations that had purchased Schlessinger's show. By

August 2000, enough LGBT community activists had begun to utilize GLAAD's "Local Laura Activism," that the organization launched "Local Laura Activism Version 2.0." The new organizing tool offered even more access to important resources for community activists interested in educating their local media about Schlessinger's defamatory past comments, as it provided them the addresses and contact information for advertisers, Paramount, and *Dr. Laura's* radio program.

Despite the opposition, *Dr. Laura* debut on September 11, 2000. With the debut of the show, community activists took on a more integral role in GLAAD's campaign. First, volunteers from across the country kept track of where Schlessinger's show would air and on what stations. This information was sent to GLAAD, which began putting daily postings on their Website, reporting where *Dr. Laura* was airing. Second, community activists began meeting with local TV stations in an effort to get a guarantee that these stations would not air episodes of *Dr. Laura* that had anti-gay content. Volunteers also continued to monitor the show, alerting GLAAD when anti-gay content was aired and on what station. Third, volunteers were integral in educating local and national advertisers about Schlessinger's defamatory comments. Due to the local educational campaigns launched in various communities, stations began moving *Dr. Laura* from its daytime slot to a post-midnight position. Additionally, most of the major advertisers began to pull their ads as they realized the depth of the controversy surrounding Schlessinger. By November 2000, *Dr. Laura* had been dropped from a daytime slot to a post-midnight slot in most of the major media markets and the lack of advertising revenue started to create financial problems for the show. Although Paramount maintained its dedication to making new episodes of *Dr. Laura*, Kraig T. Kitchin, President/COO of Premiere Radio Networks, publicly announced in March 2001 that his company had lost over $30 million on Schlessinger's show and that he should have addressed her anti-gay comments in the beginning (Premier Radio Networks, 2001). This appeared to be the final setback for *Dr. Laura*, and, on March 30, 2001, Paramount announced its decision to cancel the show (No "Laura" to watch, 2001).

The *Dr. Laura* campaign clearly illustrates GLAAD's dedication to moving beyond hostile tactics such as boycotts to embrace more cooperative and proactive strategies. In the early stages of the campaign, GLAAD met with Schlessinger and her producers to attempt to bring about change from within. When this failed to bring about the desired results, GLAAD switched to educational tactics, such as informing advertisers about Schlessinger's anti-gay views, working with TV station managers to get guarantees about not airing anti-gay statements, and meeting with Paramount executives about the content of Schlessinger's show. Educating advertisers proved to have the strongest effect, because it occurred before *Dr. Laura* went to air. Avoiding hostile tactics, such as threatening to remove financial support via boycotts, GLAAD and members of the LGBT community communicated to potential advertisers that putting their product on *Dr. Laura* would alienate a section of their consumer base, as well as align their product with anti-gay sentiments.

However, the success of the *Dr. Laura* campaign also illustrates the important role that local community activists played in the work of the national organization. The *Dr. Laura* campaign relied heavily on cooperation between GLAAD and LGBT community activists. GLAAD members and organizers from Stopdrlaura.com traveled frequently from city to city to work with community activists to form a volunteer base that could be mobilized when action, such as a letter writing campaign or local mediations with TV station managers, was needed. Although GLAAD provided resources, such as contact information for station managers and advertisers and tips for writing successful advocacy letters, community activists played a key role in educating advertisers and station managers in their local areas about Schlessinger's anti-gay remarks and the growing opposition to her show that existed in the LGBT community. Thus, by utilizing GLAAD's online organizing tool, "Local Laura Activism," community activists could not only become part of a growing GLAAD volunteer network, but could also take local ownership of a national campaign.

The successful alliance between GLAAD as a national nonprofit organization and local community activists led GLAAD to strategize about the possibilities for continuing such alliances beyond large-scale campaigns such as the *Dr. Laura* campaign. In February 2001, GLAAD announced the creation of "AM/FM Activism," an online organizing kit that would provide interested activists with the tools for launching a successful anti-defamation campaign in their local community.

"AM/FM ACTIVISM": GOING BACK TO THE COMMUNITY

Buoyed by the imminent cancellation of *Dr. Laura* in February 2001, GLAAD began to focus on how to best take advantage of the networks they had forged in the last three years with community activists who had worked on the *Dr. Laura* campaign in their local area. GLAAD realized that one way to make use of these community networks was to provide interested activists with tools for launching anti-defamation campaigns in their own areas. As a national LGBT organization, GLAAD offices across the country receive several phone calls a week from members of the LGBT community reporting on anti-gay defamation in their local area. Although GLAAD tries to provide advice to each caller, it is simply not possible for GLAAD employees to launch a large-scale campaign in every community that experiences defamation. As the online "Local Laura Activism" kit had met with such wide success, however, GLAAD decided to experiment with reworking this resource model in the form of "AM/FM Activism," an "on-line initiative that allow[s] community activists to take GLAAD's work to their community" (Testone, n.d.).

In developing "AM/FM Activism," GLAAD focused on creating an organizing tool that fit with the types of defamation most callers reported to GLAAD. Since GLAAD monitors the majority of national media, as well as cultivates and maintains ties with national film and television companies and national newspapers, members usually are abreast of national defamation issues. Examining the calls coming in from community activists, however, GLAAD realized that the majority of these calls reported defamation that had occurred on local radio talk shows. Local radio shows are able to flourish even with blatantly offensive anti-gay content, because radio remains a very cost-effective form of advertising, ensuring that even the most offensive shows still have local sponsorship. Additionally, radio talk shows fall under the realm of entertainment, and, as such, are not held to providing a balance of opinions, making it harder for local activists to have a basis for lodging complaints about anti-gay speech with the Federal Communications Commission (FCC), the organization that monitors radio content.

Getting to this type of local defamation was a key point on GLAAD's agenda. GLAAD was particularly concerned with defamation being reported from small towns, which research shows tend to have higher levels of sexual prejudice (Herek, 2000). As suggested by research on the relative isolation of gays and lesbians in small towns (Miller, 1989), GLAAD speculated that many activists in smaller communities might not have LGBT media or advocacy groups in their area, making it harder to find a community base for fighting defamation. A national organization like GLAAD does not have the resources to launch "Laura-level" campaigns in each community that is experiencing radio defamation. "AM/FM Activism," then, became a format for addressing anti-gay defamation flourishing on local, small-town radio stations.

Reworking the tools used in the *Dr. Laura* campaign for educating sponsors and advertisers, "AM/FM Activism" provides community activists with on-line access to a variety of resources and organizing strategies, as well as advice from GLAAD media experts when needed. With GLAAD behind them as a resource, community activists can build local support to address radio defamation in their community, which is considered a major goal of "AM/FM Activism." This type of support can add a significant edge to a local campaign, as it shows local radio stations and DJs that they are not simply being challenged by a handful of members from their local community; rather, they are being challenged by a national network of activists who have the skills and knowledge to successfully launch a full-scale anti-defamation campaign that could ultimately garner national attention. Additionally, by building further networks between local activists and GLAAD, the organization will have a wider volunteer action base in a variety of communities that they can work to mobilize in national defamation campaigns, creating a bridge between national and local activists.

"AM/FM Activism" Step-by-Step

Logistically "AM/FM Activism" functions like a small-scale version of the *Dr. Laura* campaign. When GLAAD is contacted by a community activist about local radio defamation, GLAAD employees direct the caller to the GLAAD Website to read about the steps in building an AM/FM campaign. Giving radio-specific examples of the different types of defamation, the handbook educates activists about how to identify what type of defamation is occurring. Once the type of defamation has been identified, activists are encouraged to think about "choosing your battles." From previous experience working with radio defamation, GLAAD is able to specify which types of defamation can successfully be addressed via educational campaigns. For example, defamation in the form of the invisibility of LGBT listeners or casual prejudice from DJs can usually be addressed successfully using "AM/FM Activism" tools. However, defamation coming from "shock jocks," DJs who make their name by humorous satire of the entire population, often cannot be resolved, as the content of these types of shows is designed to be offensive. Additionally, GLAAD discourages spending resources and time on attempting to address defamation on religious talk shows, as the likelihood of these shows altering their content is slim. If after reading these cautionary notes, however, activists see an opportunity for launching a successful campaign, they are encouraged to focus on the next step: gathering evidence.

In order to make a case against a radio show for repeated defamation, activists must have ample evidence to support their claim. For example, in the case of casual prejudice or vicious slander, tapes of offensive remarks are needed to show a pattern of anti-gay statements. Activists are advised to begin taping the show daily to document repeated anti-gay statements. Additionally, information about the DJ or talk show host, as well as the radio station and station manager, need to be gathered so that activists can learn who they are dealing with. As evidenced in the *Dr. Laura* campaign, gathering this type of information is important; GLAAD was able to show that Schlessinger had a history of making offensive statements not only about the LGBT community, but about single mothers and career women as well. Providing this history helped to bolster

GLAAD's case against Schlessinger, as they were able to document a variety of defamatory statements.

The last step before embarking on an educational campaign is to decide the desired outcome of the campaign. As with the tactics for media advocacy, the goal of educational campaigns differs based on what type of defamation has occurred. In the case of invisibility, often the goal is simply the inclusion of LGBT listeners' requests, which often is fairly easy to ensure once DJs realize they are alienating a section of their listeners. In the case of vicious slander, however, activists may seek to gain assurances from talk show hosts and station managers that the anti-gay defamation will cease or that the talk show host will issue an apology to the LGBT community. This goal is harder to realize and often involves educating advertisers and publicizing the issue through a variety of news outlets. However, GLAAD stresses that these types of campaigns are not impossible; they just need a great deal of strategic planning, the next step in "AM/FM Activism."

"AM/FM Activism" in Practice

A campaign against anti-gay defamation in a Florida case illustrates how the "AM/FM Activism" strategic plan is developed. In September 2001, a local Florida activist contacted GLAAD Atlanta to report an extreme example of defamation on a local radio talk show. The caller reported that a local radio show had a character named "Larry the Cable Guy," who frequently pontificated on national news events. Recently, "Larry" had been addressing the September 11 terrorist attacks and was referring to the Taliban as "Tali-queers," "Tali-fags," and "Afgani-fags." The local activist had attempted to address this anti-gay defamation through a call to the station manager but had received little satisfaction. When local activists are unable to get a successful resolution to their defamation complaint from station managers, GLAAD encourages them to begin a more wide-scale campaign that incorporates local LGBT media. Thus, GLAAD pointed the activist to "AM/FM Activism," encouraging him to launch an educational campaign in his community. Specifically, the activist wrote letters to the FCC and the National Association of Broadcasters, as well as contacted local LGBT media, such as the local LGBT newspaper. GLAAD also put the interested activist in contact with Equality Florida, a regional LGBT advocacy group, and provided him with contacts for Florida newspapers. In addition, the activist regularly contacted the station manager when he heard examples of defamation to make sure the station realized that the issue had not simply disappeared.

In this Florida case, one individual interested in bringing a stop to the anti-gay defamation on his local radio talk show started the educational campaign. Since the inception of the campaign, he has been able to use GLAAD as a resource also to form networks with other activists in his area. This fusion of national resources and local activism is the main goal of "AM/FM Activism," as it creates a local network that can take on local defamation and provides GLAAD with a national pool of activists that can be utilized when another large-scale campaign, such as the *Dr. Laura* campaign, emerges. As evidenced by the Florida case, having resources such as "AM/FM Activism" not only empowers individuals to effect change locally, but also creates political alliances that can play an integral role in future LGBT media activism, illustrating the importance of local-level activism as a counterpart for national advocacy.

CONCLUSION

The landscape of media advocacy has shifted radically in the last twenty years. Although the early members of what would come to be known as the Gay and Lesbian Alliance Against Defamation were forced to used hostile tactics, such as protests and boycotts, to react to anti-gay defamation, media entities now recognize the usefulness of including media advocacy groups in the production process to stop defamation before it occurs (Rossman, 2000). As illustrated by the success of the *Dr. Laura* campaign, GLAAD has moved beyond hostile tactics to embrace cooperative and proactive strategies of working with the media in order to ensure that the LGBT community has a voice in how they are represented in film, television, and newsprint. However, although GLAAD holds a position as a key player on the field of media advocacy, it does not have the resources to go beyond monitoring national media, meaning local-level anti-gay defamation often goes unaddressed. New strategies that work to bridge the gap between national-level organizations such as GLAAD and local activists willing to take on advocacy work are needed in order to address anti-gay defamation in smaller communities. Projects such as "AM/FM Activism" are the first step in creating new organizing tools that can empower interested activists to effectively monitor and educate their local media about LGBT concerns and issues Although still using national organizations as resources and allies.

Although taking up media advocacy campaigns at the local level involves a great deal of commitment and hard work, the necessity of this local addition to national media advocacy cannot be underestimated. In addition to creating local and national alliances, online resources such as "AM/FM Activism" provide interested activists and community groups with opportunities to begin to forge their own local activist networks, so that in future instances of defamation, a local response base can be mobilized. Having this local voice speaking out against anti-gay defamation can be more effective than bringing in a national organization, as it emphasizes that the opposition to defamation is coming from within the community, rather than being imposed from a national watchdog. Educational campaigns launched by local activists also are more likely to have an impact on local advertisers, as they demonstrate that these companies are alienating their local consumer base. Thus, the creation of more media advocacy strategies along the lines of "AM/FM Activism" has the potential not only to allow local activists to form alliances with national advocacy groups, but also to aid in creating a local activist network that can lay the groundwork for more committed grassroots LGBT activism in the future.

REFERENCES

"AM/FM Activism": step by step. (n.d.). Retrieved October 22, 2002, from <www.glaad.org/org/projects/amfm/index.html?record=2731>.

Garry, J. M. (2000, May 10). Update: Glaad's work regarding Dr. Laura Schlessinger. Retrieved October 20, 2001, from: <www.glaad.org/org/about/letters/index.html?record=532>.

GLAAD accomplishments. (n.d.). Retrieved October 22, 2002, from <www.glaad.org/org/about/index.html?record=64>.

GLAAD Alert. (n.d.). Retrieved October 22, 2002, from <www.glaad.org/org/publications/alerts/index.html>.

Herek, G. (2000). The psychology of sexual prejudice. *Current Directions in Psychological Science, 9*, 19-22.

Miller, N. (1989). *In search of gay America: Women and men in a time of change*. New York: Harper & Row.

Monitor and response. (n.d.). New York: Gay & Lesbian Alliance Against Defamation.

No "Laura" to watch. (2001, April 3). Glaad Laura Watch. Retrieved October 20, 2001, from <www.glaad.org/org/publications/drlaura/index.html?record=2741>.

Premiere Radio Networks loses $30 million on Dr. Laura. (2001, March 13). Glaad Laura Watch. Retrieved October 20, 2001, from: <www.glaad.org/org/publications/drlaura/index.html?record=2721>.

Rossman, G. (2000). Hostile and cooperative advocacy. In M. Sumin & G. Rossman (Eds.), *Advocacy groups and the entertainment industry* (pp. 85-104). Westport, CT: Praeger.

Russo, V. (1987). *The celluloid closet: Homosexuality in the movies*. New York: Harper & Row.

Streeter, T. (2000). What is an advocacy group, anyway? In M. Sumin & G. Rossman (Eds.), *Advocacy groups and the entertainment industry* (pp. 77-84). Westport, CT: Praeger.

Testone, G. (n.d.). A letter from GLAAD's Regional media director. Retrieved October 20, 2002, from <www.glaad.org/org/projects/amfm/index.html>.

Vaid, U. (1995). *Virtual equality: The mainstreaming of gay and lesbian liberation*. New York: Anchor Books.

A Gay and Lesbian Congregation Seeks Social Justice for Other Marginalized Communities

Lon B. Johnston
David Jenkins

SUMMARY. The Cathedral of Hope in Dallas, Texas, is the world's largest gay and lesbian congregation. As an unabashedly liberal church, the Cathedral of Hope views social justice as the foundation of theological beliefs and the heart of community building activities with other marginalized and oppressed people. These actions of social justice and community building have produced an unexpected outcome. Social justice has been returned to this congregation in the form of community affirmation, acceptance, recognition, and advocacy. Thus, one significant way for gays and lesbians to achieve social justice is to work for the same with other oppressed people, devoid of strings or hidden agendas. *[Article copies available for a fee from The Haworth Document Delivery Service:*

Lon B. Johnston, PhD, LMSW-ACP, is Assistant Professor of Social Work, School of Social Work, University of Texas at Arlington, PO Box 19129, Arlington, TX 76019 (E-mail: johnston@uta.edu).

David Jenkins, PhD, LMSW-ACP, is Associate Professor of Social Work, Department of Social Work, Texas Christian University, TCU Box 298750, Ft. Worth, TX 76129 (E-mail: D.Jenkins@tcu.edu).

The authors thank Mr. Rusty Gage, from the Cathedral of Hope, for his assistance with this project.

[Haworth co-indexing entry note]: "A Gay and Lesbian Congregation Seeks Social Justice for Other Marginalized Communities." Johnston, Lon B., and David Jenkins. Co-published simultaneously in *Journal of Gay & Lesbian Social Services* (Harrington Park Press, an imprint of The Haworth Press, Inc.) Vol. 16, No. 3/4, 2004, pp. 193-206; and: *Gay and Lesbian Rights Organizing: Community-Based Strategies* (ed: Yolanda C. Padilla) Harrington Park Press, an imprint of The Haworth Press, Inc., 2004, pp. 193-206. Single or multiple copies of this article are available for a fee from The Haworth Document Delivery Service [1-800-HAWORTH, 9:00 a.m. - 5:00 p.m. (EST). E-mail address: docdelivery@haworthpress.com].

Journal of Gay & Lesbian Social Services, Vol. 16(3/4) 2004
http://www.haworthpress.com/store/product.asp?sku=J041
© 2004 by The Haworth Press, Inc. All rights reserved.
10.1300/J041v16n03_13

1-800-HAWORTH. E-mail address: <docdelivery@haworthpress.com> Website: <http://www.HaworthPress.com> © 2004 by The Haworth Press, Inc. All rights reserved.]

KEYWORDS. Gay and lesbian, social justice, community building, faith-based community practice

Two 10-ton air conditioning units . . . $15,000 to help defray installation costs . . . a new home built on the foundation of one that burned . . . removal of debris from streets, yards, and alleys . . . 450 holiday food baskets . . . 625 Christmas gifts for children . . . 8,000 pounds of canned goods . . . 622 different medical procedures . . . $10,000 worth of school supplies and uniforms . . .

This is a partial description of both the one-time and ongoing social justice and community building actions of the world's largest gay and lesbian congregation, the Cathedral of Hope (COH) located in Dallas, Texas. Enacting this commitment to social justice, even while encountering barriers within American culture that work to deflect such actions, is one way this congregation remains vibrant and flourishes. The members of the COH are challenged by obstacles that work to reinforce the status quo while power and assets remain unjust and oppressive, obstacles such as monetary, governmental, and social restrictions (Van Soest, 1996). Members of the COH congregation continually address these barriers as they act with compassion, fight social injustice, and follow the words of Mother Theresa, "Just let them see what we do" ("Community outreach," n.d.).

This article describes the social justice actions of the members of the COH as they advocate for equality of power and assets for oppressed, marginalized, and disenfranchised people and as they challenge monetary, governmental, and social impediments that limit social justice. The serendipitous outcome of these actions has been the return of social justice to this congregation as evidenced by community affirmation, acceptance, recognition, and advocacy. First, the article briefly examines concepts of social justice, dialogue, and community building. These three concepts mirror the values of this congregation, and they also are components of this church's philosophy that challenge members to look beyond themselves and focus on marginalized and oppressed members of society. Next, the article describes the COH and details five of the church's myriad social justice and community outreach actions. The article concludes with a discussion of the ways social justice and empowerment have been returned to the church because of its own advocacy for and dialogue with marginalized, disenfranchised, and vulnerable people.

LITERATURE REVIEW

Numerous articles in the social science literature focus on community organizing and community building (Allen & Boettcher, 2000; Arches, 1999; Dunlop & Angell, 2001; Kaufman, 2001; Mizrahi & Rosenthal, 2001; Roberts-DeGennaro, 1997). Yet the literature provides limited information about community building by faith communities as a means of advocating for social justice (Johnson, Noe, Collins, Strader, & Bucholtz, 2000; Staral, 2000). Many articles focus on empowerment through social justice (Dean, 1998; Dean & Rhodes, 1998; Haynes & White, 1999; Nagda et al., 1999; Rose, 2000; Swenson, 1998; Van Soest, 1994; Van Soest, Cannon, & Grant, 2000), but, as with the literature on community building, very little research has focused on faith communities advocating for social justice.

Social Justice and Dialogue

Social justice is a core value of the COH, and, therefore, warrants elaboration and clarification. Dorothy Van Soest (1995) in the *Encyclopedia of Social Work*, identified three elements of social justice–"legal justice, commutative justice, and distributive justice"–and claimed that distributive justice, which is concerned with "what society owes a person," was the most significant of the three (p. 1811).

Van Soest (1994) also identified three alternative conceptions of justice: libertarian, utilitarian, and egalitarian. Of these three, George and Wilding (1976) argued for the egalitarian perspective because it "directly challenges the assumption that society can be rightly ordered it if is based on social and economic inequalities" (p. 71). The COH has never actually used the terms "distributive justice" or "egalitarian perspective." However, it is clear this congregation's philosophy resonates with these concepts. This church is concerned with what society owes its citizens and takes actions that go beyond simply trying to address social and economic inequality.

Employing a concept of social justice based on the egalitarian perspective, the COH has laid a conceptual foundation for community building and engagement. Many of the communities most in need of social justice, "have lost hope in the future" (Haynes & White, 1999, p. 389). Thus, the only way to honestly connect with such communities is to "build real, not artificial, bridges" (Haynes & White, 1999, p. 389) supported by the egalitarian perspective, distributive justice, and dialogue. Becker, Chasin, Chasin, Herzig, and Roth (1995) define dialogue as "a horizontal communication process aimed at fostering deeper understanding, mutual respect, empathic connection, and discovery of shared meaning among participants" (p. 145).

Community Building

The functional-community organizing model seems to be a natural expression of the egalitarian perspective and distributive justice. According to Johnson and colleagues (2000), this organizing model goes beyond advocacy and the provision of services and emphasizes actions "that change policies, behaviors, and attitudes in relation to the chosen" (p. 5) social justice issue. The rationale for actions that need to be taken is weighed against the principles of the egalitarian perspective and distributive justice. The functional-community organizing model complements the Cathedral of Hope's social justice and community building efforts because "while people in this type of community may or may not live in proximity, they share a concern about a common set of issues relating to the mission of their community" (Johnson et al., 2000, p. 5). This is an accurate description of the membership of the COH in Dallas.

Other theoretical concepts from the social work literature can be found in the Cathedral of Hope's philosophy regarding community building: strengths perspective and feminist practice. From a strengths perspective, they have no interest in employing "theories that pathologize, emphasize deficits, and 'blame the victim'" (Swenson, 1998, p. 530). Perhaps because many members of this church have experienced victim blaming and being pathologized, the congregation has no interest in depriving others of respect, which in turn eventually cuts "people off from potential internal and external resources, thus increasing their relative deprivation" (Swenson, 1998, p. 530). The COH is aware that any time the activities of a group, community, or culture are labeled as aberrant, inept, or depraved, the response is often to engaging "in boundary maintaining activities or . . . disengaging from the process altogether" (Lawson & Alameda-Lawson, 2001, p. 85). Such knowledge, often from personal experience, led the congregation to focus on resilience, resources, possibilities, and hopes of various groups with which the Cathedral builds bridges of cooperation and understanding.

One of the most important principles of feminist thought is that the personal is political (Maher & Tetreault, 1994). This thought is consistent with the belief of COH that one cannot separate personal relationships from existing social structures. Another important feminist principle that this congregation incorporates into their social justice activities is "an alternative way of understanding and using power based on collaboration and cooperation, rather than on competition" (Swenson, 1998, p. 531). Community building activities of the Cathedral are approached from a standpoint of collaboration that requires asking questions and listening, working alongside the oppressed, and sharing decisionmaking. Through the use of collaboration and cooperation, the COH tries to "harness the community's assets, expertise, and resources; to create local ownership; and to build a unified community in the process" (Mizrahi, 2001, p. 183).

The Cathedral of Hope's philosophy of social justice is based upon building bridges to other communities that focus not only on providing services, but also on policy, behavior, and attitude changes by the powers that be. The Cathedral built its philosophy of change on the egalitarian perspective and distributive justice, and upon theoretical concepts from the strengths perspective and feminist practice, without labeling their activities as such, and even possibly being unaware of these concepts found in the social work literature.

THE CATHEDRAL OF HOPE

On July 30, 1970, a group of 12 people gathered at a home in Dallas, Texas, to discuss the establishment of a Metropolitan Community Church (MCC). Because of continued growth in the 1980s, the church attempted to purchase several existing church buildings, but when the membership of those churches discovered a gay congregation was the potential buyer, they refused to sell ("The beginning," n.d.). According to Rev. Mike Piazza, senior pastor of The Cathedral of Hope (formerly known as MCC Dallas), one congregation even said they would "burn their building to the ground rather than have a gay congregation using the facility" (Cathedral of Hope, 1998).

In December of 1992, the COH held its first worship service in its newly constructed building. Membership had grown to 1,000. In a period of less than 10 years, membership tripled and stands at over 3,000 today, making the COH the world's largest predominantly gay and lesbian church ("The gay 90s," n.d.).

The vision of the Cathedral of Hope is to be "a community of hope; proclaiming God's inclusive love; removing barriers to faith; and empowering all people to grow in grace toward wholeness" ("Our vision," n.d.). Six paradigms explain how that vision is put into action, and two of these paradigms relate directly to concepts of social justice and community building:

> Paradigm number three, *We are a liberal Christian church*: By that we mean that we willingly embrace such traditionally liberal values as helping advocating for the poor, valuing the environment, recognizing as sinful such oppressive attitudes as sexism, ageism, racism, and homophobia.
>
> Paradigm number four, *Caring for those who are hurting or in need is the chief expression of what it means to be a disciple of Jesus Christ*: Caring for others is the soul of who we are. It keeps us from being consumed with ourselves. It is the antidote for the toxic effects of materialism that is consuming our society. ("Our vision," n.d.)

The "hands on" enactment of these paradigms comes from the Cathedral's outreach ministry that encourages members to move from a self-focus to an others-focus by addressing the needs of the hopeless, vulnerable, disenfranchised, and oppressed. In the year 2000, the congregation donated goods and services totaling more than $1.3 million to help bring social justice to vulnerable, disenfranchised, and oppressed people in Dallas, Texas, and in various locations around the world ("Community outreach," n.d.).

SOCIAL JUSTICE/COMMUNITY OUTREACH: "JUST LET THEM SEE WHAT WE DO"

The words of Mother Teresa, "Just let them see what we do," have been adopted as the motto of the Cathedral of Hope's social justice/community outreach programs ("Community outreach," n.d.). These words serve as a motivating force for the righting of injustices and providing of equality for no other reason than compassion for others.

Most of the Cathedral's ongoing efforts toward social justice began when a need was identified by a staff member, church member, or community representative. Then (1) representatives from the church began a dialogue and bridge-building efforts with the persons, group, or community in need; (2) questions were asked regarding what the Cathedral could do to work alongside those affected by the problem; (3) one person from the church was assigned responsibility for planning and coordinating the church's actions to alleviate the problem; (4) opportunity for involvement was advertised to church members; (5) members responded; and (6) working alongside those affected by the problem, COH members collaborated on efforts to work toward justice. Five of the COH's most significant programs are Child of Hope, the rehabilitation and building of homes, neighborhood cleanups, health clinics, and food distribution.

Child of Hope

Founded in 2000, the Child of Hope program's initial goal was to raise enough money to fund the position of a person who would work with the Dallas Independent School District and with other congregations to replicate the partnerships that the COH had developed with neighborhood elementary and middle schools. In 2001, an orphanage the Cathedral had sponsored for a number of years in the Dominican Republic was brought under the umbrella of the Child of Hope program. Thus, monies raised through this program will now be divided between public school partnerships and the Dominican orphanage.

Public School Partnerships

In 1997, the COH began a relationship with an elementary school located directly across the street from the church building. The majority of children attending this school are Hispanic and come from low-income families, and 97 percent of the children qualify for the federal free or reduced-price lunch program ("Student ethnic composition," n.d.).

The relationship with the elementary school began when a staff member from the church walked across the street and began a dialogue by asking how the Cathedral could help the school. Since then, the congregation has donated several hundred thousand dollars worth of tutoring, school supplies, and uniforms. Also, the Cathedral purchased an air conditioning system for and covered the cost of installation in this year-round school's gymnasium, planted trees on the campus, renovated the garden and grounds, and built picnic tables. In addition, the congregation donated musical instruments so the school could begin a fine arts program (R. Gage, personal communication, November 27, 2001).

Since the church became involved with the elementary school, children's test scores have risen, and the school is no longer classified as one of DISD's low performing schools. Teachers believe that tangibles such as having uniforms to wear, adequate school supplies, an improved physical environment, and tutors may have been responsible for some of the school's educational improvement. Dr. Michael Ralston, Dallas Independent School District's Director of Community Relations said, "The school's faculty and staff credit the Cathedral's volunteer tutors with being one of the reasons the school has gone from being classified as 'low-performing' to 'acceptable'" ("After delay," 2000).

In the fall of 2001, the COH began a similar partnership with a middle school a few blocks from the church building. The following note, sent to the Cathedral by a staff member at the middle school, illustrates the impact of this partnership on one child's life:

> The boy came to school with just the shirt on his back because his family had to leave San Antonio quickly and wasn't able to take any possessions. So imagine his surprise and confusion when he came to [the middle school], and they started giving him a backpack filled with school supplies. He looked at the staff person in disbelief and asked, "How much is this?" The staff person replied, "Nothing. It's given by people in the community who care about you." (M. Warejcka, personal communication, November 18, 2001)

Dominican Republic Orphanage

In 1997, the Cathedral of Hope began financial support of an orphanage and school located in Santo Domingo, Dominican Republic. Believing that the congregation should be involved in the life of the orphanage in other ways than just financially, the church sought ways to nurture the children physically, emotionally, and spiritually. Beginning in 2000, groups of church volunteers, paying their own expenses, spent a week at the orphanage getting to know the children through songs, stories, sports and games, and arts and crafts. Another visit included a health clinic providing check-ups, treatment and medical information, and daily hygiene products. A recent volunteer team was composed of educators who worked with the teachers on curriculum development. All trips have included completing repairs and renovations to the orphanage's buildings and the construction of a playground structure ("Little eyes," n.d.).

According to Becky Bridges, World Missions Coordinator at the COH, The Child of Hope program is one way of addressing social justice issues that children at the orphanage face on a daily basis. "The Child of Hope program will help children at the orphanage ... get regular healthy meals, clothing to wear to school, basic health care, and better schooling" (Bridges, 2001).

For many years the orphanage and school have been under the administration and leadership of a brother and sister who also grew up in an orphanage. In the fall of 2001, the brother, in his 30s, died. Thus, the orphanage is struggling with how to fill the vacuum left by this man's unanticipated death. The orphanage and school administrators faced the potential loss of the property that the orphanage has been leasing for several years. Using money generated through 2001-2002 Advent and Lenten offerings, the COH raised $50,000 so the orphanage and school could actually purchase the land (R. Gage, personal communication, November 27, 2001).

Rehabilitation/Building of Homes

For at least five years, The Cathedral of Hope has been involved in home renewal projects through the city of Dallas' People Helping People program. These renovations were made to bring the homes of elderly and disabled people into city code compliance. Since 2000, 34 homes have been brought into code compliance through the efforts of over 1,000 church members and community residents (R. Gage, personal communication, November 27, 2001). This is but one example of successful attempts to address social justice and build community through the provision of adequate shelter.

Neighborhood Cleanups

The first major neighborhood cleanup by the COH occurred in 1999. Over 750 volunteers from the COH and the neighborhood worked together, removing trash and other debris from alleys and streets, trimming overgrown brush and tree limbs, and cleaning the grounds of the neighborhood elementary school. At the end of the day, church and neighborhood volunteers gathered to share a meal and to continue developing relationships that had been formed that day (R. Gage, personal communication, November 27, 2001).

Similar neighborhood cleanups occurred in 2000 and 2001, with the 2001 cleanup focusing on an impoverished neighborhood in an unincorporated area of Dallas. Although residents in that neighborhood live close enough to downtown Dallas to clearly see the skyline, they have no access to city services. Their water is yellow, and values of homes range from approximately $500 to $15,000. This occurs in a city where homes in more affluent Dallas neighborhoods can be worth millions of dollars. The two main goals of the 2001 cleanup were met: (1) to restore some hope to the community and (2) to call attention to city officials regarding how badly conditions really are in the neighborhood (R. Gage, personal communication, November 27, 2001).

Health Clinics

In 1995, the Cathedral of Hope committed to funding a health clinic specifically focused on people who, for whatever reasons, had "fallen through the cracks." This financial commitment spurred the development of a clinic that still exists today, which the congregation has continued to support financially. The most recent financial support funded a position for an additional nurse (R. Gage, personal communication, November 27, 2001).

An outgrowth of the support of this health clinic has been the Cathedral's sponsorship of free health fairs that utilize the facilities of the elementary school across the street from the church building. Volunteers from the congregation, especially members who work in health care fields, administer, organize, and provide medical services to anyone in need. The most recent addition to these fairs has been a partnership formed with major medical centers in Dallas, whose staff provide a wide array of on-site health procedures during these twice-yearly events (R. Gage, personal communication, November 27, 2001). In the fall of 2001, the health fair was staffed with almost 100 volunteers who provided free medical services to 279 people, including 622 different procedures and the provision of flu shots to 175 people ("Community outreach," n.d.).

People who needed follow-up care were referred to the clinic supported by the congregation. Since the COH implemented health fairs, the medical director of the clinic reported a doubling of caseloads ("Healthcare 2001," n.d.).

Food Distribution

Since its inception in February of 2000, the Cathedral of Hope's food distribution program has involved members in monthly food and hygiene product donations for local food banks. The COH estimates that church members have donated over $100,000 worth of products in almost two years ("Community outreach," n.d.).

Like many congregations, the COH provides traditional Thanksgiving and Christmas meals, serving approximately 1,600 people each holiday. Volunteers from the Cathedral deliver the ready-to-cook meals directly to the recipients, including Bosnian refugees, persons living with AIDS, a local women's shelter, and families of children attending the congregation's adopted elementary and middle schools. Providing meals to families connected to the church's adopted schools is one other way that the COH interacts with these families and works to ultimately achieve social justice. Providing meals is not a one-time effort, but the meals are symbolic of ongoing care and concern for social justice ("Community outreach," n.d.).

RETURN OF SOCIAL JUSTICE TO THE CATHEDRAL OF HOPE

The social justice/community outreach programs of the Cathedral of Hope have always focused on people, relationships, and needs, and the building of bridges and use of dialogue to address those needs. Such a focus has mandated that the members of the COH move outside the walls of the church building and into the lives and environments of vulnerable and oppressed, as described in the previous section ("Community outreach," n.d.). The motivation for these social justice/community outreach programs has never been on "what's in it for the church or for individual members." Rather, the motivation has come out of compassion for people living where discrimination exists, injustices occur, and hope is often unknown. It is from this type of congregational commitment that the COH has experienced the unanticipated and unsought return of social justice in the form of community affirmation, acceptance, and recognition (R. Gage, personal communication, November 27, 2001).

Along with support from the community, the COH has also faced negative community responses that are intended to pathologize and emphasize deficits of the congregation, while using victim-blaming tactics. The COH has received several bomb threats over the years, and in spite of such threats, the pastoral staff has continued to lead worship services. On numerous occasions the church has been the object of demonstrations from fundamentalist, Christian groups who "greet" members as they arrive for worship. These groups carry signs with reminders of God's supposed hate for gay and lesbian people and use bullhorns to demand repentance from gay and lesbian people.

On occasion, worship services have been interrupted by protestors demanding to tell the congregation "the truth" about God's word. Staff members continually receive threatening e-mails. Recently a group of ministers in Dallas convened a conference that focused on ways of building positive relationships among all races in the community. The COH participated in these talks, and one day of the conference was scheduled to meet at the Cathedral. When participants became aware of the location of the meeting, several ministers withdrew their involvement, and the bishop of one denomination refused to let any of his pastors continue their participation.

In light of such experiences, members of the Cathedral of Hope could have focused on their shame and self-hatred. However, members chose to focus their energy in a positive manner by working for social justice for other oppressed and disenfranchised people, as described earlier. In doing so, the congregation discovered an unexpected byproduct: Efforts in community building resulted in social justice being returned to the COH. For example, in 2000, the COH was honored as the Dallas school district's "business partner of the year" for its collaboration with the neighborhood elementary school ("After delay," 2000). Such affirmation, recognition, and acceptance from outside the gay and lesbian community were the first of their kind for the Cathedral.

The challenge from the Child of Hope program to other faith-based communities to adopt and partner with local schools experienced a credibility boost when the superintendent of the Dallas school district publicly announced his support for the first Child of Hope Conference held in October, 2001 ("DISD child of hope conference set," n.d.). The partnerships formed with major medical centers during the community health fairs have resulted in new understanding and affirmation from highly respected and influential health care institutions that otherwise might never have had the opportunity to interact with gay and lesbian people in such a personal manner. Where initially the health fairs had difficulty attracting representatives from the medical fields, calls are now made to the COH from medical organizations wanting to participate in the health fairs.

In the aftermath of the September 11, 2001, terrorist attacks on New York City and Washington, D.C., the Cathedral of Hope hosted a four-hour "Gathering of Hope" service. The mayor of Dallas endorsed this gathering, and he, along with several city council members participated. An invitation was extended to anyone in the Dallas metroplex who needed help in making sense of this tragedy, and people were urged to come and go as they needed. The entire gathering was broadcast live on a local secular radio station. Participation in this event by the mayor and city council members was another indication of the affirmation and acceptance of the role that the COH plays in bringing community building and social justice to the disenfranchised and oppressed living in the city of Dallas. Such actions by city leaders would only have been dreamed of just a few years earlier ("Vigils and services," n.d.).

These actions affirm that social justice and community affirmation cannot be sought or demanded. For the predominantly gay and lesbian congregation in Dallas, Texas, known as the Cathedral of Hope, social justice has been returned in various ways because this faith-based group was willing to enter into dialogue not only with disenfranchised and oppressed people but also with community leaders and power brokers. Through such dialogue, the powerless as well as the powerful have seen the COH offering no-strings-attached social justice to vulnerable, at-risk, and disenfranchised people, for no other reason than out of compassion. The unexpected outcome has been the return of social justice to this faith-based community of gay and lesbian activists.

CONCLUSION

The Cathedral of Hope in Dallas, Texas, discovered a unique means of achieving social justice, even when the congregation's goal was not focused on social justice for itself. By acting out of compassion for vulnerable, at-risk, and disenfranchised people, and by providing opportunities for the larger Dallas community to "just let them see what we do," the COH has experienced the beginnings of social justice from others through community affirmation, recognition, and acceptance.

REFERENCES

Allen, J., & Boettcher, R. (2000). Passing a mental health levy: Lessons for the community practice professional. *Journal of Community Practice*, 7(3), 21-36.

After delay, DISD authorizes use of church's cool gift to school. (2000, May 8). *The Dallas Morning News*, p. A21.

Arches, J. L. (1999). Challenges and dilemmas in community development. *Journal of Community Practice*, 6(4), 37-55.

Becker, C., Chasin, L., Chasin, R., Herzig, M., & Roth, S. (1995). From stuck debate to new conversation on controversial issues. *Journal of Feminist Family Therapy*, 7(1/2), 143-163.

The beginning, Coming to our own & the gay 90s. Retrieved November 13, 2001, from <www.cathedralofhope.com/history.htm>.

Bridges, B. *Cathedral weekly news* (December 23, 2001), *15*(51), 7.

Cathedral of Hope. (1998). *A Cathedral of Hope* [Video recording]. (Available from The Cathedral of Hope, 5910 Cedar Springs, Dallas, TX 75235)

Community outreach. Retrieved November 13, 2001, from <http://www.cathedral ofhope.com>.

Dean, H. E. (1998). The primacy of the ethical aim in clinical social work: Its relationship to social justice and mental health. *Smith College Studies in Social Work*, 69, 13-21.

Dean, R. G., & Rhodes, M. L. (1998). Social constructionism and ethics: What makes a "better" story? *Families in Society: The Journal of Contemporary Human Services, 79*(3), 254-262.
DISD child of hope conference set. Retrieved October 12, 2001, from <www.dallasisd.org.
Dunlop, J. M., & Angell, G. B. (2001). Inside-outside: Boundary-spanning challenges in building rural health coalitions. *Professional-Development, 4*(1), 40-48.
The gay 90s. Retrieved November 13, 2001, from <www.cathedralofhope.com>.
George, V., & Wilding, P. (1976). *Ideology and social welfare*. London: Routledge & Kegan Paul.
Haynes, D. T., & White, B. W. (1999). Will the "real" social work please stand up? A call to stand for professional unity. *Social Work, 44*, 385-391.
Healthcare 2001, Retrieved November 23, 2001, from <www.cathedralofhope.com>.
Johnson, K., Noe, T., Collins, D., Strader, T., & Bucholtz, G. (2000). Mobilizing church communities to prevent alcohol and other drug abuse: A model strategy and its evaluation. *Journal of Community Practice, 7*(2), 1-27.
Kaufman, R. (2001). Coalition activity of social change organizations in a public campaign: The influence of motives, resources and processes on levels of activity. *Journal of Community Practice, 9*(4), 21-42.
Lawson, M. A., & Alameda-Lawson, T. (2001). What's wrong with them is what's wrong with us. *Journal of Community Practice, 9*(1), 77-97.
Little eyes, little hands, and lots of big smiles. Retrieved November 13, 2001, from <www.cathedralofhope.com/dr/index.htm>.
Maher, F. A., & Tetreault, M. K. T. (1994). *The feminist classroom*. New York: Harper Collins.
Mizrahi, T. (2001). The status of community organizing in 2001: Community practice context, complexities, contradictions, and contributions. *Research in Social Work Practice, 11*(2), 176-189.
Mizrahi, T., & Rosenthal, B. B. (2001). Complexities of coalition building: Leaders' successes, strategies, struggles, and solutions. *Social Work, 46*, 63-78.
Nagda, B. A., Spearmon, M. L., Holley, L. C., Harding, S., Balassone, M. L., Moise-Swanson, D., & de Mello, S. (1999). Intergroup dialogues: An innovative approach to teaching about diversity and justice in social work programs. *Journal of Social Work Education, 35*, 433-449.
Our vision. Retrieved November 13, 2001, from <www.cathedralofhope.com>.
Roberts-DeGennaro, M. (1997). Conceptual framework of coalitions in an organizational context. *Journal of Community Practice, 4*(1), 91-107.
Rose, S. M. (2000). Reflections on empowerment-based practice. *Social Work, 45*, 403-412.
Staral, J. M. (2000). Building on mutual goals: The intersection of community practice and church-based organizing. *Journal of Community Practice, 7*(3), 85-95.
Student ethnic composition [districtwide]. Retrieved November 23, 2001, from <www.dallasisd.org>.
Swenson, C. R. (1998). Clinical social work's contribution to a social justice perspective. *Social Work, 43*, 527-537.

Van Soest, D. (1994). Strange bedfellows: A call for reordering national priorities from three social justice perspectives. *Social Work, 39,* 710-717.

Van Soest, D. (1995). Peace and social justice. In R. L. Edwards (Ed.), *Encyclopedia of social work* (19th ed., Vol. 3, pp. 1810-1817). Washington, DC: NASW Press.

Van Soest, D. (1996). Impact of social work education on student attitudes and behavior concerning oppression. *Journal of Social Work Education, 32,* 191-202.

Van Soest, D., Canon, R., & Grant, D. (2000). Using an interactive website to educate about cultural diversity and societal oppression. *Journal of Social Work Education, 36,* 463-479.

Vigils and services: Attack on America. Retrieved September 14, 2001, from <archive.dallasnews.cm/cgi-bin/display>.

From Movement Demands to Legislation: Organizing in the LGBT Community in Mexico City

Mirka J. Negroni

SUMMARY. In August 1999, the First Meeting of Lesbians and Lesbian Feminists was held in Mexico City. From this meeting evolved an organized effort for expanded lesbian and gay rights in Mexico City. This article, which, of necessity, is seen through the author's dual role as participant/observer, or insider/outsider, attempts to trace the initial blossoming of two movement ideas–a lesbian kiss-in and legal recognition of same-sex relationships–and their eventual transformation into a major news media event and a proposed piece of city legislation. *[Article copies available for a fee from The Haworth Document Delivery Service: 1-800- HAWORTH. E-mail address: <docdelivery@haworthpress.com> Website: <http://www.HaworthPress.com> © 2004 by The Haworth Press, Inc. All rights reserved.]*

KEYWORDS. Gay and lesbian, social justice, legislation, movements, Mexico City

---

Mirka J. Negroni, BA, MPA, is a research associate at the National Institute for Public Health, School of Public Health, Avenida Universidad 655, Cuernavaca, Morelos CP 62508, Mexico (E-mail: mirka@intertepoz.com).

[Haworth co-indexing entry note]: "From Movement Demands to Legislation: Organizing in the LGBT Community in Mexico City." Negroni, Mirka J. Co-published simultaneously in *Journal of Gay & Lesbian Social Services* (Harrington Park Press, an imprint of The Haworth Press, Inc.) Vol. 16, No. 3/4, 2004, pp. 207-218; and: *Gay and Lesbian Rights Organizing: Community-Based Strategies* (ed: Yolanda C. Padilla) Harrington Park Press, an imprint of The Haworth Press, Inc., 2004, pp. 207-218. Single or multiple copies of this article are available for a fee from The Haworth Document Delivery Service [1-800-HAWORTH, 9:00 a.m. - 5:00 p.m. (EST). E-mail address: docdelivery@haworthpress.com].

Although there is limited documentation, the contemporary movement for lesbian, gay, bisexual, and transgender (LGBT) rights in Mexico has a long and active oral history that can be traced to the politically active 1970s, when various groups began giving a public face to the gay and lesbian movement in Mexico. One of first gay and lesbian groups in Latin America was the *Frente de Liberacion Homosexual* (the Homosexual Liberation Front), organized in 1971 in response to the firing of a Sears employee because of his supposedly homosexual behavior. Currently, LGBT people in Mexico have limited protections, but some important battles have been won, including the passage of Article 281 bis in Mexico City which prohibits discrimination based on sexual orientation. Unlike Nicaragua or Puerto Rico, Mexico has never had laws that penalize homosexuality or lesbianism. But many people faced police oppression in the form of extortion in exchange for not telling parents or coworkers of their lesbianism or homosexuality. People in Mexico have organized in a variety of ways, through local organizations, marches, and the development of a Commission to Denounce Hate Crimes. Mexico has a thriving LGBT movement, with organizations in various large cities throughout the republic and numerous gay and lesbian publications. The vast majority of LGBT organizing has been at the local level, with national efforts often coming apart before they begin.

The main LGBT issues around which people in Mexico have mobilized include the right to have places for recreation. Major opposition to LGBT rights is often based on the incredible strength of the Catholic Church in Mexico, and a major opponent has been *Provida*, an antiabortion organization that spends a significant amount of time denouncing all attempts to ensure any space for Mexico's LGBT citizens. In 1998 during the forum for Sexual Diversity and Human Rights, precursor to the inclusion of sexual orientation in Article 281 bis, *Provida* staged a protest outside the City Assembly. They have also been one of the few groups openly hostile to the *Sociedades de Convivencia* project discussed in this article. There have also been important supporters, such as local political leaders, feminist groups that are not lesbophobic, and many of the leftist intelligensia in the country. Despite the support of some political leaders and the advances in the Mexico City legislature, it is important to note that the conditions for LGBT people in the country vary greatly; anti-gay rhetoric is still acceptable in parts of the country where the influence of the Catholic Church is strongest. I would not venture to claim that I know what the hopes of Mexico's LGBT communities are, but on a personal level I would love to have my relationship recognized so that my partner could enjoy my workplace benefits. I and others want the media to cover events in our lives in a responsible manner. I want more lesbian characters in the soap operas with dignified story lines. I want local television stations to broadcast all of *Buffy the Vampire*

Slayer, and not only the episodes before one of the main characters came out as a lesbian. I want more lesbians, gay men, and transsexuals in the New Mexican Cinema. I believe lesbians with children want to live without the fear that their children might be taken away. Many lesbians and gay men want to form families–some with children, some without–and all want to do this without fear of government intervention.

In this context, the current movement for protective rights for LGBT families is not divorced from the hopes and wants of the larger LGBT movement. However, we must remember that for many lesbian feminists raised in the socialist movement, family rights may not be part of their work agenda; instead, they may prefer to focus on ending workplace discrimination or police violence.

LGBT STORYTELLING: HOW DO WE DOCUMENT OUR LIVES?

As with lesbian, gay, bisexual, and transgender rights movements everywhere, the movements in Mexico have experienced difficulties in documenting their activities and tracing their successes and their failures. Attempts are currently being made to compile a comprehensive history of the LGBT movement (see, for example, Mogrovejo, 2000b, 2001; "Un amor," 2000).

Accounts of past events are forever plagued by the perspective of the teller. Historians face the same difficulties that all researchers face, such as decisions about what to include and what to leave out. I am neither a historian nor, in the case of the LGBT movement, a researcher. I write about LGBT organizing in Mexico City with various disclaimers. First, this account is made by a non-Mexican–in fact, I am a Puerto Rican who lives in Mexico through an accident of love and migration. Second, I do not believe in definite accounts of anything; the best we can do is to "say it how we saw it," recognizing that we leave out other people's truths. Third, I am a firm believer in the need for gender parity in organizing, despite all the difficulties arising when women and men work together toward LGBT rights. Like all stories, this one has to begin somewhere, and for me it begins with the *Primer Encuentro Metropolitano de Lesbianas y Lesbianas Feministas* (First Metropolitan Meeting of Lesbians and Lesbian Feminists).

Primer Encuentro Metropolitano de Lesbianas y Lesbianas Feministas

The *Primer Encuentro Metropolitano de Lesbianas y Lesbianas Feministas* was held in August 1999 in Mexico City. Over the course of three days, more than 200 persons attended. They came from various states in Mexico, though the majority of the women were from Mexico City. Themes for each day's panel discussion included Autonomy, Organizations and Other Diversities, and Dialogue and Representation. The third day was devoted to a discussion of what we can agree on and where we can work together. The *Encuentro* also included a lesbian video screening each day, as well as other cultural events. The *Encuentro* was a watershed event for me and a great number of lesbian activists, because it brought together women who did not often work together. The lesbian movement in Mexico has seen some acrimonious disagreement between lesbian groups, and this meeting provided an opportunity for questions and answers with the leaders of the movement, real and self proclaimed.

I facilitated the final day's table. Despite all of our political and personal differences, we came up with a (very short) list of demands from the *Encuentro* to the world outside. Most of the demands had to do with city ordinances or events and were sent over e-mail to newspapers and to other lesbian groups. We agreed to continue meeting after the conference to try and make some of these demands real, to discuss other ideas that were mentioned at the meeting but which were included not in the list of demands, and to provide a forum where groups could inform each other about what they were doing. Unfortunately, these meetings did not continue beyond a couple of times. The dissolution of the meetings came over a disagreement about having a lesbian march, with claims from the long-time organizers that this would destroy the more than 20-year-old Gay Pride March in Mexico City. Although the meetings did not fully succeed, many of the demands contained in the document were picked up by various lesbian groups. Among these was the idea of a registry for gay and lesbian common law couples *(parejas de hecho)*, a proposal made by the *Enlace Lésbico Femenista* (a coalition of lesbian groups and independents) at the final meeting day. The registry would benefit gay and lesbian couples left out of the common law provisions when the federal legislature changed the wording of the common law statute to include only relationships between a man and a woman.

MEETING BETWEEN ENOÉ URANGA AND ENLACE LÉSBICO

Enoé Uranga, an open lesbian recently elected to the Mexico City Assembly, attended a meeting with members of *Enlace Lésbico Feminista* held on November 12, 2000, at the home of two of the members of the group. The Assemblywoman met with many groups during those early days of her term, in an attempt to collect the demands of the LGBT communities. From a long list of concerns raised to Assemblywoman Uranga, the idea of a registry of unions and a lesbian kiss-in were two of the many that she took up as immediate priorities. Assemblywoman Uranga had already stated her interest in promoting same-sex relationship rights in articles in the lesbian press (Mogrovejo, 2000a). Enoé committed to working on a piece of legislation to present to the City Assembly, and the members of *Enlace Lésbico* agreed to work with her and others toward launching an idea originally called a *Levantamiento Amado* (A Loving Uprising). They agreed that a kiss-in seemed like an appropriate launch for a campaign to secure rights for same-sex couples, and the idea of a kiss-in on Valentine's Day was agreed upon at the meeting.

Shall We Meet?

As is always the case in LGBT organizing, the meetings began. We had a meeting to discuss what the law that Enoé Uranga would introduce should and should not include. Parental rights were the first to fall, as it was clear to almost everyone–even some lesbians with children–that Mexico was not ready to accept LGBT parents. Lawyers working with the Assemblywoman conducted exhaustive research to look at similar legislation in other countries. In an attempt to be inclusive, the law would cover many different types of families, not just LGBT families that were not currently recognized by law. So rather than support a domestic-partner law such as the ones that had been passed in other countries, this one could include more than two people who did not necessarily have to have a romantic or sexual relationship. We decided we needed to meet with others who might be supportive; so to an already large number of LGBT organizations, we added women's groups, sexuality groups, and human rights groups, among others. Some groups began leaving almost as soon as they had arrived; others wanted a gay-and-lesbian-specific law, and as soon as that was taken out, they left. Some women got tired of the misogyny of some of the men, who were often disrespectful and argumentative, interrupting women.

We had meetings to decide what to call this thing: "Domestic partnership" was rejected because of the implication of domesticity and the way in which "partners" implies a business-like relationship in Spanish. After much discussion, the wording of "*Sociedad de Convivencia*" (Society for Living Together) was agreed upon.

PRD Proposes Solidarist Unions

To complicate matters, the Democratic Revolutionary Party (PRD for the initials in Spanish of the political party, *Partido de la Revolución Democrática*) launched the idea of a law for solidarist unions, *Uniones Solidarias*, in December 2000–right around the time of the budget debates in the City Assembly (*De Unión Solidaría a Sociedad de Convivencia*, n.d.). Solidarist unions would give civil marriage rights to gays and lesbians. That the proposal was made so close to budget discussions (which had raised serious questions about the financial administration of the city under the PRD), made it apparent that the move was simply an attempt to take media attention away from the city's financial problems. Few LGBT activists supported the legislation publicly; most saw it as a no-win situation. Nevertheless, the new proposal did provide the proponents of the *Sociedades de Convivencia* with a series of problems, as the public and the media began to confuse the two. Although the *Uniones Solidarias* legislation was never formally presented, the lobbying work for the *Sociedades de Convivencia* legislation was made more difficult by the existence of competing ideas.

Presentation of the Sociedades de Convivencia Legislation

Notwithstanding the previous setbacks, on January 18, 2001, in a presentation (Mogrovejo, 2001) in the Benito Juarez Forum of the Mexico City Assembly, the *Sociedad de Convivencia* legislation was finally presented by Assemblywoman Uranga to a room full of LGBT activists and friends. Briefly, the proposed *Sociedad de Convivencia* legislation called for minimum assurances in areas of inheritance rights and housing rights for same-sex and other couples based on their willingness to live together and provide jointly for their well-being not based necessarily on a sexual relationship (to read the original proposed legislation, see *Iniciativa de Ley de Sociedad De Convivencia*, n.d.). One decision that was made rather early on, as stated above, was not to include adoption, a decision made in an effort to have legislation that was winnable.

Some elements–such as the fact that the law would cover not only couples, but also potentially any number of people in a relationship–seemed particularly innovative, but other elements drew strong criticisms from some feminist lesbians (Barranco, 2001). Some argued that it should include access to health care (a critical point for discussion because the Mexico City provides only limited health services, while health care is a federal right under Mexican law). Others complained that making these relationships somewhat equivalent to common law arrangements made no sense for same-sex couples, given that common law regulations refer specifically to unions between men and women. All in all, it is important to note that some of the critics have failed to recognize that we were dealing with a city law, and even in one of the biggest cities in the world, the responsibilities and recognition that a city law can give are limited.

FEBRUARY 14, 2001:
BELLAS ARTES INUNDATED WITH LGBT FAMILIES

At the same time that the legislative proposal for the *Sociedades de Convivencia* was being developed, the idea of a symbolic union on Valentine's Day was being planned. On February 7, 2001, a press conference was held to promote the law and to talk about the event that would serve as the beginning of a public relations campaign to inform the public about the law. With the theme, *"Por el derecho a la diferencia: La Sociedad de Convivencia"*/"For the right to difference: the Society for Living Together," the legislation was officially presented to the public on February 14, 2001. The event became a political and cultural festival to provide the opportunity for lesbian, gay, bisexual, transgender, and heterosexual couples to publicly and symbolically register their unions under the concept of the *Sociedad de Convivencia*.

This event was an effort to educate Mexican society as a whole about the need for legal protection of the large diversity of families that exist today, while informing the public about this citizens' initiative headed by the independent legislative representative Assemblywoman Enoé Uranga. Several well-known personalities in Mexican society participated in the celebration, including several popular actors, political analysts, award-winning authors, important gay activists, and other major political figures.

The *Red de Apoyo a las Sociedades de Convivencia*, a loose network of organizations that supported the initiative, had decided to use the area outside of Bellas Artes because we worried that the Zocalo, or City Plaza, where many events are held, would be simply too big. Bellas Artes also provided a more beautiful backdrop and a more likely photo opportunity. We need not have worried at all, as it turned out the Esplanade in front of Bellas Artes was almost dangerously small. We do not know exactly how many people joined us there to launch a campaign to reform the city's Civil Code to include *Sociedades de Convivencia*. It is estimated that between 3,000 and 5,000 people were present at this historic event.

We should have known that our call for action and our support would be more than we had anticipated, when even the very conservative newspaper *Reforma* mentioned the event in its February 14 edition (Uranga, 2001); on February 15, we were front-page news in this bastion of Mexican conservatism (Calixto, 2001). *Reforma* even went so far as to host a Web chat on the subject. In fact, the media coverage on radio and television and in print journalism was unexpectedly wide and overwhelmingly supportive, including coverage in major Mexican newspapers, including *La Jornada, Excelsior, Milenio*, and *Publico* (Bertrán, 2001; Pavón and Páramo, 2001; Román, 2001; Téllez, 2001). As had been feared, some of the media confused the *Sociedades de*

Convivencia and the *Uniones Solidarias* in their coverage. There was international coverage by *Telemundo* and *Univision* on both their television transmissions and their Web pages. The news even made the *Boston Globe* (Lloyd, 2001).

At the registration table, couples were in line to register their names in a book and receive a Certificate of their Union. Numbered cards were distributed to couples who wanted to register. Only 100 cards had been printed and these were all gone in less than 30 minutes. Couples gathered asking for their cards. The folks on the ground could not move, and all the media possible were there: radio, television, cable, newspapers, and international media. Truly, no one could believe how many people wanted to participate in the event; the open call had far surpassed our expectations. More than 300 same-sex couples registered that day. Gay men and lesbians supported a legislative proposal through their own visibility. But there were also a few heterosexual couples, happily sharing this day without any prejudice, among them a man and a woman who came with their three small children, who yelled out in celebration when their mom and dad signed their union and gave each other a kiss.

POSTMORTEM ON FEBRUARY 14, 2001

The Valentine's Day event was a significant success on many levels; it grabbed media attention, showed a large demand for the legislation, and made the issue a public debate. In terms of an organizing tool, I believe many of us think it could have been improved. The stage was filled with people who had shown up at the last minute, not the organizers who had spent weeks in meetings putting the event together. We forgot to thank all the people who had worked tirelessly to get word to the media to bring people to the event. We concentrated on presenting artists and actors instead of the people who had come to support the event.

Though some of the lesbian groups left the day-to-day organizing at this point, other groups came in. The differences inherent in organizing a major event versus the sometimes boring lobbying work needed to pass legislation in a cantankerous City Assembly separated many from the group. The Assemblywoman and others from her team worked tirelessly and met with all 66 members of the Assembly to introduce the bill. Other events, not as massive as the one on the February 14, were planned to keep the proposed legislation in people's minds. The law was sent through an exhaustive review process by lawyers and magistrates, and even the Supreme Court of the City. Throughout this process small changes were made to the law, though it remained the same in spirit. In its final version the proposed legislation was changed to cover only couples, after it became evident that larger unions would be difficult to legislate. The law currently covers the barest minimum of items such as succession rights, legitimate guardianship, and food pensions (Y. Ramirez, personal communication, February 25, 2002).

The legislation was officially presented to the Assembly on April 24, 2001, with the support of 41 of the 66 legislators (Medina, 2001). After its presentation, the proposed legislation was sent to the Mexican Human Rights Commission and the Commission for Legislative Studies and Parliamentary Practices. These commissions must vote on the proposed legislation before it can be presented for a vote to the Assembly floor (Y. Ramirez, personal communication, February 25, 2002). Originally, the Commissions were set to vote in September, and then the vote was moved to the end of November. In October, the Supreme Court of the City approved the law.

Citizens' Colloquia on the Sociedades de Convivencia

On November 6, 7, and 8, a series of citizens' colloquia were held to prepare for and gather citizen input leading to the vote. They also gave an importunity to show significant support from sectors outside the LGBT movement for this initiative. The first panel was entitled, *"The legal recognition of social diversity in the construction of a state of law."* The second panel was entitled, *"The Law in the cultural battle against discrimination: An international perspective,"* and it brought together representatives from Belgium, Holland, France, South Africa, and Germany to share their experiences in the legal recognition of diversity and respect. The final panel was entitled *"The culture of diversity battles intolerance"* and included sexologists and psychotherapists arguing the importance of laws such as the one proposed. The Colloquia were successful in terms of their ability to draw people and to keep the item in the press.

The Treacherous Road to Voting in the Asamblea Legislativa (Legislative Assembly)

In further preparation for a vote on the legislation, Mexican and international activist networks, including the International Gay and Lesbian Human Rights Commission (IGLHR),were called upon to write to members of the assembly and to support the legislation in a variety of ways, International support was useful, both in easing the fears of some of the more nervous members of the City Assembly, by showing them they were not alone in this, but also in putting pressure on them. The meeting of the Joint Commissions was set for November 23 to vote to send the legislation to the Assembly floor for a vote. Members of the leftist PRD and the conservative PAN (*Partido Acción Nacional*) political parties refused to attend the meeting, in effect postponing the vote until 2002.

FEBRUARY 14, 2002:
THE SECOND TIME AROUND

A second day of symbolic registration of unions was held on February 14, 2002. The stage this time was the Benito Juárez Hemiciclo, a fitting site given Benito Juárez's commitment to the lay state. (Liberal and anticlerical, Juaréz was Minister of Justice when he produced the "Juárez Law," abolishing clerical immunity by limiting jurisdiction of ecclesiastical courts to ecclesiastical cases. He later became Mexico's first indigenous president.) The event was much better organized this time: the "judge" wore robes, and the tables were set up high where they would not be trampled on. However, many of the lesbian organizations that had participated early on in the process were missing. Some were disappointed with the wording of the legislation, and others, uninterested in the ins and outs of a long legislative process, had pulled away from the process. Others got tired of the misogynist attitude of some of the men pushing for the legislation.

On the other hand, many welcomed the event with its festive atmosphere. Some people wanted an opportunity to come together and celebrate, and 4,000 people did just that. However, many more men than women attended, a disturbing statistic given the fact that women started this idea and that a woman led the fight to make it happen. The news coverage, though perhaps not as extensive as the first time around, was overwhelmingly sympathetic to the cause. And though some of the newspapers missed the important revindication of human rights and simply published a picture with a short byline, the majority covered the event accurately and respectfully (Bravo, 2002; Estévez, 2002; Flores, 2002; Pavón, 2002a, 2002b). It is also important to note that even a year after the idea of the *Uniones Solidarias* had died out, the confusion with the *Sociedades de Convivencia* continued, despite all the media education efforts.

Unfortunately, I cannot help but wonder if we have not lost an important opportunity here to work better together as a community. In preparation for this article, I sent out a letter to members of the *Red Cuidadana de Apoyo para la Sociedades de Convivencia* and other LGBT e-mail lists, with three simple questions regarding their perspectives on *Sociedades de Convivencia*. Only two men answered. Of the over 200 organizations that support the legislation, few took the time to reflect upon what this legislative process has meant to the movement.

In late June, the law was brought to a vote in the Assembly. Unfortunately, at the last minute a member of the conservative political party, *Partido Acción Nacional* (PAN) voted to delay the vote for a year and one month. Enoé Uranga is committed to continue to fight for this piece of legislation and is currently questioning the legality of the motion. Other members of the *Red Ciudadana* are taking on members of *Provida* in the media to debate the merits of the legislation. However, it is difficult to know were we go from here. Many have charged the Catholic Church with influencing the votes of some of the members of the left PRD who voted against the measure. How can we counter that influence? How do we hold Assembly members accountable? Some of these questions go well beyond the LGBT movement to questions of political accountability and the separation of church and state, which are of interest to and have implications for many social change movements.

CONCLUSION

The process, which began with a proposal from a few lesbian groups, has gone beyond that nucleus to include a great many other players. Unfortunately, the move from movement demand to legislation left out some of the activists who originally proposed the idea. The difficulties of gender parity in organizing were evident throughout the process, but women have stayed firmly at the head of this movement. The proposed legislation is certainly a step forward for Mexico City and the country, but even its staunchest supporters admit it is only a first step. What is unclear to me is whether or not the LGBT movements will be able to push for this first step in a convincing manner–and then be able to push for the other steps necessary to making full rights for LGBT people in Mexico a reality in the long term.

In order to sustain the pursuit of LGBT rights, it will be necessary to reflect on a number of important issues that arose from the experience with the *Sociedad de Convivencia*. For example, why did an idea that came from the lesbian movement and which was led by a lesbian legislator lose much of its lesbian following? What are the challenges of *real* gender parity in organizing? How do activists and legislators work together? Are organizing and lobbying such different arenas? How does one build skills in both to work collectively?

REFERENCES

Barranco, I. (2001) ¿Sociedad de Convivencia o Conveniencia? *LeSVOZ, 21,* 14-16.
Bertrán, A. (2001, February 15) Se unen entre arroz, curiosos y ramos de flores 'Queremos Que Nos Miren.' *Reforma,* p. 5B.
Bravo, E.M. (2002, February 15) Amor sin barreras. *Crónica,* p. 23.
Calixto, J. (2001, February 15) La sociedad de convivencia, formula *gay. Milenio Diario,* p. 1.
De Unión Solidaría a Sociedad de Convivencia. (n.d.) Retrieved August 20, 2002, from <http://members.tripod.com/ofmexico/id88.htm>.

Estévez, O. (2002 February 15) Foto. *El Economista*, p. 42.
Flores, C. (2002 February 15) Se casan lesbianas y gays. *Novedades* 2F.
Iniciativa de Ley de Sociedad De Convivencia. (n.d.) Retrieved August 20, 2002, from <www.hartas.com/mp/soc_convivencia.htm>.
Lloyd, M. (2001, February 16) In Mexico, a mass gay wedding. *Boston Globe*, p. A8.
Medina, A. (2001, June 7). Extracto del reportaje: Reconocer todas las formas de convivencia. Retrieved August 20, 2002, from <www.laneta.apc.org/convivencia/>.
Mogrovejo, N. (2000a) Entrevista Exclusiva con Enoé Uranga. *LeSVOZ, 16*, 15-18.
Mogrovejo, N. (2000b) *Un Amor Que Se Atrevió A Decir Su Nombre: La lucha de las lesbianas en su relación con los movimientos homosexual y feminista en América Latina*. Mexico: Plaza Valdés, S.A. de C.V.
Mogrovejo, N. (2001) En base al amor y la libertad Iniciativa de Ley Sociedad de Convivencia. *LeSVOZ, 20*, 6-7
Pavón, C. (2002a) Piden Homosexuales Ley de Convivencia. *El Universal*, p. 1.
Pavón, C. (2002b) Toman Gays el Hemiciclo a Juárez: Salen del clóset y se casan. *Metro*, p. 3.
Pavón, C., & Páramo A. (2001, February 15) Concretan unión 500 parejas gay. *Reforma*, p. 1B.
Román, J. A. (2001, February 15) Inaceptable, bendición a parejas del mismo sexo. *La Jornada*, p. 48.
Téllez, C. (2001, February 15) Más de 500 parejas de Homosexuales y Lesbianas se Unieron; Piden los Consideren Sociedades de Convivencia. *Excelsior*, p. 26A.
Un amor que sé atrevió a decir su nombre: Grito de rebeldía que rompe con los simulacros de la comunidad lésbica de México. (2000) *LeSVOZ, 14*, 24-26.
Uranga, E. (2001, February 14) Celebran Hoy 'bodas gay.' *Reforma*, p. 7b.

Index

AARP, 136
Abstinence-only-until-marriage "sex education," 140
Abuse, alcohol, prevention of, in GLB community, 154-157
Abzug, B., 56
ACLU. *See* American Civil Liberties Union (ACLU)
Acquired immunodeficiency syndrome (AIDS), in GLB community, prevention of and care and support for, 160
Act on Registered Partnership for Homosexual Couples, 149
Activism
　AM/FM, 181-192. *See also* "AM/FM activism"
　Internet as space for, 172-175
ACT-UP, 169
Adam, B.D., 86
AEGIS. *See* American Educational Gender Information Service (AEGIS)
Affilia, xv
"Afgani-fags," 190
AFL-CIO, 59
AIDS. *See* Acquired immunodeficiency syndrome (AIDS)
Alcohol abuse, prevention of, in GLB community, 154-157
Alinsky, S., 12-14
American Civil Liberties Union (ACLU), 11, 57, 58, 63
　of Kentucky, xix, 7
American Civil Liberties Union (ACLU) Gay and Lesbian Rights Projects, 132

American Educational Gender Information Service (AEGIS), 167,169,172
American Enterprise Institute, 130
America Online, 174
American Society on Aging, 136
"AM/FM activism," 181-192
　background of, 185-187
　going back to community, 187-191
　in practice, 190-191
　step-by-step, 189-190
Anti-Discrimination Act of 2001, 55
Anti-discrimination laws, coalition building and electoral organizing in passage of, in Connecticut, 35-53
Anti-discrimination statutes, in Maryland
　continued resistance to, 62-64
　organizing to amend, 55-68
　　dynamics of, 64-66
　　finding sponsor and rallying support in, 57-60
　　lessons learned from, 66-67
　　political process of, 57-62
　　processes involved in, 64-66
　　strategy for, 60-62
　passage of bill, 62-64
Anzaldua, G., xvi
Asamblea Legislativa, voting in, treacherous road to, 215
Ashcroft, J., 133
Association of Community Organization and Social Administration, xv
Association of Federal, State, County, and Municipal Employees, 59
Ayala, G., 143

Bailey, R.W., 132
Baltimore Justice Campaign, 58
Barrett, K., 143
Baruch College, at the City University of New York, xvii
Becker, C., 195
Bellas Artes, inundated with LGBT families, 213-214
Benefit(s), Social Security, 143
Benito Juarez Forum, of Mexico City Assembly, 212
Benito Juarez Hemiciclo, 216
"Beyond Tolerance, Building a Better Community for Our Youth," 109
Bicklin, D.P., 125
Bill 7 Award, 82
Black Queer Youth, 93
Boes, M., 107
Bonelli, J., xv, 35,37,39,40-41,44,46,47,48
Boston Globe, 214
Boulden, W.T., 102
Boy Scouts, 143
Bradford, J., 143
Brandeis University, Florence Heller School of Social Welfare at, xvii
Brescia University, xix
Brett, L., 51
Bridges, B., 200
Brouillet, A., 42
Buffy the Vampire Slayer, 208-209
Bush, A., 140
Bush administration, xxi-xxii, 145
Bush, G.W., 130,132,133,134,140,142
Bush-Cheney administration, 130
Business community, in community education, 26
Button, J.W., 3

Cahill, S., xv, xxiii, 129
Calhoun, S., 121,124,125
Canada
  lesbians and gay men in, context of, 85-87
  queer youth in, 87-88
  social service response to trans youth in, 87-88
  Supreme Court of, 87
Canadian Charter of Rights and Freedoms, 87
Canadian Human Rights Code, 85
Canadian military, 85
Caro, E., 40,41,42,46,47,48
Carver School of Social Work, The Southern Baptist Theological Seminary, xviii
Cathedral of Hope (COH), Dallas, Texas, 193-206. *See also* Gay and lesbian congregation, social justice sought by, for other marginalized communities
  community building by, 196-197
  described, 197-198
  food distribution by, 201-202
  health clinics of, 201
  rehabilitation/building of homes, 200
  return of social justice to, 202-204
Catholic Church, 51,217
Census 2000's Same-Sex Household Data: A Users' Manual, 144
Center for Lesbian and Gay Studies, at City University of New York, 132
Central Toronto Youth Services (CTYS), xvii, 83-84
C-FAIR (Committee for Fairness and Individual Rights), 5,7
Chamber of Commerce, 62
Chancellor's Award, xvi
Change, organizing for, 1-15
Chao, E., 130
Chasin, L., 195
Chasin, R., 195
Cheney, D., 130
Child of Hope program, 198,200

Children's Alliance, xviii
CitizenLink Website, 115-116
Citizens' Colloquia, on *Sociedades de Convivencia,* 215
City University of New York
  Baruch College at, xvii
  Center for Lesbian and Gay Studies at, 132
Civil Rights Movement of 1960s, 65
Clinton administration, xxi-xxii
Clinton, B., 130,132
Clinton-Gore administration, 130
Coalition building, in community education, 25-26
Coalition for Services for Lesbian and Gay Youth, 88
Cole, S., 173,175
Coleman, E., 153
Colorado State University, xvii
Colt Firearms, 46
Columbia University, xvi
Coming Out Day, 67
Commission for Legislative Studies and Parliamentary Practices, 215
Commission to Denounce Hate Crimes, 208
Committee for Fairness and Individual Rights (C-FAIR), 5,7
Committee for Legislative and Political Action, of GLCCB, 59
Committee on Fairness, of Louisville Board of Aldermen, 10
Communication, among GLB population, organizing for changes in, 161-163
Community(ies)
  business, in community education, 26
  female-to-male, 169
  GLB, Norwegian, 149
  GLBT, demographics and policy priorities of, problems associated with, 134-135
  going back to, "AM/FM activism" and, 187-191
  LGBT, 19-20,182,183,184
    in Mexico City, organizing of, 207-218. *See also* Lesbian, gay, bisexual, and transgender (LGBT) community, in Mexico City, organizing of
  for LGBTT youth of Toronto, 81-98. *See also* Lesbian, gay, bisexual, transsexual and transgender (LGBTT) youth, building community for Toronto's; Supporting Our Youth (SOY)
  religious, in community education, 26
  rural, gay experience of, 101-102
Community Advisory Committee, 83
Community building, 196-197
Community Coalition, 118
Community education
  at Rightville Community Resource Center, 118-123
  in social justice, 30-31
  visibility and, 23-28
    business community in, 26
    coalition building in, 25-26
    religious community in, 26
    research's role in, 25
    timing of, 23
    working with media in, 23-25
"Community Organizing 101," 67
Community outreach, in social justice, 30-31
Community Resource Center (CRC), 118, 122
Community support, in social justice, 30-32
Community-based alliances
  across differences, building of, 105-106
  described, 106-107

between GLBTQQA youth and adults in rural settings, building of, 99-112
Community-building response, to queer and trans youth in Canada, 89-90
Connecticut, anti-discrimination laws in, coalition building and electoral organizing in passage of, 35-53
Connecticut Citizen Action Group, 44
Connecticut Civil Liberties Union, 51
Connecticut Coalition for Lesbian and Gay Civil Rights, xv, 37,52
Connecticut General Assembly, 36
Connecticut Legislature, 51
Connecticut Positive Action Coalition, xv
Connecticut State Federation of Teachers, 44, 45-46
Connecticut Women's Education and Legal Fund, 51
Constituent Action Network, 60
Council on Social Work Education Committee on Sexual Orientation and Gender Expression, xvi
Courier-Journal, 9
CRC. *See* Community Resource Center (CRC)
Creating Change: Public Policy, Sexuality and Civil Rights, xix
Creating Change Award, 17,32
Criminal Code, 86-87
Criminal offense, to partnership, 148-149
CTYS. *See* Central Toronto Youth Services (CTYS)
Currah, xviii

Defense of Marriage legislation, 51
D'Emilio, J., 132
Democratic National Committee, 137, 139
Democratic Revolutionary Party, 211
Democrats for Change, 42-44
Democrats for Change Democratic Town Committee, 36
Denny, D., 171,172
Department of Health and Human Services, 130,135
DePaul University, xix
Development and Diversity, xv
Dialogue, defined, 195
Diaz, R., 143
Dignity USA, 59
Dobson, J., 115
Dominican Republic orphanage, 199-200
Dr. Laura, 183,185-187
Dr. Laura campaign, 183,185-187,188, 189,191
Drug use, alcohol, prevention of, 154-157

Eberly, D., 140
Education, community
 at Rightville Community Resource Center, 118-123
 in social justice, 30-31
 visibility and, 23-28. *See also* Community education, visibility and
Elder Abuse and Neglect Survey, 134
Elder Abuse study, 135
Elderly, GLBT, public policy issues affecting, 136-139
Ellis, J., 143
Employment Non-Discrimination Act (ENDA), 56
Encyclopedia of Social Work, 195
ENDA. *See* Employment Non-Discrimination Act (ENDA)
Enlace Lésbico, Enoé Uranga and, meeting between, 210-212
Enlace Lésbico Femenista, 210
Enoé Uranga, Enlace Lésbico and, meeting between, 210-212

Equality
 GLBT think tanks' importance to, 129-146
 virtual, limits of, 131-134
Ethnicity, Muslim, GLB, 160-161
Excelsior, 213

Faculty Scholars Program, at University of Kentucky, xvi
"Fairness = Everyone," 6
"Fairness: No More, No Less," 6
Fairness Alliance, 17
Fairness Amendment, 4-5, 9
Fairness Campaign, 2, 4-8,9,10,11,12, 13,21-23
 process of, 22
 structure of, 22
"Fairness Does a City Good," 6
Fairness Ordinance, 6,9,11,13,20,21
 in Lexington-Fayette County, Kentucky, 17
Family Ministry, xvi
Fatherhood initiatives, 139-140
Faulkner, A.O., xv, 113
FCC. *See* Federal Communications Commission (FCC)
February 14
 2001, 213-215
 2002, 216-217
Federal Communications Commission (FCC), 188
Federico Memorial Lecture for the Association of Baccalaureate Social Work Program Directors, xvi
Female to Male International (FTMI), 167
Female-to-male (FTM) community, 169
Figueroa, J., 42,43,46
First Meeting of Lesbians and Lesbian Feminists, 207
Florence Heller School of Social Welfare, at Brandeis University, xvii

Focus on the Family, 115
Food distribution, by COH, 201-202
Foothills Youth Group, 119,120,122
For Fairness Campaign, 63
Ford Foundation, xxiv
 Governance and Civil Society Unit in Peace and Social Justice Program at, xix
Fragmentation, resistance to, four female transgender students of color speak about school, 69-79
Free State Justice (FSJ), 55-56,57,58, 60, 61, 63
Frente de Liberacion Homosexual, 208
Fruit Loopz @ Pride, 82,83
FSJ. *See* Free State Justice (FSJ)
FTM (female-to-male) community, 169
FTMI. *See* Female to Male International (FTMI)

GAIN. *See* Gender Advocacy Internet News (GAIN)
Gale, C., 42-43
Gardner-Webb University, xviii
Gates Millennium Scholar, xvi
Gay
 lesbian
 bisexual
 transgender
 queer, questioning, and ally (GLBTQQA) youth
 described, 100-101
 GLBTQQA adults and, community-based alliances between, in rural settings, 99-112
 and queer (GLBTQ) persons, 100
 rural, supportive services for, 102-103

and transgender (GLBT)
community
demographics and policy
priorities of,
problems associated
with, 134-135
welfare reform's threat to,
139-141
and transgender (GLBT)
elders, public policy
issues affecting,
136-139
and transgender (GLBT)
rights, 2
and transgender (GLBT)
rights movement,
xxi
and transgender (GLBT)
think tanks, in
equality and
liberation
advances in, 135-145
importance of, 129-146
and transgender (GLBT)
youth
rural settings for,
changing context of,
103-105
school and, 114-115
and bisexual (GLB)
communities
alcohol abuse prevention in,
154-157
challenges facing, 160-161
coming out and coming in
process, facilitation
of, 158-160
drug use prevention in,
154-157
HIV/AIDS prevention, care,
and support in, 160
meeting needs of, 153-161
Norwegian, 149
and bisexual (GLB) population

communication and
partnership in,
organizing for
changes in, 161-163
health and social service
needs in
assessment of
legal framework in,
148-149
Norwegian experience,
147-164. *See also*
under Norway
capacity building in, 162-163
living conditions of, 150-153
Muslim ethnic minority in,
160-161
Lesbian, Bisexual, and Transgender
(GLBT) Community Center
of Baltimore and Central
Maryland, 58
Lesbian and Straight Education
Network (GLSEN), 105,
119-120
Lesbian and Straight Education
Network's (GLSEN) School
Climate Survey, 100
Gay & Lesbian Outreach to Elders
(GLOE), 138
Gay and Lesbian Advocates and
Defenders, 132
Gay and Lesbian Alliance Against
Defamation (GLAAD), xxiv,
181-192
Gay and lesbian congregation, social
justice sought by, for other
marginalized communities,
193-206. *See also* Cathedral
of Hope (COH), Dallas,
Texas
literature review, 195-197
Gay and Lesbian Human Rights
Commission, xvii
Gay and Lesbian or Bisexual Alliance
(GLOBAL), 4

Gay and Lesbian Rights Movement, early days in, 37-52
Gay and Lesbian Strategic studies, 145
Gay experience, of rural communities, 101-102
Gay men, in Canadian context, 85-87
Gay-straight alliance (GSA), 105
GEA. See Gender Education & Advocacy (GEA)
Gender Advocacy Internet News (GAIN), 167
Gender Education & Advocacy (GEA), 167, 172
GenderPAC (GPAC), 167, 169
General Assembly, 115
George, V., 195
Gingrich, N., 131
GLAAD. See Gay and Lesbian Alliance Against Defamation (GLAAD)
GLAAD Alert, 184
GLB population. See Gay, lesbian, and bisexual (GLB) population
GLBBC, Committee for Legislative and Political Action of, 59
GLBT. See under Gay, lesbian, bisexual and transgender (GLBT)
GLBT Community Resource Center, 116,117,118
GLBTQ persons. See Gay, lesbian, bisexual, transgender, and queer (GLBTQ) persons
GLBTQQA youth. See Gay, lesbian, bisexual, transgender, queer, questioning, and ally (GLBTQQA) youth
GLCCB, 63
Glendening, P., 58,63
GLHRC. See Greater Louisville Human Rights Coalition (GLHRC)
GLOBAL. See Gay and Lesbian or Bisexual Alliance (GLOBAL)

GLOE. See Gay & Lesbian Outreach to Elders (GLOE)
GLSEN. See Gay, Lesbian and Straight Education Network (GLSEN)
Gore, A., 132
Governance and Civil Society Unit, in Peace and Social Justice Program, of Ford Foundation, xix
Governor's Special Commission to Study Sexual Orientation Discrimination in Maryland, xvi
GPAC. See GenderPAC (GPAC)
Grabarz, J., 51
Grassroots, meets homophobia, 113-128
Grassroots effort, context for, 115-118
  local area in, 116
  school district in, 116-117
Greater Hartford Lesbian and Gay Task Force, 38
Greater Louisville Human Rights Coalition (GLHRC), 3-4
Greif, G.L., xv-xvi, 55,61
Griot Circle, 138
Grise-Owens, E., xvi, 1,20
GSA. See Gay-straight alliance (GSA)
Guitierrez, N., xvi, 69

Hagan, B., 40
Hammond, I., 118,119
Harbeck, K.M., 114
Hartford City Council, 37,39,41,46,48
Hartford Democratic Party, 41
Hartford Gay Pride celebration, 42
Hartford Organizing, 38-42
Harvard University, xvii
"Hate Hurts," 6
Haynes, K.S., 66
Health clinics, of COH, 201
Health needs, of GLB population, assessment of, Norwegian experience, 147-164

Heels Club, 169
Heritage Foundation, 130,140
Herndon, K., 7
Herzig, M., 195
HIV infection. *See* Human immunodeficiency virus (HIV) infection
HIV Prevention for the Kentucky Department for Health Services, xix
Hixson, S., 56,57,58
Homan, M.S., 124
Home of the Innocents, xviii
Homophobia, grassroots meet, 113-128
Homosexual Liberation Front, 208
Honnold, J., 143
Horn, W., 130,140
Human immunodeficiency virus (HIV) infection, in GLB community, prevention of and care and support for, 160
Human Relations Commission, 5
Human Relations Committee, 59-60
Human rights activity, in Rightville, Colorado, history of, 117-118
Human Rights Campaign, 59,63,132, 182
Human Rights Commission, 21,31,117
Hyde, S., 49
Hyman, J.B., 11

IAM. *See* International Association of Machinists (IAM)
IFGE. *See* International Foundation for Gender Education (IFGE)
IGLHR. *See* International Gay and Lesbian Human Rights Commission (IGLHR)
Immigration Act of Canada, 85
In Your Face (IYF), 167
Inciativa de Ley de Sociedad de Convivencia, 212

Income Inflation: The Myth of Affluence Among Gay, Lesbian, and Bisexual Americans, 145
Institute for American Values, 140
Institute for Gay and Lesbian Strategic Studies, 143
  at University of Massachusetts, 132
Institute for the Study of Sexual Minorities, in Military, at University of California, 132
Interfaith Council, 125
International Association of Machinists (IAM), 45,46
International Foundation for Gender Education (IFGE), 167,171
International Gay and Lesbian Human Rights Commission (IGLHR), 215
Internet
  as space for activism, 172-175
  as tool for organizing, 171-172
  transgender organizing on, 165-179. *See also* Transgender organizing, on Internet
ITA. *See* It's Time America (ITA)
It's Time America (ITA), 167, 169
IYF. *See* In Your Face (IYF)

Jackson, J., 9,39,50
Jefferson County Department for Human Services, xix
Jefferson County Fiscal Court, 10
Jefferson, M., 118,119,120,125
Jenkins, D.A., xvi, 193
Johns Hopkins University, 169
Johnson, L., 65
Johnston, K., 196
Johnston, L.B., xvi, 193
Joint Commission(s), 215
Joint Commission on Accreditation of Health Care Organizations, 136-137
Jones, K., xv

Jorgensen, C., 166
Juan Figueroa Campaign, 42-44
Juang, xviii
"Juarez Law," 216
Judicial Proceedings Committee, 60, 61
"Just let them *see* what we do," 198-202
Justice
   journey toward, 1-15
      beginning of, 2-5
      lessons learned from, 12-14
      partners on, 9
   social, one community's path to, 17-33. *See also* Social justice, one community's path to

KBHC. *See* Kentucky Baptist Homes for Children (KBHC)
Keating, A., xvi
Kent School of Social Work, at University of Louisville, xix
Kentucky Alliance Against Racist and Political Repression, 4, 7
Kentucky Baptist Homes for Children (KBHC), 8,9
Kentucky Court of Appeals, 11
Kentucky Derby Parade, 6
Kentucky Fairness Alliance (KFA), 6, 21
   implementation of contemporary social movement strategies and tactics for social changes by, 18
Kentucky Fairness Alliance (KFA)–Bluegrass, 20
Kentucky Rainbow Coalition, 4
Kentucky Supreme Court, 8
KFA. *See* Kentucky Fairness Alliance (KFA)
King, M.L., Jr., 65
Kirkens SOS, 161-162
Kirkley-Bey, M., 40,41

Kitchin, K.T., 186
Kontekst Kommunikasjon, xix, xviii

La Jornada, 213
Lambda Legal Defense and Education Fund, 132
"Larry the Cable Guy," 190
"Laura-level" campaigns, 188
League of Women Voters, 63
LEAP. *See* Legislative Electoral Action Program (LEAP)
Leaving Our Children Behind: Welfare Reform and the GLBT Community, xv, 140
Legislative Black Caucus, 63
Legislative Education Action Program, 52
Legislative Electoral Action Program (LEAP), 36, 44
LEO. *See Louisville Eccentric Observer (LEO)*
Lepischak, B., xvii, 81
Lesbian(s)
   in Canadian context, 85-87
   local agency's firing of, 8-9
Lesbian, gay, bisexual
   and transgender (LGBT) civil rights and social and political activism, 18
   and transgender (LGBT) community, 19-20,182,183, 184
   in Mexico City, organizing of, 207-218
   and transgender (LGBT) families, *Bellas Artes* inundated with, 213-214
   and transgender (LGBT) rights, in Mexico, 208
   and transgender (LGBT) storytelling, 209-210
   transsexual and transgender (LGBTT) youth, building

community for Toronto's, 81-98. *See also* Supporting Our Youth (SOY)
  challenges facing, 95-96
  framework for, 91-96
  implementation of new initiatives in, 93-95
  volunteer base development for, 91-93
"Lesbian, Gay, Bisexual, and Transgender Older Persons," 136
Lesbian and Gay Association, 149,150, 154,158,159,161
Lesbian and Gay Rights Coalition Political Action Committee (LGPAC), 44-46
Lesbian Avengers, 169
Lesbian Health Conference, 144
Levantamiento Amado, 211
Lexington-Fayette Urban County Human Rights Commission, 20
LGBT. *See* Lesbian, gay, bisexual, and transgender (LGBT)
LGBTT youth. *See* Lesbian, gay, bisexual, transsexual and transgender (LGBTT) youth
LGPAC. *See* Lesbian and Gay Rights Coalition Political Action Committee (LGPAC)
Liberation, GLBT think tanks' importance to, 129-146. *See also* Gay, lesbian, bisexual, and transgender (GLBT) think tanks, in equality and liberation, importance of
Lifetime Achievement Award in Community Organization, xv
Lindsey, A., xvii, 113
Little, S., 46,48
"Living Conditions and Life Quality Among Lesbian Women and Gay Men," 150
Living whole, 69-79

LLEGO. *See* National Latina/o Lesbian, Gay, Bisexual and Transgender Organization (LLEGO)
Lobbying, 27-28
"Local Laura Activism," 185,186
"Local Laura Activism Version 2.0," 186
Local Ordinance 199-94, 20
Louisville Board of Aldermen, 4
  Committee on Fairness of, 10
Louisville Eccentric Observer (LEO), 8,10,12
Louisville Fairness Campaign, 23
Louisville Youth Group, xix, 4
Louisville/Jefferson County Human Relations Commission, 3
Love Makes a Family, 51

Magre, S., 9,10
Make Your Family Count!, 143
Mantilla, E., 49
March for Justice, 4,6
Marriage promotion, 139
Maryland, anti-discrimination statutes in, organizing to amend, 55-68. *See also* Anti-discrimination statutes, in Maryland, organizing to amend
Maryland Anti-Discrimination Act, 57, 58,60,66-67
Maryland Chapter of the National Association of Social Workers (MD-NASW), 58
Maryland General Assembly, 56
Maryland Legislative Council of Social Workers, 58-59
Maryland Senate, 59
Maryland State Teachers Association, 59,63
Maryland's House Judiciary Committee, 59

MCC. *See* Metropolitan Community Church (MCC)
McClennan, D.L., xvii, 55
MD-NASW. *See* Maryland Chapter of the National Association of Social Workers (MD-NASW)
Media, as factor in community education, 23-25
Media advocacy, process of, 184-187
Medicare, 137
Mentoring and Housing Program, 83
Metro Council, 11
Metropolitan Community Church (MCC), 197
Mexican American Legal Defense Fund, 141
Mexican Human Rights Commission, 215
Mexico City, organizing LGBT community in, 207-218. *See also* Lesbian, gay, bisexual, and transgender (LGBT) community, in Mexico City, organizing of
Mexico City Assembly, Benito Juarez Forum of, 212
Mickelson, J.S., 66
Milenio, 213
Minter, xviii
Mother Teresa, 198
Muslim(s), GLB, 160-161

NAACP, 141
Nangeroni, N., 173,175
National Association of Broadcasters, 190
National Association of Social Workers, xviii
National Association of Social Worker/Texas Special Interest Committee on Gay, Lesbian, and Bisexual Issues, xvi

National Center for Lesbian Rights, 59
National Conference on Gender (NCG), 167
National Family Caregiver Support Program, 139
National Gay and Lesbian Journalist's Association, 182
National Gay and Lesbian Task Force (NGLTF), 17,32,59,129-130, 132,141,145,182
  Policy Institute of, xix, 136,142, 144,145
National Gay and Lesbian Task Force (NGLTF) Creating Change Conference, xxii
National Institute for Public Health, Cuernavaca, Morelos Mexico, xvii
National Latina/o Lesbian, Gay, Bisexual and Transgender Organization (LLEGO), xvii
National media tools, at local level, 181-192. *See also* "AM/FM activism"
National Opinion Research Center's General Social Survey, 135
National Organization for Women (NOW), 44
National Transgender Advocacy Coalition (NTAC), 172
NCG. *See* National Conference on Gender (NCG)
Negroni, M.J., xvii, 207
Neighborhood cleanups, 200-201
New England Health Care Employees-District 1199-SEIU, 44,46
New School for Social Research, xvi
New York Association for Gender Rights Advocacy (NYAGRA), 167
New York Times, 136
New York Times Magazine, 8,10,12
Newsweek, 136

NGLTF. See National Gay and
    Lesbian Task Force
    (NGLTF)
NGLTF Creating Change Conference.
    See National Gay and
    Lesbian Task Force
    (NGLTF) Creating Change
    Conference
NGLTF Policy Institute, 132,136
1987 March for Justice, 14
Nobel Peace Prize, 65
Norton, 133
Norway
    GLB communities in, 149
    GLB population in, health and
        social service needs in,
        assessment of, 147-164. See
        also Gay, lesbian, and
        bisexual (GLB) population,
        health and social service
        needs in, assessment of
    welfare state in, set-up of, 149-150
Norwegian Foundation for Health and
    Rehabilitation, 158
Norwegian Psychiatrist Association,
    149
NOW. See National Organization for
    Women (NOW)
NTAC. See National Transgender
    Advocacy Coalition (NTAC)
Nuestras Voces study, 143
NYAGRA. See New York Association
    for Gender Rights Advocacy
    (NYAGRA)

Ontario Trillium Foundation, 84, 90,
    97
Ontario's Human Rights Code, 82-83
*Organizing in Hard Times: Labor and
    Neighborhoods in Hartford,*
    xviii-ix
Otis, M.D., xvii-xviii, 17
Outing Age, 136-139

Outreach, community, in social justice,
    30-31
*Overcoming the Odds: Raising
    Academically Successful
    African American Females,*
    xvi
Owens, L.W., xviii, 1
Owensboro Gay Alliance, xix

PAN *(Partido Acción Nacional),* 215,
    216
Paramount Domestic Television, 185,
    186
Parents, Families, and Friends of
    Lesbians and Gays (PFLAG),
    4,58,63,119-120
Park, P., 167
Parliament of Canada, 85
Partido Acción Nacional (PAN), 215,
    216
Partido de la Revolución Democratica,
    211
Partnership, among GLB population,
    organizing for changes in,
    161-163
Party Town Committee structure, 43
Peace and Social Justice Program,
    Governance and Civil
    Society Unit in, of Ford
    Foundation, xix
Pedreira, A., 8, 10, 12
People for Change (PFC), xv, 36,
    38-42, 52
People for Change (PFC) party, xviii
People for the American Way, 59
People Helping People program, 200
Perrotti, J., 125
Perry, C.S., 48,49
Personal Responsibility and Work
    Opportunity Reconciliation
    Act, 140
Peters, M., 49
PFC. See People for Change (PFC)

PFLAG. *See* Parents, Families and Friends of Lesbians and Gays (PFLAG)
Piazza, M., 197
Pink Ink Literary Café, 82
Policy Institute, 143
  of National Gay and Lesbian Task Force, xix
Policy Institute of the National Gay and Lesbian Task Force, xv, 133,135-136
Popular Music and Society, xviii
Premiere Radio Networks, 186
Presbyterian U.S.A. National Headquarters, 3
Pride & Prejudice program, xvii
Pride 2001, 83
Pride Day, 110
Pride Senior Network, 138
Pride Week celebrations, 83
Primer Encuentro Metropolitano de Lesbianas y Lesbianas Feministas, 209-210
Prism, 99,100,108-110
Progressive Student's League, 4
Promotion(s), marriage, 139
Provida, 208
PRPAC. *See* Puerto Rican Political Action Committee (PRPAC)
Public, 213
Public school partnerships, 199
Puerto Rican Political Action Committee (PRPAC), 42, 44

Queer youth, in Canada, 87-88
  community-building response to, 89-90
QueerNation, 169

Racial and Economic Justice Initiative, 140
Rainbow Book Club, 82
Rainbow Coalition, 39
Ralston, M., 199

Reagan, R., 39,131
Rector, R., 130
Red e Apoyo a las Sociedades de Convivencia, 213, 216
Redistricting and the GLBT Community: A Strategy Memo, 142
Reforma, 213
Religious community, in community education, 26
"Religious Minorities: Empowerment Through Reconciliation," xvii
Religious Task Force, 51
Republican Congressional leadership, 142
Research, role in community education, 25
Riehl, R., 39,47
Rienzo, B.A., 3
Rightville Coalition for Human Rights, 117,118
Rightville Community Resource Center
  committee tasks at, 119
  community education at, 118-123
  creating resources through utilizing volunteers at, 125-126
  cultivating and utilizing allies at, 125
  developing curriculum and training corps at, 123
  educational packets at, 119-120
  enlisting established community leadership at, 125
  meeting with Sam Calhoun, 121
  meetings with school principals brings promise of cooperation at, 122
  opportunities to provide training at, 122-123
  personal stories from youth, 120
  slow change at, acceptance of, 126
  Social Change Committee at, 118, 119

success of, factors in, 124-126
tailoring strategy and tactics to specific community situation at, 124-125
Rivera, R.R., 56
Robertson, P., 11
Rofes, E., 114
Roosevelt, E., xxii
Roth, S., 195
Royal Canadian Mounted Police, 85
Rules for Radicals, 12
Rural communities, gay experience of, 101-102
Rural settings, community-based alliances between GLBTQQA youth and adults in, building of, 99-112
Russo, V., 182
Rutgers University School of Social Work, xv

SAGE. *See* Senior Action in a Gay Environment (SAGE)
San Francisco Chronicle, 130
San Francisco State University, 143
Sandkjaer, B., xviii, 147
Schilt, K., xviii, 181
Schlessinger, L., 183,185,186,190
School(s)
  four female transgender students of color speak about, 69-79
  GLBT youth and, 114-115
Senate Judicial Proceedings Committee, 59,62,63
Senior Action in a Gay Environment (SAGE), 138
September 11, 2001, terrorist attacks on New York City and Washington, D.C., 203
SERL. *See* Survey Evaluation and Research Lab (SERL)
Service Employees International Union State Council, 46

"Sex education," abstinence-only-until-marriage, 140
Sex Reassignment Surgery (SRS), 166
Shapiro, E., xviii, 165
Shepard, M., 8-9, 108
Simmons, L., xviii, 35,48
Smith, G.A., 174
Snively, C.A., xix, 99
Social Change Committee, 121
  at Rightville Community Resource Center, 118,119
  tasks of, 119
Social Discrimination and Health, 143
Social Discrimination and Health: The Case of Latino Gay Men and HIV Risk, 143
Social justice
  and dialogue, 195
  one community's path to, 17-33
    background of, 18-20
    celebration and reflection, 31-32
    community climate of, 18-19
    education and, 23-28. *See also* Community education, visibility and
    local history in, 20
    making case in public forum, 28-30
    strategies for maintaining community support and involvement in, 30-32
  partnership in community-wide, efforts for, 31
  pursuit of, 22-23
  return of, to COH, 202-204
Social justice organizations, 27
social justice/community outreach, 198-202
Social Security, 130,134,137,138,139
Social Security benefits, 143
Social service needs, of GLB population, assessment of, Norwegian experience,

147-164. *See also* Gay, lesbian, and bisexual (GLB) population, health and social service needs in, assessment of
Social service response, to trans youth, in Canada, 87-88
Sociedades de Convivencia, 211,216, 217
  Citizens' Colloquia on, 215
Sociedades de Convivencia legislation, presentation of, 212
Sociedades de Convivencia project, 208,212 213
Solidarist unions, 211-212
SOY. *See* Supporting Our Youth (SOY)
Special Commission to Study Sexual-Orientation Discrimination, in Maryland, 56
SRS. *See* Sex Reassignment Surgery (SRS)
Stanford University, 169
Staples, L., 124
State Commission on Human Rights and Organizations, 51
Steinsvag, B-A, xix, 147
Storksen, I., xix, 147
Strategies to Overcome Oppression and Discrimination for Marginalized Groups, xvii
Support, community, in social justice, 30-32
Supporting Our Youth (SOY), 91-98. *See also* Lesbian, gay, bisexual, transsexual and transgender (LGBTT) youth, building community for Toronto's
  overview of, 82-84
  sponsor of, 83-84
Supportive services, for rural GLBTQ persons, 102-103
Supreme Court of Canada, 87
Supreme Court of the City, 214
Survey Evaluation and Research Lab (SERL), of Virginia Commonwealth University, 143-144
Swan, W.K., 65

TakeBackMaryland, 64
"Tali-fags," 190
"Tali-queers," 190
Teachers college Columbia University, xvi
Telemundo, 214
Terrorist attacks on New York City and Washington, D.C., September 11, 2001, 203
Texas Christian University, xvi
The 2000 National Election Study and Gay and Lesbian Rights: Support for Equality Grows, 142
"The Other Mother and Second Parent Adoption," xvii
The Southern Baptist Theological Seminary, Carver School of Social Work at, xviii
The Union Institute and University, xv
3rd District Democratic Town Committee, 43
This Bridge We Call Home: Envisioning the Spirit of This Bridge Called My Back, xvi
Timing, as factor in community education, 23
Toronto, LGBTT youth of, building community for, 81-98. *See also* Lesbian, gay, bisexual, transsexual and transgender (LGBTT) youth, building community for Toronto's; Supporting Our Youth (SOY)
"Trans Movements: From Gender Clinics to Internet Organizing," xviii
Trans youth
  in Canada, community-building response to, 89-90

social service response to, in
Canada, 87-88
'Trans'cending barriers, 165-179. *See also* Transgender organizing, on Internet
Trans_Fusion Crew, 93
Transgender Nation, 167,169
Transgender organizing
on Internet, 165-179
literature review of, 168
methods of, 167-168
role of, 170-175
social history of, 168-170
Transgender Rights: Culture, Politics, and Law, xviii
Transgender students, of color, female, speak about school, 69-79
TransShare, 167
Tri-Ess, 169
Trinity College, 47
2000 Census, 144
2000 National Election, 142
2000 National Election Study, 131

UAW. *See* United Auto Workers (UAW)
Uniones Solidarias, 211-212,214,216
United Auto Workers (UAW), 44,50
University of Bergen, xix
University of California
Institute for the Study of Sexual Minorities in Military at, 132
Los Angeles, xviii, 143,169
at Santa Barbara, xviii
University of Chicago National Opinion Research Center, 134
University of Connecticut School of Social Work, xv, xviii
University of Kentucky, xvii-xviii
Faculty Scholars Program at, xvi
University of Louisville, 4
Kent School of Social Work at, xix
University of Maryland, 61
Baltimore County, xvii

University of Maryland School of Social Work, xv
University of Massachusetts, Institute for Gay and Lesbian Strategic Studies at, 132
University of Michigan, xv, 57
University of Minnesota, 169
University of Missouri, Columbia, xix
University of Oklahoma, xvii
University of Pennsylvania, xv-xvi
University of Texas
at Arlington, xvi
at Austin, xviii
University of Wyoming, xvii
Univision, 214
UNSPOKEN RULES, xvii
Uranga, Assemblywoman, 210-211
Uribe, V., 114
U.S. Administration on Aging Website, 136
U.S. Census, 134, 143
U.S. Court of Appeals, for Sixth Circuit, 11
U.S. Department of Justice, 11
U.S. Supreme Court, 115

Vaid, U., xix, xxiv, 64-65,130,133
Valentine's Day event, 213-215
Van Soest, D., 195
Van Wormer, K., 107
Vessels, J., xix, 1
Virginia Commonwealth University, SERL of, 143-144
Virginia Price's Hose, 169
"Virtual equality," limits of, 131-134
Virtual Equality: The Mainstreaming of Gay and Lesbian Liberation, xix,133
Visibility
in community education, 23-28. *See also* Community education, visibility and
in social justice, 30-31

Voter News Service, 132,134-135
Voting Rights Act, 65

Wald, K.D., 3
Wallace, C., 6
Ward-Pugh, T., 10
Weicker, L., 36,51
Welfare reform, threat to GLBT families and individuals, 139-141
Welfare state, in Norway, set-up of, 149-150

Wells, J., 107
Westheimer, K., 125
Wilding, P., 195
Winfrey, O., 19
"Women and the New American Welfare," xv
World Missions Coordinator, at COH, 200

Yang, A., 142,143
York University, xvii

SPECIAL 25%-OFF DISCOUNT!

Order a copy of this book with this form or online at:
http://www.haworthpress.com/store/product.asp?sku=4980
Use Sale Code BOF25 in the online bookshop to receive 25% off!

Gay and Lesbian Rights Organizing
Community-Based Strategies

___ in softbound at $18.71 (regularly $24.95) (ISBN: 1-56023-275-7)
___ in hardbound at $29.96 (regularly $39.95) (ISBN: 1-56023-274-9)

COST OF BOOKS ___	❑ **BILL ME LATER:** ($5 service charge will be added)
Outside USA/ Canada/ Mexico: Add 20%. ___	Bill-me option is good on US/Canada/Mexico orders only; not good to jobbers, wholesalers, or subscription agencies.
POSTAGE & HANDLING ___	
US: $4.00 for first book & $1.50 for each additional book	❑ Signature ___
Outside US: $5.00 for first book & $2.00 for each additional book.	❑ Payment Enclosed: $ ___
SUBTOTAL ___	❑ PLEASE CHARGE TO MY CREDIT CARD:
In Canada: add 7% GST. ___	❑ Visa ❑ MasterCard ❑ AmEx ❑ Discover ❑ Diner's Club ❑ Eurocard ❑ JCB
STATE TAX ___	Account # ___
CA, IN, MIN, NY, OH, & SD residents please add appropriate local sales tax.	Exp Date ___
FINAL TOTAL ___	Signature ___
If paying in Canadian funds, convert using the current exchange rate, UNESCO coupons welcome.	*(Prices in US dollars and subject to change without notice.)*

PLEASE PRINT ALL INFORMATION OR ATTACH YOUR BUSINESS CARD

Name		
Address		
City	State/Province	Zip/Postal Code
Country		
Tel	Fax	
E-Mail		

May we use your e-mail address for confirmations and other types of information? ❑Yes ❑ No
We appreciate receiving your e-mail address. Haworth would like to e-mail special discount offers to you, as a preferred customer. **We will never share, rent, or exchange your e-mail address.** We regard such actions as an invasion of your privacy.

Order From Your Local Bookstore or Directly From
The Haworth Press, Inc.
10 Alice Street, Binghamton, New York 13904-1580 • USA
Call Our toll-free number (1-800-429-6784) / Outside US/Canada: (607) 722-5857
Fax: 1-800-895-0582 / Outside US/Canada: (607) 771-0012
E-Mail your order to us: Orders@haworthpress.com

Please Photocopy this form for your personal use.
www.HaworthPress.com